Mindfulness

FOR

DUMMIES

A Wiley Brand

2nd Edition

by Shamash Alidina

FOR

DUMMIES

A Wiley Brand

Mindfulness For Dummies®, 2nd Edition

Published by: **John Wiley & Sons, Ltd.,** The Atrium, Southern Gate, Chichester, www.wiley.com

This edition first published 2015

© 2015 John Wiley & Sons, Ltd, Chichester, West Sussex.

Registered office

John Wiley & Sons Ltd, The Atrium, Southern Gate, Chichester, West Sussex, PO19 8SQ, United Kingdom

For details of our global editorial offices, for customer services and for information about how to apply for permission to reuse the copyright material in this book please see our website at www.wiley.com.

Wiley publishes in a variety of print and electronic formats and by print-on-demand. Some material included with standard print versions of this book may not be included in e-books or in print-on-demand. If this book refers to media such as a CD or DVD that is not included in the version you purchased, you may download this material at www.dummies.com. For more information about Wiley products, visit www.wiley.com.

Designations used by companies to distinguish their products are often claimed as trademarks. All brand names and product names used in this book are trade names, service marks, trademarks or registered trademarks of their respective owners. The publisher is not associated with any product or vendor mentioned in this book.

For general information on our other products and services, please contact our Customer Care Department within the U.S. at 877-762-2974, outside the U.S. at (001) 317-572-3993, or fax 317-572-4002. For technical sup-port, please visit www.wiley.com/techsupport.

A catalogue record for this book is available from the British Library.

ISBN 978-1-118-86818-8 (paperback); ISBN 978-1-118-86819-5 (ebk); ISBN 978-1-118-86820-1 (ebk)

Printed in Great Britain by TJ International, Padstow, Cornwall

10 9 8 7 6

Contents at a Glance

Table of Contents

Foreword

● ●

Sitting down to start a book has many similarities to sitting down to a great meal. There is a warm felt sense of anticipation (in body and mind) of a pleasant experience. There is curiosity in the mind. There is an awareness of a certain 'hunger' for what is about to be taken in. And there we are, fully present to what we encounter before us: whether it is the visual experience of the design of the book or the plate presentation of the meal, whether it is the aroma of a desired food or the fresh smell of a newly-printed and opened book. Perhaps this captures something of your experience as you read these words, but on the other hand, as they say, 'your mileage may vary'. Take a moment to stop and notice what your experience ACTUALLY is right now in this very moment. What is the quality of your mind? What do you notice in your body? Are you aware of your breath moving in and out of your body, essentially 'breathing itself'?

Few things are more elementally basic and simple, yet so hard to convey in words and instructions, than mindfulness. At its essence it is simply being present, to our experience, our whole experience, and nothing but our experience. Yet you can read that previous sentence dozens, even millions of times, and still not know (at a level well below words) how to systematically practice it and bring it into your life with all its stresses and challenges. The only way to truly know mindfulness and cultivate it in one's life is to practice it like your life depends on it. Because in many ways it does. The degree to which you can be fully present to your experience, letting go of judgment when it is not useful and truly seeing things as they are, really determines the degree of suffering and stress you will experience in this crazy life of ours.

So the biggest difference between sitting down to this book and sitting down to a fine meal in a gourmet restaurant is that this book, as wonderful, instructional and inspirational as it is, is simply the menu and not the meal itself. We've all seen many beautiful menus in amazing restaurants the world over, but not one of them would have tasted anything like the meals they described! Those menus, like *Mindfulness for Dummies*, simply (but elegantly) point to the **real** heart of the matter: the *practice* of mindfulness. A practice that has the potential to nourish and fulfill us in ways that nothing else truly can, and bring equanimity, kindness and balance into every corner of our busy, full lives.

So, the invitation is to approach this book as Derek Wolcott (in his poem *Love After Love*) suggests we approach our very existence: 'Sit. Feast on your life.'

Steven D. Hickman, Psy.D., Clinical Psychologist, Assistant Clinical Professor, University of California at San Diego, Department of Psychiatry, Director, UCSD Center for Mindfulness

Introduction

● ●

*W*hen I was about eight years old, I discovered an amazing fact – I'm actually alive, on this planet, in this universe! And so is everyone else. The fact that there's a universe at all is amazing, but that I'm in it too . . . that was mind blowing. I started going round telling everyone, but they didn't share my excitement. I saw adults mechanically going to work and doing the shopping, and friends playing games, but I was conscious of an incredible sense of existence happening that they weren't able to share. It was like an amazing set of fireworks was exploding, but everyone was looking the wrong way.

As I grew up, I began to lose my grip on this sense of wonder until I stumbled upon mindfulness and a range of philosophies. I was relieved to find others who'd contemplated similar questions to me, and to learn a way of managing my stress at the same time. I continue to enjoy asking the big questions, and find that mindfulness beautifully compliments my natural tendency to be philosophical.

In this book you can discover how to re-ignite your perception of this mystery called life, so you aren't just existing to complete to-do lists, but are actually living. You find out how to practise mindfulness, so you can integrate a new way of being into your everyday life, helping you to cope with managing stress, challenging emotions, and increasing your general sense of wellbeing in a rich variety of different ways.

About This Book

Mindfulness For Dummies provides you with the tools to practise mindfulness on your own. Each chapter is brimming with insights about what mindfulness is, how to practise mindfulness quickly and easily, and how to deepen your experience. I wrote this book with the beginner in mind, but the knowledge goes far deeper, and experienced mindfulness practitioners will find lots of new aspects to ponder. As the research on mindfulness continues to develop rapidly, I've chosen to explain in detail the core mindfulness practices and approaches that have been tested many times before and found to be effective.

Foolish Assumptions

In writing this book, I made a few assumptions about who you are:

- ✔ You're keen to learn more about mindfulness, but don't know exactly what it is, and how to practise it.
- ✔ You are willing to have a good go at trying out the various mindfulness exercises before judging if they'll work for you.
- ✔ You're interested in the many different applications of mindfulness.
- ✔ You're not afraid of a bit of mindfulness meditation.

Beyond those, I've not assumed too much, I hope. This book is for you whether you're male or female, 18 or 88.

Icons Used in This Book

Sprinkled throughout the book you'll see various icons to guide you on your way. Icons are a *For Dummies* way of drawing your attention to important stuff, interesting stuff, and stuff you really need to know how to do.

The audio tracks that can be found on www.dummies.com and that accompany this book include a selection of guided mindfulness exercises for you to try. Find these exercises by looking for this icon.

This is stuff you need to know: whatever else you carry away from this book, note these bits with care.

Have a go at different mindfulness exercises and tips with this icon.

Take careful note of the advice under this icon, and you'll avoid unnecessary problems – ignore at your peril.

Find some precious pearls of wisdom and meaningful stories next to this icon.

Beyond the Book

In addition to the content in the print or e-book you're reading right now, this book also comes with some access-anywhere goodies on the web. Check out the free Cheat Sheet at www.dummies.com/cheatsheet/Mindfulness for a simple summary of all the key points contained in this book. This really handy sheet can be printed out for you to carry with you throughout the day, so you can dip into it for some mindfulness anytime you need to.

You can also access three unique articles about mindfulness, in addition to this book. To read those, visit www.dummies.com/extras/mindfulness.

And last but most importantly, this book also includes lots of high quality, downloadable mindfulness exercises. These exercises are available online as audio tracks. They are referred to through the book, as marked with the icon Play This, and vary in lengths from 3 minutes to 25 minutes.

To download the audio tracks to your device, go to www.dummies.com/extras/mindfulness.

Alternatively, you could even play them straight from your smart phone when you have wifi access. Be sure to bookmark the link so you can easily access the mindfulness audio tracks anytime you need them. Listening to the guided mindfulness exercises is the easiest way most people practise mindfulness as beginners.

Where to Go from Here

I've put this book together so that you can dip in and out as you please. I invite you to make good use of the Table of Contents – or the index – and jump straight into the section you fancy. You're in charge and it's up to you of course. If you're a total beginner, or not sure where to start, take a traditional approach and begin with Part I.

I wish you all the best in your mindfulness quest and hope you find something of use within these pages. Happy mindfulness!

Part I

Getting Started with Mindfulness

For Dummies can help you get started with lots of subjects. Visit www.dummies.com to learn more and do more with *For Dummies*.

In this part . . .

- ✔ Discover what mindfulness is and explore its meaning.
- ✔ Take a journey into the benefits of mindfulness living.
- ✔ Find out just what makes mindfulness so popular.

Chapter 1

Discovering Mindfulness

Mindfulness means paying attention on purpose, in the present moment, infused with qualities like kindness, curiosity and acceptance.

Through being mindful, you discover how to live in the present moment in an enjoyable way rather than worrying about the past or being concerned about the future. The past has already gone and can't be changed. The future is yet to arrive and is completely unknown. The present moment, this very moment now, is ultimately the only moment you have. Mindfulness shows you how to live in this moment in a harmonious way. You find out how to make the present moment a more wonderful moment to be in – the only place in which you can create, decide, listen, think, smile, act or live.

You can develop and deepen mindfulness through doing mindfulness meditation on a daily basis, from a few minutes to as long as you want. This chapter introduces you to mindfulness and mindfulness meditation and welcomes you aboard a fascinating journey.

Understanding the Meaning of Mindfulness

Mindfulness was originally developed in ancient times, and can be found in Eastern and Western cultures. Mindfulness is a translation of the ancient Indian word *Sati*, which means awareness, attention and remembering:

✓ **Awareness.** This is an aspect of being human that makes you conscious of your experiences. Without awareness, nothing would exist for you.

✔ **Attention.** Attention is a focused awareness; mindfulness training develops your ability to move and sustain your attention wherever and however you choose.

✔ **Remembering.** This aspect of mindfulness is about remembering to pay attention to your experience from moment to moment. Being mindful is easy to forget. The word 'remember' originally comes from the Latin *re* 'again' and *memorari* 'be mindful of'.

Awareness from the heart

The Japanese character for mindfulness is illustrated below:

This Japanese character combines the words for 'mind' and 'heart' and beautifully captures the essence of mindfulness as not just awareness, but awareness from the heart.

Say that you want to practise mindfulness to help you cope with stress. At work, you think about your forthcoming presentation and begin to feel stressed and nervous. By becoming *aware* of this, you *remember* to focus your mindful *attention* to your own breathing rather than constantly worrying. Feeling your breath with a sense of warmth and gentleness helps slowly to calm you down. See Chapter 6 for more about mindful breathing.

Dr Jon Kabat-Zinn, who first developed mindfulness in a therapeutic setting, says:

> 'Mindfulness can be cultivated by paying attention in a specific way, that is, in the present moment, and as non-reactively, non-judgementally and openheartedly as possible.'

You can break down the meaning even further:

- ✔ **Paying attention.** To be mindful, you need to pay attention, whatever you choose to attend to.

- ✔ **Present moment.** The reality of being in the here and now means you just need to be aware of the way things are, *as they are now*. Your experience is valid and correct just as it is.

- ✔ **Non-reactively.** Normally, when you experience something, you automatically react to that experience according to your past conditioning. For example, if you think, 'I still haven't finished my work,' you react with thoughts, words and actions in some shape or form.

  Mindfulness encourages you to *respond* to your experience rather than *react* to thoughts. A reaction is automatic and gives you no choice; a response is deliberate and considered action. (Chapter 12 delves deeper into mindful responses.)

- ✔ **Non-judgementally.** The temptation is to judge experience as good or bad, something you like or dislike. I want to feel bliss; I don't like feeling afraid. Letting go of judgements helps you to see things as they are rather than through the filter of your personal judgements based on past conditioning.

- ✔ **Openheartedly.** Mindfulness isn't just an aspect of mind. Mindfulness is of the heart as well. To be open-hearted is to bring a quality of kindness, compassion, warmth and friendliness to your experience. For example, if you notice yourself thinking, 'I'm useless at meditation,' you discover how to let go of this critical thought and gently turn your attention back to the focus of your meditation, whatever that may be. For more on attitudes to cultivate for mindfulness, see Chapter 4.

Looking at Mindfulness Meditation

Mindfulness meditation is a particular type of meditation that's been well researched and tested in clinical settings.

Meditation isn't thinking about nothing. Meditation is paying attention in a systematic way to whatever you decide to focus on, which can include awareness of your thoughts. By listening to your thoughts, you discover their habitual patterns. Your thoughts have a massive impact on your emotions and the decisions you make, so being more aware of them is helpful.

In mindfulness meditation, you typically focus on one, or a combination, of the following:

✔ The feeling of your own breathing

✔ Any one of your senses

✔ Your body

✔ Your thoughts or emotions

✔ Whatever is most predominant in your awareness

This book and accompanying downloadable audio (MP3s) include guided meditations.

Mindfulness meditation comes in two distinct types:

✔ **Formal meditation.** This is a meditation where you intentionally take time out in your day to embark on a meditative practice. Time out gives you an opportunity to deepen your mindfulness practice and understand more about your mind, its habitual tendencies and how to be mindful for a sustained period of time, with a sense of kindness and curiosity towards yourself and your experience. Formal meditation is mind training. Chapter 6 contains more about formal meditation.

✔ **Informal meditation.** This is where you go into a focused and meditative state of mind as you go about your daily activities such as cooking, cleaning, walking to work, talking to a friend, driving – anything at all. Think of it as everyday mindfulness. In this way, you continue to deepen your ability to be mindful, and train your mind to stay in the present moment rather than habitually straying into the past or future. Informal mindfulness meditation means you can rest in a mindful awareness at any time of day, whatever you're doing. See Chapter 8 for more ways to be mindful informally.

When I say 'practise' with regard to meditation, I don't mean a rehearsal. To practise meditation means to engage in the meditation exercise – not practising in the sense of aiming one day to get the meditation perfect. You don't need to judge your meditation or perfect it in any way. Your experience is your experience.

Using Mindfulness to Help You

You know how you get lost in thought? Most of the day, as you go about your daily activities, your mind is left to think whatever it wants. You're operating on 'automatic pilot' (explained more fully in Chapter 5). But some of your automatic thoughts may be unhelpful to you, or perhaps you're so stuck in those thoughts you don't actually experience the world around you. For example, you go for a walk in the park to relax, but your mind is lost in thoughts about your next project. First, you're not really living in the present moment, and second, you're making yourself more stressed, anxious or depressed if your thoughts are unhelpful. (Chapters 12 and 13 explore overcoming unhelpful thoughts.)

Mindfulness isn't focused on fixing problems. Mindfulness emphasises acceptance first, and change may or may not come later. So if you suffer from anxiety, mindfulness shows you how to accept the feeling of anxiety rather than denying or fighting the feeling, and through this approach change naturally comes about. As an old saying goes: 'What we resist, persists.' Mindfulness says: 'What you accept, transforms.'

This section explores the many ways in which mindfulness can help you.

In mindfulness, acceptance means to *acknowledge* your present-moment experience. Acceptance doesn't mean resignation or giving up.

Allowing space to heal

When you have a physical illness, it can be a distressing time. Your condition may be painful or even life-threatening. Perhaps your illness means you're no longer able to do the simple things in life you took for granted before, like run up the stairs or look after yourself in an independent way. Illness can shake you to your very core. How can you cope with this? How can you build your inner strength to manage the changes that take place, without being overwhelmed and losing all hope?

High levels of stress, particularly over a long period of time, have been clearly shown to reduce the strength of your immune system. Perhaps you went down with flu after a period of high stress. Research on care-givers who experience high levels of stress for long periods of time shows that they have a weaker immune system in response to diseases like flu.

Mindfulness reduces stress, and for this reason is one way of managing illness. By reducing your stress you improve the effectiveness of your immune system, and this may help increase the rate of healing from the illness you suffer, especially if the illness is stress-related.

Mindfulness can reduce stress, anxiety, pain and depression, and boost energy, creativity, the quality of relationships and your overall sense of wellbeing. The more you do mindfulness, the better: monks who've practised mindfulness all their lives have levels of wellbeing, measured in their brains, way above anything scientists thought was possible.

Chapter 14 is all about how mindfulness can help to heal the body.

Enjoying greater relaxation

Mindfulness can be a very relaxing experience. As you discover how to rest with an awareness of your breathing or the sounds around you, you may begin to feel calmer.

However, *the aim of mindfulness is not relaxation*. Relaxation is one of the welcome by-products.

Mindfulness is the development of awareness of your inner and outer experiences, whatever they are, with a sense of kindness, curiosity and acceptance. You may experience very deep states of relaxation when practising mindfulness, or you may not. If you don't, this doesn't mean you're practising mindfulness incorrectly. You just need a little patience.

Why is relaxation not the aim of mindfulness? Try being totally relaxed for the next few minutes. What if you can't relax? If you aim for relaxation, you're going to succeed or fail. If you feel you're failing, you're just going to become more tense and stressed, which is exactly what you don't want. In mindfulness, you can't fail, because you don't have some experience you have to achieve. You simply practise paying attention to whatever your experience is, as best you can, and whatever happens, happens. You gain an understanding from your experience. Mindfulness is very forgiving!

Table 1-1 shows the difference between relaxation and mindfulness exercises.

Table 1-1	Relaxation versus Mindfulness	
Exercise	*Aim*	*Method*
Mindfulness	To pay attention to your experience from moment to moment, as best you can, with kindness, curiosity and acknowledgment	To observe your experience and shift your attention back to its focus if you drift into thought, without self-criticism if you can
Relaxation	To make muscles relaxed and to feel calm	Various, such as tightening and letting go of muscles

Improving productivity

To be mindful, you usually need to do one thing at a time. When walking, you just walk. When listening, you just listen. When writing, you just write. By practising formal and informal mindfulness meditation, you're training your brain, with mindful attitudes like kindness, curiosity and acknowledgement.

So, if you're writing a report, you focus on that activity as much as you can, without overly straining yourself. Each time your mind wanders off to another thought, you notice what you were thinking about (curiosity), and then without criticising (remember you're being kind to yourself), you guide your attention back to the writing. So, you finish your report sooner (less time spent thinking about other stuff) and the work is probably of better quality (because you gave the report your full attention). The more you can focus on what you're doing, the more you can get done. Wow – mindfulness can help you improve your productivity!

You can't suddenly decide to focus on your work and then become focused. The power of attention isn't just a snap decision you make. You can train attention, just as you can train your biceps in a gym. Mindfulness is gym for the mind. However, you don't need to make a huge effort as you do when working out. When training the mind to be attentive, you need to be gentle or the mind becomes less attentive. This is why mindfulness requires kindness. If you're too harsh with yourself, your mind rebels.

Awareness also means that you notice where energy is being wasted. If you have a habit of worrying or thinking negatively, you can become aware of such thoughts and learn to stop them.

Stress is the biggest cause of absenteeism (not turning up to work). Mindfulness is one way of managing your stress levels and therefore increasing productivity, because you're more likely to stay healthy and be able to work in the first place. (Perhaps that's not a benefit, after all!)

Your work also becomes more enjoyable if you're mindful and when you're enjoying something you're more creative and productive. If you're training your mind to be curious about experience rather than bored, you can be curious about whatever you engage in.

Eventually, through experience, you begin to notice that work flows through you, rather than you doing the work. You find yourself feeding the children or making that presentation. You lose the sense of 'me' doing this and become more relaxed and at ease. When this happens, the work is effortless, often of a very high quality and thoroughly enjoyable – which sounds like a nice kind of productivity, don't you think?

Developing greater wisdom

Wisdom is regarded highly in Eastern and Western traditions. Socrates and Plato considered philosophy as literally the love of wisdom (*philo-sophia*). According to Eastern traditions, wisdom is your essential nature and leads to a deep happiness for yourself and to helping others to find that happiness within themselves too.

You can access greater wisdom. Mindfulness leads to wisdom, because you learn to handle your own thoughts and emotions skilfully. Just because you have a negative thought, you don't believe the thought to be true. And when you experience tricky emotions like sadness, anxiety or frustration, you're able to process them using mindfulness rather than being controlled by them.

With your greater emotional balance, you're able to listen deeply to others and create fulfilling, lasting relationships. With your clear mind, you're able to make better decisions. With your open heart, you can be happier and healthier.

Mindfulness leads to wisdom because of your greater level of awareness. You become aware of how you relate to yourself, others and the world around you. With this heightened awareness, you're in a much better place to make informed choices. Rather than living automatically like a robot, you're con-sciously awake and you take action based on reflection and what's in the best interest of everyone, including yourself.

I consider the Dalai Lama as an example of a wise person. He's kind and compassionate, and thinks about the welfare of others. He seeks to reduce suffering and increase happiness in humanity as a whole. He isn't egocentric, laughs a lot and doesn't seem overwhelmed with all his duties and the signifi-cant losses he's experienced. People seem to thoroughly enjoy spending time with him. He certainly seems to live in a mindful way.

Think about who you consider to be wise people. What are their qualities? I'd guess you find them to be conscious and aware of their actions, rather than habitual and lost in their own thoughts – in other words, they're mindful!

Discovering your observer self

Mindfulness can lead to an interesting journey of personal discovery. The word *person* comes from the Latin word *persona*, originally meaning a char-acter in a drama, or a mask. The word *discovery* means to dis-cover or to uncover. So in this sense, personal discovery is about uncovering your mask.

As Shakespeare said: 'All the world's a stage, and all the men and women merely players.' Through mindfulness practice, you begin to see your roles, your persona or mask(s) as part of what it means to be you. You still do everything you did before: you can keep helping people or making money or whatever you like doing, but you know that this is only one way of seeing things, one dimension of your being.

You probably wear all sorts of different masks for different roles that you play. You may be a parent, daughter or son, partner, employee. Each of these roles asks you to fulfil certain obligations. You may not be aware that it's possible to put all the masks down through mindfulness practice.

Mindfulness is an opportunity to just be yourself. When practising mindfulness meditation, you sometimes have clear experiences of a sense of being. You may feel a deep, undivided sense of peace, of stillness and calm. Your physical body, which usually feels so solid, sometimes fades into the background of your awareness, and you have a sense of connection with your surroundings.

Some people become very attached to these experiences and try hard to repeat them, as if they're 'getting closer' to something. However, over time you come to realise that even these seemingly blissful experiences also come and go. Enjoy them when they come, and then let them go.

Through the practice of mindfulness, you may come to discover that you're a witness to life's experiences. Thoughts, emotions, and bodily sensations come and go in your mindfulness practice, and yet a part of you is just observing this all happening – awareness itself. This is something very simple that everyone can see and experience. In fact, being naturally yourself is so simple, you easily overlook it.

According to Eastern philosophy, as this witness, you're perfect, whole and complete just as you are. You may not feel as if you're perfect, because you identify with your thoughts and emotions, which are always changing. Ultimately you don't need to do anything to attain this natural state, because you are this natural state all the time – right here and right now.

For these reasons, mindfulness is not about self-improvement. At the core of your being, you're perfect just the way you are! Mindfulness exercises and meditations are just to help train your brain to be more focused and calm, and your heart to be warm and open. Mindfulness is not about changing you: it's about realising that you're perfectly beautiful within, just the way you are.

Eckhart Tolle, author of *A New Earth: Create a Better Life*, says:

> '*What a liberation to realize that the "voice in my head" is not who I am. Who am I then? The one who sees that.*'

Once you discover that you're the witness of all experience, you're less disturbed by the ups and downs of life. This understanding offers you a way to a happier life. It's that little bit easier to go with the flow and see life as an adventure rather than just a series of struggles.

Starting the Mindfulness Adventure

Mindfulness isn't a quick fix, but the adventure of a lifetime. Imagine mindfulness as being like a journey on a boat. You're an explorer looking for new and undiscovered land. Along the way I'll explain how mindfulness mirrors such a journey.

Beginning the voyage

The journey begins, and you set sail. You're not sure what you're going to find, and you may not be too sure why you're going in the first place, but that's part of the excitement and adventure. You may think that you're finally doing something you really enjoy and can gain from. This is what you wanted to do, and you're on the boat now. At the same time, you're a bit anxious about what may happen – what if things don't work out?

The beginning of the mindfulness journey may feel like this for you. You may be thinking, 'Finally, I've found what I need to do,' and you're keen to find out how to do it, being curious and in anticipation. At the same time, you may feel unsure that you can 'do' mindfulness: you suspect you don't have the patience/focus/discipline/inner strength. You have *ideas* about the journey of mindfulness. At the moment you may suffer from *x* and *y*, and after reading this book you want to have reduced those painful feelings. You may have clear goals you want to achieve and hope mindfulness is going to help you to achieve those goals.

Having a long-term vision as to what you hope to achieve from mindfulness is helpful, but concentrating too much on goals is unhelpful. Mindfulness is ultimately a goalless activity. Mindfulness is process-oriented rather than goal-oriented. You're not actually going anywhere. This is the paradox of mindfulness. If you get overly obsessed with the goals, you focus on the goal rather than the process. However, mindfulness is the journey itself. You aren't going to reach the present moment sometime in the future: you can only be in the present moment *now*. More important than anything else is how you meet this moment. If you can train yourself to be open, curious, accepting, kind and aware of this moment, the future takes care of itself. So, as you steer your boat, keep aware and awake. See Chapter 3 for more about vision in mindfulness.

Overcoming challenges

As you continue your mindfulness journey, before long the initial excitement begins to wear off. You experience rough seas and pirates! Some days, you wish you hadn't started this journey in the first place. Perhaps you should have just stayed at home.

Regularly practising mindfulness can be challenging. What was new and exciting to begin with no longer feels fresh. You may sense a resistance to sit down and meditate, even for a short period, but without knowing why. Don't worry: this is very common. When you overcome the initial resistance, you may discover the practice isn't as bad as you imagined meditating to be. As soon as you start, you feel okay and even enjoy it. You also feel great afterwards, because you managed to overcome the initial resistance of your mind to do something for your own health and wellbeing.

Each time you struggle with the thoughts and feelings in your mindfulness practice, you're generally not accepting or acknowledging them as the natural state of your mind. Lack of acknowledgement usually means criticism of yourself or of the whole process of mindfulness. If you persevere, you discover slowly but surely the importance of accepting your thoughts and emotions and the situation you're in and not blaming anyone for that situation, including yourself. In mindfulness, acceptance always comes first; change follows.

Another common challenge is understanding the right attitude to bring to your mindfulness practice. Unhelpful but common attitudes include:

- I'm going do this and must get it right.
- I should focus 100 per cent.
- I'm going to try extremely hard.

Having done a bit of mindfulness meditation, you get thoughts like 'I can't focus at all' or 'My mind was all over the place. I can't do it' or 'That was a bad meditation.' However, as you continue your journey of mindfulness, your attitudes begin to shift towards thoughts such as:

- I'm going to bring an attitude of kindness and curiosity, and acknowledge whatever my experience is, as best I can.
- I won't try too hard, nor will I give up. I'll stay somewhere in the middle.
- My mind is bound to wander off. That's okay and part of being mindful.
- There's no such thing as a bad meditation.

Reaching the other side

One day, a young man was going for a walk when he reached a wide river. He spent a long time wondering how he would cross such a gushing current. Just when he was about to give up his journey, he saw his teacher on the other side. The young man shouted from the bank: 'Can you tell me how to get to the other side of this river?'

The teacher smiled and replied: 'My friend, you are on the other side.'

You may feel that you have to change, when actually you just have to realise that perhaps you're fine just the way you are. You're running to achieve goals so that you can be peaceful and happy, but actually you're running away from the peace and happiness. Mindfulness is an invitation to stop running and rest. You're already on the other side.

As your attitudes change, mindful exercises and meditations becomes easier, because you're bombarded by fewer judgemental thoughts during and after the practice. And even if you do have judgemental thoughts, you treat them like all the other thoughts you experience and let them go as best you can.

Exploring the journey of a lifetime

After sailing for a long time, you finally see some land in the distance that's more beautiful than anything you've seen in your exploration. You decide to stop when you get there. The land looks so new and fresh, but at the same time very familiar and cosy. As you draw closer, you discover that you're approaching your own house. Of all the places you've been and all the adventures you've had, you feel most at home here, the place you left! However, the journey hasn't been fruitless. You've discovered much along the way and had to travel that journey to discover what you most treasure.

Ultimately in mindfulness, you realise that you don't need to search for anything at all. Everything is okay just the way things are. You're already home. Each moment is magical, new and fresh. Each moment is a treasure never to be repeated again, ever. Your awareness is always shining, lighting up the world around you and inside you effortlessly. Awareness has no off or on switch: awareness is always effortlessly on. Although you experience ups and downs, pleasures and pain, you no longer hang onto things as much, and you therefore suffer less. This isn't so much a final goal as an ongoing journey of a lifetime. Life continues to unfold in its own way, and you begin to grasp how to flow with life.

Buddha is quoted as saying:

> 'The secret of health for both mind and body is not to mourn for the past, worry about the future, or anticipate troubles, but to live in the present moment wisely and earnestly.'

The journey of mindfulness is to discover how to live this way.

A taste of mindfulness: Mindfulness of Senses

You may like to experience a little mindfulness. You could read endlessly about what a coconut tastes like, but you won't really know till you taste it yourself. The same goes for mindfulness.

The beauty of this simple mindfulness exercise is that it covers everything you need to know about mindfulness. I have adapted the exercise from a technique I discovered at a 'school of practical philosophy' many years ago. I would like to pass on the gift to you.

This exercise is best done by listing to Track 2 from the audio. Find a comfortable posture for you. You can sit up in a chair, a couch or lie down on a mat – whatever you prefer. Begin by noticing the colours entering your eyes. Notice the tones, shades and hues. Enjoy the miracle of sight that some people don't have. Then, gently close your eyes and be aware of the sense of touch. The sensations of your body. The feeling of your body naturally and automatically breathing. Feel areas of tension and relaxation. Next, be aware of scent. Then move on to any taste in your mouth.

Next, become aware of sounds. Sounds near and far. Listen to the sound itself, not so much your thoughts about the sounds. Let go of all effort when listening – allow the sounds to come to you. Finally drop into your observer self – the awareness that lights up all your senses. Rest in that background awareness, whatever that means for you. The feeling of 'being'. The feeling of 'I am' that we all have. Just let go of all effort to do something, and just be. . .and when you're ready, bring this mindful exercise to a close and stretch your body if you wish.

Consider these questions:

What effect did that exercise have on your body and mind? What did you discover?

If you want to become more mindful, you could simply practise this exercise a few times a day. The exercise is simple but powerful and transformative when practised regularly.

Chapter 2

Enjoying the Benefits of Mindfulness

*T*he enjoyment that comes from mindfulness is a bit like the enjoyment that comes from dancing. Do you dance because of the cardiovascular benefits or for boosting your brain by following a tricky dance routine? When you dance with a goal or motive in mind, it kind of spoils it a bit, doesn't it? Dancing for the sake of dancing is far more fun. But of course, dancing for the sheer pleasure of it doesn't reduce the benefits on your mind and body of dancing – they're just the icing on the cake.

In the same way, be mindful for the sake of being mindful. Mindfulness is about connecting with your senses, being curious, exploring the inner workings of the human mind. If you're too concerned about reaping the benefits of mindfulness, you spoil the fun of it. The journey of mindfulness isn't to reach a certain destination: the journey *is* the destination. Keep this in mind as you read about the various benefits of mindfulness described in this chapter, and let the dance of mindfulness unfold within you. The benefits of mindfulness – relaxation, better mental and emotional health, and an improved relationship with yourself and others – are just the added bonuses along the way. Read on to discover how mindfulness can help you.

Relaxing the Body

The body and mind are almost one entity. If your mind is tense with anxious thoughts, your body automatically tenses as well. They go together, hand in hand.

Why does your body become tense when you experience high levels of stress? The reason is mechanical and wired in the human body. When you experience stress, a chain reaction starts in your body, and your whole being prepares to fight or flee the situation. So a lot of energy surges through your body; because your body doesn't know what to do with this energy, you tense up.

The aim of mindfulness isn't to simply make you more relaxed. Mindfulness goes far deeper than that. Mindfulness – a mindful awareness – is about becoming aware and exploring your moment-by-moment experience, in a joyful way if at all possible.

So if you're tense, mindfulness means becoming aware of that tension. Which part of your body feels tense? What shape, colour and texture is that tension? What's your reaction to the tension; what are your thoughts? Mindfulness is about bringing curiosity to your experience. Then you can begin breathing into the tense part of your body, bringing kindness and acknowledging your experience – again, not trying to change or get rid of the tension. And that's it. Rest assured, doing this often leads to relaxation. See Chapter 12 for more on stress reduction.

Getting back in touch

As a baby, you were probably very much in touch with your body. You noticed subtle sensations, and may have enjoyed feeling different textures in the world around you. As you grew up, you learnt to use your head more and your body less. You probably aren't as in touch with your body as you were as a young child. You may not notice subtle messages that the body gives you through the mind. I'm sure that some people see the body as simply a vehicle for carrying the brain from one meeting to another!

In fact, the messages between your mind and body are a two-way process. Your mind gives signals to your body, and your body gives signals to your mind. You think, 'I fancy reading that mindfulness book,' and your body picks it up. You feel hungry, and your body signals to your mind that it's time to eat. What about the feeling of stress? If you notice the tension in your shoulders, the twitch in your eye, or the rapid beating of your heart, again your body is sending signals to your mind.

What if your mind is so busy with its own thoughts that it doesn't even notice the signals from your body? When this happens, you're no longer in touch with or looking after your body. Hunger and thirst, tiredness and stress – you're no longer hearing clearly your instinctual messages. This leads to a further disconnection between bodily signals and your mind, so things can get worse. Stress can spiral out of control though this lack of awareness.

Mindfulness emphasises awareness of your body. An important mindfulness meditation is the body scan (described in full in Chapter 6). In this meditation, you spend 10–30 minutes simply being guided to pay attention to different parts of your body, from the tips of your toes to the top of your head. Some people's reaction is, 'Wow, I've never paid so much attention to my body; that was interesting!' or 'I now feel I'm moving back into my body.'

The body scan meditation can offer a healing experience. Emotions you experienced in the past but weren't ready to feel, perhaps because you were too young, can be suppressed and trapped in the body. Sometimes, people suffer for years from a particular physical ailment, but doctors are unable to explain the cause of it. Then, through counselling or meditation, the suppressed emotion arises into consciousness, which releases the emotion. The tightness in the body or the unexplained 'dis-ease' sometimes disappear with the release of the emotion. This is another example of how interconnected mind and body really are, and of the benefits of getting back in touch with the body. Chapter 14 has more on healing the body through mindfulness.

The cracked pot

Once upon a time there was a water bearer who carried two pots of water to his teacher each day. Each day he would walk to the nearest stream, fill both pots with water, and walk back, one pot on each side of a pole he carried across his neck. One pot was cracked, and so by the time the water bearer reached his teacher, it was only half full. This continued for two years, with the water bearer only bringing one and a half pots of water. The perfect pot was proud of its achievements. The cracked pot was sad that it could only do half the job it was supposed to do. One day, the cracked pot said to the water bearer, 'I feel so upset and ashamed. I'm imperfect and I can't hold a full pot of water. What use am I to anyone?' The water bearer told the cracked pot to look on the ground as he carried it. The cracked pot noticed the most beautiful wild flowers and plants on its side of the path. The water bearer explained, 'When I realised you were cracked, I decided to plant seeds on one side of the path, and every day, as you leak, you water that side of the path. If you weren't cracked, these gorgeous flowers wouldn't be here for all to enjoy.'

Sometimes you may think you're not perfect, or your mindfulness practice is not perfect, but how do you know? This story goes to show that even a cracked pot can be seen as perfect just as it is. In the same way, you're perfect just the way you are, with all your imperfections – they're what make you unique.

Boosting your immune system

If something's wrong with your body, normally your immune system fights it. Unfortunately, one aspect of the stress response is your immune system not working as hard. When threatened, your body puts all its resources into surviving that threat; energy required for digestion or immunity is turned off temporarily.

Stress isn't necessarily bad for you. If your stress levels are too low, you're unable to perform effectively and get bored easily. However, if you're stressed for sustained periods of time at high levels, your body's natural immune system is going to stop working properly.

The latest research has found that if you have a positive attitude towards stress, seeing stress as energising and uplifting, the stress seems to have little negative effect on your body. So even your attitude towards stress has an effect.

Mindfulness enables you to notice subtle changes in your body. At the first sign of excessive stress, you can bring a mindful awareness to the situation and discover how to dissipate the stress rather than exacerbate it. By being mindful, you can also remember to see the positive, energising benefits of stress rather than just its negatives. In this way, mindfulness can really benefit your immune system.

Reducing pain

Amazingly, mindfulness has been proven to actually reduce the level of pain experienced by people practising it over a period of eight weeks. I've had clients who couldn't find anything to help them manage and cope with their pain until they began using mindfulness meditation.

When you experience pain, you quite naturally want to block that pain out. You tighten your muscles around the region and make an effort to distract yourself. Another approach is that you want the pain to stop, so you react towards the pain in an angry way. This creates greater tension, not only in the painful region but in other areas of the body. Sometimes you may feel like fighting the pain. This creates a duality between you and your pain, and you burn energy to battle with it. Or perhaps you react with resignation: the pain has got the better of you and you feel helpless.

Mindfulness takes a radically different approach. In mindfulness, you're encouraged to pay attention to the sensation of pain, as far as you can. So, if your knee is hurting, rather than distracting yourself or reacting in any other way, you actually focus on the area of physical pain with a mindful awareness.

This means you bring attitudes like kindness, curiosity and acknowledgment towards the area of pain, as best you can. This isn't easy at first, but you can get better with practice. You can then consider the difference between the sensation of the physical pain itself and all the other stuff you bring to the pain. You begin to understand the difference between *physical* pain and *psychological* pain. The physical pain is the actual raw sensation of pain in the body, whereas the psychological pain is the stress, anxiety, and frustration generated. Through mindfulness, you begin to let go of psychological pain so that only the physical pain is left. When the psychological pain begins to dissolve, the muscle tension around the physical pain begins to loosen, further reducing the perception of pain. You begin to be able to accept the pain as it is in this present moment. Read Chapter 14 for more about mindfulness and physical healing.

Slowing down the ageing process

Have you ever wondered why people die of old age? What exactly is the ageing process? Scientists have discovered that ageing occurs quite naturally in your cells. The scientists (Elizabeth Blackburn and colleagues) who discovered this won the Nobel Prize in medicine back in 2009 for this finding.

All your cells contain *DNA* – the information needed to reproduce each cell. These bundles of DNA are protected with small caps called *telomeres*, which are like the protective ends of shoelaces. The caps prevent the chains of DNA from fraying.

The older you get, the more these caps shorten. Eventually they disappear completely and your cells are unable to reproduce. That's called dying of old age.

This wearing out of the caps at the ends of DNA bundles is associated with many diseases of old age like cancer, heart disease, diabetes and arthritis. Previously, scientists thought that this shortening of telomeres was inevitable.

The good news, however, is that the lower your level of stress, the slower these telomeres wear out. Research on groups that practice mindfulness meditation has shown that telomeres can actually be lengthened. This is an incredible finding. A mental discipline of mindfulness affected the microscopic genes in the bodies of those in the study and effectively reduced the rate of ageing. Those mindful meditators who felt the most positive benefit were the ones with the most improved telomere lengths.

So, no more need for Botox, anti-ageing cream or plastic surgery. Just practise mindfulness – it's cheaper and you'll probably look more beautiful and live to a ripe old age!

Don't try harder

A martial arts student went to his teacher and said earnestly: 'I'm devoted to studying your martial system. How long will it take me to master it?' The teacher's reply was casual: 'Ten years.' Impatiently, the student answered: 'But I want to master it faster than that. I'll work very hard. I'll practise every day – ten or more hours a day if I have to. How long will it take then?' The teacher thought for a moment and replied: 'Twenty years.'

What does this story mean to you? To me, it shows that hard work and attaining a goal don't necessarily go together. Sometimes, especially when practising something like mindfulness, you need simply to let things unfold in their own time. If you're anxious, you may just block your understanding. Mindfulness is about letting go, not trying harder.

Calming the Mind

Your mind is like the ocean: occasionally wild, and at other times calm. Sometimes your mind goes from thought to thought without stopping to rest. At other times, your thoughts come more slowly and have more space between them.

Mindfulness isn't so much about changing the rate of your thoughts, but about noticing the thoughts arising in the first place. By taking a step back from thoughts, you can hover above the waves. The waves are still there, but you have more possibility of watching the show rather than being controlled by the thoughts themselves.

Think of your mind like a good friend. If you invited your friend to your home, how do you treat her? Should you force her to drink coffee, eat three chocolate biscuits, and listen to you talk about your day even if she doesn't want to? She may prefer tea and plain biscuits, and want to talk about her day too. You *ask* her what she'd like, in a kind and friendly manner. In the same way, treat your mind like a friend. Invite your mind to pay attention to your breath or the work you're doing. When you notice that your mind is restless, acknowledge this. Smile and gently ask your mind to re-focus. The gentle approach is the only way. Then your mind will naturally clear in its own time.

Listening to your thoughts

Everything man-made around you was originally a thought in someone's head. Many people consider thought to be all-powerful. All your words, all your actions and activities – everything is motivated by thought. So, being aware of the kind of thoughts going through your mind makes sense.

Have you ever noticed how you have the same sort of thoughts going around and around in your head? The brain easily gets into habitual patterns as your thoughts travel their paths within your brain. *Neurons that fire together, wire together.* Each time you have a particular thought or carry out a particular action, you slightly increase the chance of having the same thought again. Through repeated thinking or action, the connection between neurons strengthens. If you aren't mindful of these thoughts or actions, you may have all sorts of negative, untrue, unhelpful thoughts or behaviours that influence your life without you even being aware of them or questioning the truth or validity of them.

For example, let's say a client gives you negative feedback for some work you did. The thought 'I'm not good enough for this job' or 'That person is so stupid' may keep going around and around your head. You feel rough, your sleep is impacted and you can't properly focus on today's tasks. That's not a great help. But fret not: mindfulness to the rescue!

Mindfulness encourages you to watch your thoughts, emotions, and actions; then you're better able to notice unhelpful thoughts and question their truth. Additionally, just being mindful of thoughts and emotions with a sense of warmth seems to naturally dissipate them. They become far less of a problem. Turn to Chapter 6 for a sitting meditation that includes mindfulness of thoughts and emotions.

Your brain is telling you stories

Scientists are interested in how the sense of self is created in your brain. You know that you're alive, but how? That's what scientists are studying.

Researchers discovered that your brain is constantly telling you stories. Stories about who you are, what your relationship is to the people you're with, where you're going, what you're going to do this week, and so on. Let's call this your story-telling self. But what if you're telling yourself negative stories? Stories about how you're not good enough and that you're undeserving of happiness and success. It can become a real energy drain.

Fortunately, I've got good news for you. The story-telling self isn't always in operation. There's also a present-moment self. When this part of your brain is activated, you're living in the here and now, connected with your senses. People who practise mindfulness exercises can increase the amount of time they operate with this present-moment self, and can help themselves to become happier people!

So watch out when your mind is telling stories about you, especially discouraging stories, and then smile and turn your attention to one of your senses. By smiling, you're helping yourself see the positive side of your situation rather that setting up a battle in your mind. And connecting with your senses helps to disengage the ruminative, story-telling brain from taking over your mind.

Making better decisions

Every moment of every day you make decisions, whether you're aware of them or not. You made a decision to read this chapter. At some point, you'll decide to stop and do something else. Even if you decide to make no decisions, that's a decision too! More significant decisions you have to make have a bigger impact, and a 'good' decision is highly desirable. All you do and have at the moment is mostly due to the decisions you made in the past.

Awareness of your body can help you make better decisions: a gut feeling is a signal from your belly telling you what to do, and has been found in some experiments to be faster and more accurate than logical thinking. Research shows a mass of nerves in the gut that's like a second brain. This intuition is routinely used by top CEOs of corporations to make critical decisions.

Richard Branson, founder of the Virgin Group, says he makes most of his decisions based on gut instinct. If he relied on pure logical thinking and advice from accountants, he wouldn't have started Virgin Atlantic, Virgin Galactic or many of his other ventures. Relying on his feelings, and not just pure reason, has made him both a multi-billionaire and great philanthropist.

Why is gut feeling so effective? Your unconscious mind has far more information than your conscious mind can handle. Making decisions just based on conscious logical thought misses out on the huge capacity of the subconscious brain. Mindfulness helps to deepen your level of awareness, and helps you to begin to tap into your intuitive, subconscious side.

Coming to your senses

One of the key ways of becoming more mindful and of calming the mind is to connect with your senses: sight, sound, touch, smell, and taste. Consider the expressions, 'That was *sens*ible,' 'I *sense* something's wrong,' and 'She's come to her *senses*.' People's use of the word 'sense' shows we appreciate and value being in touch with our organs of perception. You know innately the value of connecting to your senses if you want to make a *sens*ible decision.

What's the benefit of purposefully connecting with your senses? Well, if you aren't paying attention to the stimulation coming through your five senses, you're only paying attention to your thoughts and emotions. You're not aware of anything else. Your thoughts are mainly based on your experiences from the past – from memory. You may imagine something new, but on the whole your mind reworks past experiences or projects ideas into the future based on your past experiences. Emotions are also influenced by your thoughts. So, without paying attention to your senses, you're stuck with your own thoughts and emotions based on the past instead of the present.

By purposefully connecting with one of your senses – say, touch – you begin naturally to calm your mind a little. In mindfulness you can begin by focusing on your breathing. Focus on your belly stretching or your chest expanding, or perhaps the movement of the air as it enters and leaves your body. By focusing on a particular sense, in this case the sense of touch, you're focusing your attention. Rather than your mind wandering wherever it pleases, you're gently training it to stay on one object, namely your breathing. And in the same way as you train a puppy to walk along a path and not keep running off, each time your attention strays, you bring it back, just as you would gently pull the puppy back to the path. You're discovering how to be gentle with yourself, as well as finding out how to focus your attention. See Chapter 6 for a short mindful breathing meditation.

By coming to your senses mindfully, you are:

✔ Training your attention to focus

✔ Being kind to yourself when your mind wanders off

✔ Realising that you have a certain amount of choice about what you pay attention to

✔ Understanding that you can deliberately choose to shift attention away from thinking and into the senses

✔ Calming your mind and developing a sense of clarity

Creating an attentive mind

Attention is essential in achieving anything. If you can't pay attention, you can't get the job done, whatever the job is. Mindfulness trains your attention by sustaining your attention on one thing, or by switching the type of attention from time to time.

Daniel Goleman, author of the book *Emotional Intelligence: Why It Can Matter More Than IQ*, recently published a book called *Focus: The Hidden Driver of Excellence*. He explains just how important focus is in every domain of our lives. He also identified a research study that imaged the brains of people practising mindfulness of breath (try it yourself in Chapter 6). Researchers found four different stages while the brain went through the following mental workout:

1. **Focus on your breathing.** The part of the brain that deals with focus is activated.

2. **Notice that your brain is on a train of thought.** The part of the brain that notices that your attention has drifted off into a train of thought is activated.

3. **Let go of that train of thought.** The part of the brain that enables you to let go of your thoughts is activated.

4. **Refocus on your breathing.** The part of the brain used to re-focus on the object you wish to focus on is re-activated.

The parts of the brain dedicated to each of these processes were strengthened through repeated mindfulness practice.

If you do this exercise regularly, you'll become more adept at focusing on whatever you need to pay attention to – whether it's writing an email, listening to a loved one or watching a sunset.

Your attention can be focused in different ways (shown in Figure 2-1):

✔ Narrow attention is focused and sharp, like the beam of a laser. You may use this type of attention when chopping vegetables or writing a letter.

✔ Wide attention is more open and spacious, like a floodlight. When you're driving, ideally your attention is open so you notice if a car moves closer to you from the side, or if children are playing farther ahead.

✔ Outer attention is attention to the outer world through your senses.

✔ Inner attention is an awareness of your thoughts and feelings.

✔ Observer or witness awareness is your capacity to know what type of attention you're using. For example, if you're drawing a picture, you're aware that your attention is narrow. If you're walking through the countryside, you're aware that your attention is wide. For more on witness awareness, see the section 'Becoming Aware: Discovering Yourself' below.

Empty your cup

A professor once went to visit a teacher of mindfulness. The professor was a world-famous scholar of mindfulness and had studied all the different methods. He knew all the Eastern scriptures and Western science on the subject. He could answer any question on mindfulness with ease and a sense of pride.

The teacher asked if he would like a cup of tea, and the professor said yes. The teacher began filling the cup until it was full, and kept going. The tea was overflowing, and the teacher continued to pour. 'What are you doing! The cup is already full!' exclaimed the professor, panicking. 'You are like this cup,' said the teacher calmly. 'How can I teach you anything of real value until you empty your cup?'

If you want to benefit from mindfulness, you need to put aside all your ideas about it, especially if you think you know what mindfulness is all about. Opinions, ideas, and beliefs block the beauty and simplicity of mindfulness.

All the different mindfulness meditations you read about in this book train your mind to be able to sustain attention in the various different ways mentioned in the preceding list.

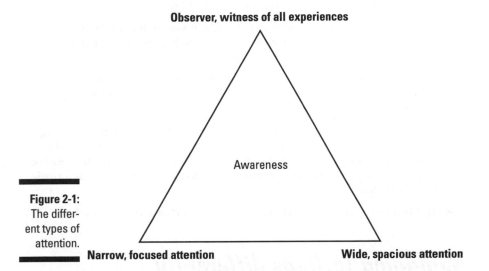

Observer, witness of all experiences

Awareness

Figure 2-1:
The different types of attention.

Narrow, focused attention   **Wide, spacious attention**

Soothing Your Emotions

Emotions are tremendously influential on your behaviour and thoughts. If you're feeling low, you're probably far more reluctant to go out with friends, or laugh at a joke, or work with zest. If you're feeling great, you're on top of things; everything feels easy, and life flows easily.

How do you deal with emotions? Are you swept up by them, and do you just hope for the best? Mindfulness offers the opportunity to soothe yourself and step back from emotional ups and downs.

Understanding your emotions

What's an emotion, a feeling, or mood?

You experience emotion partly from a survival point of view. If you don't feel scared when faced with a raging bull, you'll find yourself in lots of trouble. Other emotions, like happiness, help to create social ties with those around you, increasing your security. Even depression is thought to have evolved for your protection, reducing motivation and therefore the chance of experiencing harm or wasting energy through pursuing an unattainable goal.

Emotion comes from a Latin word meaning 'to move out'. If you observe emotions, you can discover certain important characteristics:

✔ **Emotions are always changing.** You aren't stuck with one emotion all your life, at the same intensity.

✔ **Emotions are a very physical experience.** If you're feeling anxious, you may feel a tingling in your stomach. If you're feeling angry, you may feel your breathing and heart rate go up.

✔ **You can observe your own emotions.** You can sense the difference between yourself and your emotions. You're not your emotions, you're the observer of your emotions.

✔ **Emotions make a huge impact on your thoughts.** When you're feeling down, you're likely to predict negative things about yourself or other people. When you're feeling happy, you're more likely to think positive thoughts, predict positive outcomes, and look upon the past in a positive light too.

✔ **You tend to perceive emotions as pleasant, unpleasant, or neutral.**

Managing feelings differently

Take a few minutes to consider the following emotions and how you deal with them:

✔ Anger

✔ Anxiety

✔ Fear

✔ Depression

Your approach may be to either avoid the emotion and pretend it isn't there, or to express your feelings to whoever is nearby. Mindfulness offers an alternative – a way of meeting emotions that enables you to see them in a different light. The idea is to acknowledge and give mindful attention to difficult feelings, rather than avoid or react to them. Surprisingly, this tends to dissipate the strength and the pain of the emotion. See Chapters 12 and 13 for ways of dealing with a variety of different emotions.

My first experience of mindfulness was exciting, because my emotional state was quickly changed to a sense of calmness and joy. In fact, I didn't even know I was previously stressed! The feeling of stress was just my normal state of mind. I was amazed that such a short mindfulness exercise could have such a powerful effect. I immediately had a desire to share this new-found technique with others.

The guesthouse

This superb poem by Rumi (1207–1273) captures the attitude you're moving towards when dealing with emotions mindfully.

> This being human is a guesthouse.
>
> Every morning a new arrival.
>
> A joy, a depression, a meanness,
>
> some momentary awareness comes
>
> as an unexpected visitor.
>
> Welcome and entertain them all!
>
> Even if they're a crowd of sorrows
>
> who violently sweep your house
>
> empty of its furniture,
>
> still, treat each guest honourably.
>
> He may be clearing you out
>
> for some new delight.
>
> The dark thought, the shame, the malice,
>
> meet them at the door laughing,
>
> and invite them in.
>
> Be grateful for whoever comes,
>
> because each has been sent
>
> as a guide from beyond.

Knowing Thyself: Discovering Your Observer Self

Before examining my sense of self and relationship with the world, I used to believe that I was a tiny, isolated human being living in the corner of a city on a planet called Earth, fighting to survive and hopefully thrive. However, through mindfulness I began to discover a totally different and satisfying dimension of myself that I'd overlooked. Mindfulness helps you to see things from a more holistic perspective. Having a sense of a deeper dimension and connection with the world around you puts the waves of life's challenges into a much bigger context. If you're the ocean, what trouble do waves give you?

Inscribed above the ancient Greek temple of Apollo at Delphi is the phrase 'Know thyself,' a vitally important concept for Greek philosophers like Socrates. But self-reflection isn't advocated so much in the twenty-first century!

Who are you? What is this incredible thing called life? These are the questions I've often grappled with. While making money and spending time with friends was fun, it lacked any sense of depth. So I found myself in a mindfulness class. Life was too wonderful and mysterious to be lived without meaning or purpose.

The lion and the sheep

Mindfulness naturally leads to self-examination – examination of who's doing the mindfulness in the first place. The following story may help to illustrate the realisation that can take place.

A lion cub accidentally strayed away from its mother, and ended up with a flock of sheep. The lion cub grew up with the other sheep, ate what the other sheep ate, and behaved like them too. As the lion grew up he continued to behave in the same way, frightened of the subtlest sounds. However, something just didn't feel right. One day, he looked into a still pool of water and saw a beautifully clear reflection of himself. He was a lion, not a sheep. Because he'd believed himself to be like the other sheep,

he behaved and thought like one. Now that he saw who he truly was, everything changed, and yet he was just the same as he always was. He returned to his pride and lived according to his true nature.

In the same way, if you identify yourself with thoughts like 'I can never talk to her!' or emotions like 'I am depressed,' you're like the lion identifying itself as a sheep. Mindfulness shows you that you're much bigger that fleeting thoughts and emotions; you're also awareness itself. Then you see thoughts as just thoughts and emotions as just emotions. They're not reality: they're just a passing experience.

Mindfulness helps you to put things in perspective. If you go from place to place, rushing to finish all that stuff on your to-do list, and when you're done are so exhausted that you just collapse in front of the television, you may have a bit of a problem discovering who you truly are in the meantime. By taking some time to be mindful, you're giving yourself the opportunity to stop and look at all these incessant thoughts and emotions that come and go, and discover the sense of being that's behind the mind chatter. A part of yourself that's peaceful, joyous and whole.

This book describes one approach to discovering your sense of self that I've found immensely liberating and fascinating. Self-discovery is a personal journey, so you may have a totally different way of understanding your deep, inner being.

Read each of these paragraphs as slowly as you can. Notice your judgements and desire to agree or disagree with the statements. Try doing neither, and instead just read and reflect.

✔ **Are you just your body?** Your body is made up of hundreds of millions of cells. Cells are dying and re-forming all the time. Every few years, pretty much all the cells in your body are replaced with new ones – so your body is completely different to the one you had as a baby. Right now, you're digesting food, your nails and hair are growing, and your immune system is fighting any diseases within you. It's all just happening – you're not doing it. Even if your body becomes totally paralysed, the sense of you being here will still be present. The very fact that you say 'my body' suggests that the body is something you *have*, rather than your core self.

✔ **Are you just your thoughts?** Thoughts keep coming, no matter how mindful you are. The fact that you can be aware of your thoughts means that you are separate from them. If you were your thoughts, you wouldn't be able to notice them. The fact that you can observe your thoughts means they're separate and a space lies between you and what you think. In mindfulness practice, you can step back from your thoughts from time to time, but you can't control thoughts. Do you even know what you're going to think in the next few minutes? No. But can you be *aware* of your thoughts? Yes.

✔ **Are you just your emotions?** Just as you can observe thoughts, you can also observe your emotions. Doesn't this mean you're separate from your emotions? Emotions arise and eventually pass away. If you were your emotions, then your emotions would never pose any problem at all. You would be able to control emotions and wouldn't choose to have negative feelings.

So, what are you? What's left? Let's call it the observer self. There's no specific word in the English language for this. If you're the observer, you can't be that which you observe. In this sense you can say *you are awareness.* Thoughts and ideas, emotions and images, desires, fears and actions arise *in you* but you're aware of them all. Everything arises *in awareness*, in being. That's what you are. You aren't just the thought 'I'm Shamash' or 'I'm Jane;' you're that sense of presence that underlies experience.

Some of the attributes of awareness or the observer self are:

✔ **You're always aware.** Sometimes that awareness is lost in thoughts and dreams; sometimes it's connected with the senses.

✔ **Awareness happens by itself.** Awareness is different to attention. Attention or *mindful* awareness is something to be cultivated and trained, which is what most of this book is about, but *pure* awareness is your inner self. To be aware takes no effort. You don't need to *do* awareness. Awareness is effortlessly operating right now as you read. You can't turn off or run away from awareness!

✔ **Awareness comes before thought.** As a baby, you had awareness without words and ideas. Thoughts and concepts come after awareness.

✔ **In terms of awareness, you're both 'no-thing' and everything.** Without awareness, nothing would exist for you. With awareness, you're a part of every experience you have. This sounds contradictory, but look into these concepts yourself. Ask yourself what your daily experience would be like without awareness.

Having read all these attributes of awareness, what's your reaction? Whether you believe these ideas or not isn't important; what *is* important is examining and exploring these ideas for yourself. As Socrates said, 'The unexamined life is not worth living.' I've personally found looking deeper into my identity to be completely transformative and liberating – mindful self-discovery is the ultimate exploration for me!

Spend a few minutes resting as an observer of your moment-to-moment experience. This can turn out to be an incredibly peaceful experience. That's a meditation in itself. No need to react to your thoughts, emotions, or any other sensations. Just watch the experiences arise and fall again. Be the observer self. And if you find yourself trying too hard, don't forget to smile! That'll remind you that this is a non-doing process – not just another thing that requires a lot of effort. To experience this further, see the sitting mediation in Chapter 6. It's called 'open awareness'.

The story of the stonemason

Once upon a time a stonemason paused to rest from his hard work for a few minutes at the side of an enormous rock. He saw a lord and his servants pass underneath the shade of the trees nearby.

When the stonemason saw this rich lord with all his luxuries and comfort, his work suddenly felt much harder. 'Oh, if only I were a rich man,' he thought, 'I'd be so happy!' Suddenly a voice answered from the mountain: 'Your wish shall become reality; a rich man you shall be!'

When the stonemason returned home, he found a beautiful palace where his simple home had stood. The poor man was overflowing with joy, and before long his old life was completely forgotten. One day, when he was walking in the marketplace, he felt the Sun burn on his face, and he wished he was as mighty as the Sun itself. Immediately he became the Sun.

As the Sun, he felt all-powerful. His light shone around the entire world, and his rays beamed on kings and cobblers alike. But before long, a cloud moved in front of him and obscured his light. 'What's this?' he wondered. 'A cloud is mightier than me! Oh, how I wish I were a cloud.'

And a cloud he became. He blocked the Sun's beams, and for weeks he poured rain until the rivers overflowed their banks and the crops of rice stood in water. Towns and villages were destroyed by the sheer power of the rain, but he noticed that only the great rock on the mountainside remained unmoved. 'What's this?' he cried. 'A rock is mightier than me! Oh how I wish I were a rock.'

And the rock he became, and he gloried in the power. Proudly he stood, and neither the heat of the Sun nor the force of rain could move him. 'This is the best!' he said to himself. But soon he heard a strange noise at his feet, and when he looked down he saw a stonemason breaking him up, piece by piece. Then he cried in his anger: 'Oh, if only I were a stonemason!'

In that instant, he became the stonemason once again, and remained content as he was for the rest of his life.

Part II
Preparing the Ground for Mindful Living

Doing

More likely to be restless, dissatisfied, conceptual, focused on outer world, avoiding negative experiences and goal orientated.

Being

Your inner sense of awareness, allowing, acceptance, peace, stillness and silence which is ever present, underneath the doing.

For some online extras about mindfulness, head online and visit www.dummies.com/extras/mindfulness.

In this part . . .

✔ Create a solid foundation on which to build a life filled with everyday mindfulness.

✔ Explore how motivation and commitment to mindfulness can benefit your life.

✔ Learn to go with the flow.

Chapter 3

Nurturing Your Motivation

*O*ne of the best ways of boosting your capacity to be mindful is to practise mindfulness meditation every day. Establishing a daily habit of mindfulness isn't always easy, but it's well worth the effort. With a clear and strong motivation to practise, you can develop the firm commitment necessary to engage in mindfulness regularly. Once the habit of daily mindfulness is created, the routine becomes as natural as having a shower – you now have a way of training and resting your mind every day, not just your body.

This chapter explores what your deep intentions of mindfulness are and it includes a range of exercises and how you can you use them to motivate your daily mindfulness practice.

Exploring Your Intentions

The word 'intention' comes from the Latin *intendere*, meaning to direct attention. Intention is purpose – what you hope to achieve from a certain action. If you're driving to work and your intention is to get there on time no matter what happens, you may drive recklessly and dangerously. If you're driving to work and your intention is to get there safely, you try to drive with a more focused attention, and at a safe and reasonable speed. Here's a more startling example. Imagine someone cutting you with a knife – such as a surgeon who has to insert a blade and cut you open. Because the intention of the surgeon is to help restore your health, you're probably willing to undergo this seemingly horrendous procedure. However, a murderer may also use a blade, but with a far less positive intention and you're unlikely to be so willing!

Intention shapes the nature of the whole action itself. Although the action may be the same (as with the example of cutting someone open), the intention itself strongly influences your moment-by-moment experience and state of mind. For this reason, the right intention is vitally important in mindfulness meditation. I'd go so far as to say that the nature of the intention itself strongly influences the quality of your meditative practice.

Clarifying intention in mindfulness

Dr Shauna Shapiro of Santa Clara University, together with several colleagues, came up with a helpful model to suggest how mindfulness works. The researchers identified three key components: *intention*, *attention* and *attitude*. The components are required together and feed into each other when you engage in mindfulness. The components link in well with the often-used definition of mindfulness, which is: *paying attention in a particular way: on purpose, in the present moment and non-judgementally*. Breaking this down, you have:

- ✔ Paying attention – *attention*
- ✔ On purpose – *intention*
- ✔ In a particular way – *attitude*

These three components work together seamlessly to create the moment-to-moment experience that is mindfulness. Figure 3-1 shows the components of mindfulness working together.

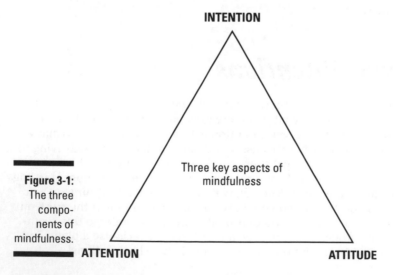

INTENTION

Three key aspects of mindfulness

ATTENTION   ATTITUDE

Figure 3-1: The three components of mindfulness.

Intention is a component that often gets lost when people consider mindfulness, and yet it's vitally important. Intention sets the scene for what unfolds in the practice itself.

Intention evolves. One study has shown that people's intention in mindfulness is usually stress reduction, and moves on to greater understanding of their thoughts and emotions, and finally towards greater compassion. For example, you may begin practising meditation to reduce your anxiety and when that subsides, you practise to attain greater control over your emotions and eventually to be a more compassionate and kind person to your family and friends. What's *your* intention?

Mindfulness is being developed to relieve the suffering caused by a whole host of different conditions, from eating disorders to anxiety in pregnancy, from reducing students' stress to speeding up the healing process for psoriasis. These are all a wonderful flowering of applications of mindfulness, but keep in mind the original purpose and vision of mindfulness as a way of relieving *all* suffering, both yours and others', and developing a greater sense of compassion. Such a large and positive vision enlarges the practice of mindfulness for those who share those possibilities.

Finding what you're looking for

The following exercise – what I call a 'mindful visualisation' – can give you great insight into your true and deep intentions in practising mindfulness. When I first used this exercise, I was surprised and fascinated by the insights into my own deep motives.

Afterwards, do the writing exercise described in the next section.

Discovering your intention: Mindful visualisation

This exercise is best done by listing to Track 3 from the audio. Find a comfortable position: seated in a chair or sofa, or lying down. Choose a position in which you feel cosy and comfortable. Close your eyes.

> Imagine that you're sitting by the side of a beautiful lake. The place can be somewhere you've been before or seen before, or may be completely created in your imagination – it doesn't matter which. Find a place where you feel calm and relaxed. The lake may have majestic trees around one side and stunning mountains in the distance. The temperature is just about perfect for you, and a gentle breeze ensures that you feel refreshed. A flock of birds are flying across the horizon, and you can sense a freshness in the air. Your body feels relaxed and at ease.

You look down and notice a pebble. You pick it up and look at it. It has a question engraved on it. The question is: 'What do I hope to get from mindfulness?' You look carefully at the question as you hold the pebble gently in your hand.

You throw the pebble out into the lake. You watch the pebble as it soars through the air in an arc, almost in slow motion, and eventually makes contact with the surface of the water. You see the circular ripples radiate out. As the pebble contacts with the water, you continue to reflect on the question: 'What do I hope to get from mindfulness?'

The pebble moves down into the water. You're able to see the pebble as it sinks deeper and deeper into the water. As it continues to smoothly fall downwards in the deep water, you continue to watch it, and you continue to reflect on the question: 'What do I hope to get from mindfulness?' You keep watching as the pebble falls, and you keep reflecting on the question.

Eventually, the pebble softly makes contact with the bottom and settles there. The question 'What do I hope to get from mindfulness?' is still visible. Reflect on that question for a few more moments.

Bring the exercise to a close, noticing the physical sensations of your body, taking a slightly deeper breath and, when you're ready, slowly opening your eyes. If you keep a journal, record what you discovered in it. This may help to reveal further insights as you write.

No right or wrong answers exist for this 'intention' meditation. Some people get clear answers about what they hope to get out of practising mindfulness, and others reflect on the question, yet no answers arise. Some people find that the answers they get at the surface of the lake are the more obvious ones but, as the pebble falls deeper, their reasons to practise clarify and deepen too. If the meditation was helpful, great; if not, don't be concerned – there are other exercises to do later in this chapter.

Discovering your intention: Sentence completion

Take a piece of paper or your journal, and write as many answers as you can to the following questions in one minute, without thinking about them too much:

I want to practise mindfulness because . . .

I'm hoping mindfulness will give me . . .

If I'm more mindful I'll . . .

The real reasons I want to practise mindfulness are to . . .

Ultimately mindfulness will give me . . .

Mindfulness is . . .

These sentence-completion exercises may help to clarify your motivation and intentions for mindfulness.

Now read and reflect on your answers. Did any of your answers surprise you? Why is that? You may like to come back to these answers when you're struggling to motivate yourself to meditate; reading your answers then can be a way of empowering yourself to practise some meditation.

Developing a vision

A *vision* is a long-term aspiration: something you're willing to work towards. By having a clear vision, you have an idea of where you need to get to. Think of it in terms of any journey you make, for which you need to know two things: where you are now, and where you need to get to.

Mindfulness is about being in the present moment and letting go of goals. Why think about visions and intentions? Why not just be in the here and now and forget about aspirations? Well, the vision gives you the energy, the motivation and the strength to practise mindfulness, especially when you really don't feel like practising.

For example, your mind may be jam-packed with thoughts, ideas and opinions to such an extent that you can't easily calm down. Your vision may be to be a calm and collected person, someone who never really worries about things too much, and who others come to for advice. With this in mind, you know why you're practising mindfulness and *are committed* to sticking at it. This doesn't mean that the goal of each and every mindful meditation is calmness, and that if you're not calm you've failed; a vision is bigger than that – a long-term objective rather than a short-term goal.

If you're not too sure what your vision is, come back to this section after doing some mindfulness exercises or after dipping into other areas of this book. Doing this may give you a clearer idea of a vision to work towards. The practice of mindfulness itself helps to develop an unambiguous vision as you begin to experience some benefits.

Try the following two exercises to help clarify your vision.

Writing a letter to your future self

This is a wonderful way to develop a long-term vision of what you hope to achieve through mindfulness.

Reflect on your future self in five or ten years. This is your chance to let go and dream. How will you feel? What sort of person do you hope to be? How do you cope with challenges in your life?

Write a letter to yourself about it, or if you're a visual person, draw pictures. This vision gives your brain something to work towards, and the opportunity to begin discovering a path for you to tread to get there.

Pin the letter up on the wall at home, or ask a good friend to post the letter back to you any time in the next year. Most people feel great receiving a letter from themselves dropping through the post, and the self-reflection always seems to arrive at the right time in your life.

You can even send an email to yourself from your future self. The website www.futureme.org allows you to do this for free.

Attending your own funeral

Try to overcome any reluctance about this exercise, because it's very moving and powerful. Imagine being at your own funeral service. You're aware of family and friends around you. Consider each person and imagine everyone saying what you'd *like* them to say about you. Really hear the positive things they're saying about you and your life. What do they value about you? What sort of aspects of your personality would you like them to talk about? What have they admired about you? After the exercise, think about it. How did you feel? What did people say about you?

The exercise helps to put things into context and clarifies your values – what's really important to you. How can you use what was said to create a vision of the kind of person you want to become? How can that vision help motivate your mindfulness practice?

Ask yourself the following question every day for a couple of weeks: 'If today were the last day of my life, would I want to do what I'm about to do today?' Whenever the answer is no for too many days in a row, you know that you need to change something. Even if you don't explicitly ask this question, you get a flavour of the value of considering death in order to help you wake up and focus on what's most important in life.

Practising mindfulness for everyone's benefit

If you're clear about the personal benefits of mindfulness, and practise mindfulness for your own benefit, that's great. However, you can also experiment with practising mindfulness for others. Shifting your intention can make the experience more enjoyable. Just like if you do some volunteer work, you're doing the work to help others, so you can practise mindfulness meditation in a way that's of service to others.

How does mindfulness benefit others? Well, the more you practise mindfulness, the more likely you are to be kind, attentive and helpful to others. You'll probably be less snappy and irritable. You'll be in control of your temper and have the energy and willingness to help others with their difficulties. All these qualities are not just great for you – they're great for anyone you come into contact with.

Here are a few people you can think of who may benefit from your mindfulness practice:

✔ Your partner or close family

✔ Your friends

✔ Your colleagues at work

✔ The village, town or city where you live

Pick one group that resonates with you. See if you can practise your mindfulness from the perspective of helping that particular group of people through your increased mindful awareness and friendly demeanour.

This approach works for all activities. For example, when I remember that I'm writing this book for your benefit, I feel far more motivated. I want to write it as best I can to help you to be healthier, happier and more peaceful. It feels great! If I was writing and *just* thinking about how it may make me more popular or wealthy, the action becomes far less joyous.

Preparing Yourself for Mindfulness

Having a positive attitude towards mindfulness is helpful. You're probably new to mindfulness, therefore you don't know whether it'll work for you. But being open to the possibility that you'll find value in mindfulness helps, just like when learning any new skill like golf, French or flower arranging!

If you go into mindfulness thinking 'This probably isn't going to help me,' as you practise and meet obstacles, you may just give up.

As Henry Ford said:

'Whether you think you can, or you think you can't – you're right.'

So think you can! It's worth listening to Henry Ford: he revolutionised the car industry. You may not agree with Ford's invention, but he achieved what many thought was impossible. Mindfulness can be just as revolutionary in your own life, if you have the right attitude. By having a positive attitude, you're giving yourself permission to find more peace and joy in your life.

When you cultivate a long-term vision for why you want to practise mindfulness, let it be just that: long term. Let go in the here and now as you engage in the practice. Don't worry too much about whether you're moving towards your goal. Trust that the process of mindfulness meditation, practised by millions of people and supported scientifically by thousands of research papers, will take care of itself if you give it time, and stop questioning its value as far as you can.

Looking Beyond Problem-Solving

Mindfulness isn't a quick fix. You need to practise mindfulness on the good days and the bad ones – on days when you feel things are going okay, as well as when you feel anxious, stressed or depressed. Mindfulness is best cultivated slowly and steadily, day by day, so that when things become difficult or challenging for you, you can remember and use mindful awareness to bring your attention to your breathing and soothe your mind.

Who knows? We shall see

One day, a student graduated with a first class honours degree from a top university. His friends and family celebrated and said how lucky he was. He was sure to land a great job. He replied: 'Who knows? We shall see.'

As soon as the party was over, the country slipped into a deep recession. People were getting laid off left, right and centre. No company was employing anyone. He applied for more than 50 jobs to no avail. He didn't even get interviewed. His parents and partner felt sorry for him. He said: 'Who knows? We shall see.'

He decided to start up a business selling phones. At first, it didn't seem to work, but suddenly, as demand picked up, the business started to makes lots of money. He sealed a massive deal and eventually become a millionaire. He bought a new house overlooking the sea. Others were amazed at his turn of fortune. He said: 'Who knows? We shall see.'

Unfortunately, all his savings were lost when a big bank failed. His house was repossessed and he had to move back with his parents. All those around him said how sorry they were about how things worked out. He smiled and said: 'Who knows? We shall see.'

He read in the paper that the couple who were now living in his old house were completely flooded. Due to rising sea levels, the foundations of the house became weak and had to be demolished. The insurance company didn't pay out and the couple lost everything. Everyone said how lucky the man was to leave when he did. He smiled and said: 'Who knows? We shall see.'

This story illustrates that you can judge problems in life as 'good' or 'bad', but you're not really seeing the big picture. No one knows what's going to happen next and things may turn out to be okay. Try to keep an open mind in both your apparent fortune and misfortune.

Think of regular mindfulness meditation like putting on a safety belt in a car. You put the belt on every time you travel just in case you're in an accident. You don't put the belt on just before you crash – you'd be too late. The car journey is the same, whether you have a belt on or not, but the main difference is the preparation for what may happen. The safety belt of mindfulness helps to slow things down, so you can enjoy the view and come to a safe stop when things become challenging.

There will always be days when you forget to practise mindfulness, or just can't find the motivation to do so. When this happens, your job is to be tremendously forgiving. Be really nice to yourself. Just like when children get a low grade in a subject – there's no point shouting at them. Instead, you encourage them. Pick them up. Tell them to try again, step by step, nice and slowly. Give yourself the same gentle encouragement when you struggle to be mindful – that's the only way to get back into the practice.

Honing Your Commitment

Commitment is a pledge you make for a course of action. In this case your commitment is to mindfulness, developed through meditation and practised every day. Once you've decided to practise meditation, to commit is to follow through with your beliefs consistently. Commitment is also persistence with purpose. To achieve anything of significance, you need certain key commitments to stick to. Without commitment you can be easily swayed by passing feelings, and before long you forget the practices that you thought about doing, or they become too far out of reach for you to resume them in your life.

How do you make a commitment? The truth of the matter is that commitment is hard work. Just look at the number of people who struggle to stick to their New Year resolutions. However, the very fact that you make a commitment is the first step. Just because you failed to achieve your commitment doesn't mean you should give up altogether. Say you want to stop eating chocolate. The first few days are fine, but then after a week you see a delicious bar of your favourite chocolate lying on the kitchen table to tempt you, and without thinking you begin devouring it. As you put the wrapper in the bin, you think that you've 'failed' and you may give up on the resolution altogether. Instead, realise that during the first seven days since your resolution not to eat chocolate, you haven't eaten chocolate for six days. That's pretty good going: six out of seven, or a 86% success rate! Try again tomorrow.

Commitment is most challenging when times are hard. When you've had a tough day, when everything seems to be going wrong, when the last thing you want to do is sit down and meditate, ironically that's when you need commitment most. Challenging days test your commitment to your original decision to practise every day. However, if you don't practise, even though you had every desire and squeezed every ounce of your commitment to practise but just didn't manage it, bring an attitude of curiosity and acceptance to the situation rather than beating yourself up. What's done is done. You wanted to practise but you didn't. The question is: 'What happened?' What thoughts and feelings led to your inaction? What's going through your mind right now as you ask yourself these questions?

Mastering self-discipline

The word 'discipline' has negative connotations for some people, and can be a bit of a turn-off, which is a shame because self-discipline is important for a healthy lifestyle. Self-discipline is the ability to get yourself to do a certain action despite your emotional state at the time.

Imagine what you can achieve with perfect levels of self-discipline. No matter what you choose to do, you'll be able to do it. Say you want to become fitter. You just make that decision and you're guaranteed to follow through with the necessary regular exercise to ensure that your desired outcome happens. This little example goes to show how amazingly powerful self-discipline can be and why it's worth cultivating.

However, on its own, discipline can create a sense of cold, clinical action, almost too devoid of emotion. By combining this sense of discipline with your intentions and helpful attitudes (covered in Chapter 4), you can create a useful source of inspiration for your mindfulness practice.

Here are some tips for boosting your self-discipline for daily mindfulness meditation:

- ✔ **Forgive yourself for the odd slip.** Remember, meditation is a long-term process. Don't just give up because of a lapse. If at first you don't succeed, find out why and try again!

- ✔ **Take things step by step.** Research has found that willpower is like a muscle. Willpower can become fatigued if you use it too much in a day, but can be strengthened over time. So don't try to transform your whole life in a day. You may want to start with a very short daily mindfulness practice.

- ✔ **Believe in yourself.** You can do it. Even if you suffer from attention disorders or you're ill, you can practise mindfulness, so believe that you're capable of making a commitment. Any tiny step is valid.

- ✔ **Ask for support.** Perhaps you can practise meditation with a partner or friend. Joining a meditation group can be a valuable support too.

✔ **Reward yourself.** You've probably given yourself a hard time on many an occasion for not doing something right, or well, or not being good enough, so why not reward yourself for doing something you're proud of? Creating a daily discipline of meditation is hard, so if you do manage for a week or even a few days, treat yourself to a little something!

Making a commitment that's right for you

One of the reasons people find it hard to stick to a commitment is because they're too ambitious. If you've never gone jogging before and you suddenly decide to run the marathon tomorrow, one of two things happens: you give up or you finish in a very injured and unhappy state. The knock-on effect is that you hate running or think that you're useless at it.

If you decide you're going to meditate for two hours a day for the rest of your life, no matter what happens, that may be tough. You need to take things easy and begin slowly. How do you decide the right commitment for you? Well, it depends what you want to get out of meditation. You can start with an eight-week commitment of practising mindfulness meditation for 30 minutes per day, and see how that goes. (See Chapter 9 for more about the eight-week routine.)

Maybe ten minutes a day is more appropriate for your lifestyle, or even regular three-minute meditations throughout the day. Perhaps you suffer from chronic pain or depression or want to develop yourself to a high level and wish to make a bigger commitment. That's fine, of course, but start fairly modestly and build up your practising time. Meditation has no ideal minimum or maximum time for which to practise it. And ultimately, your whole life can be a meditation. Any time you do whatever you're doing consciously, with a non-judgemental atten-tion, you're being mindful.

If you think that life is going well for you, and you just get slightly stressed from time to time and want something to relax and focus you a bit more, then perhaps ten minutes of formal mindfulness meditation practice may be fine for you. If you suffer from medium to high levels of stress, anxiety, depression, or ill health, turn to Chapters 12–14 for advice on the right commitment for you.

Once the regular discipline of meditation becomes a habit, the effort of practice becomes less. Cast your mind back to when you first learnt to brush your teeth. It was probably a real chore. Yes, it's good for your teeth, but you weren't interested – you wanted to play a game or watch TV, not waste your time brushing your teeth. But now, if you don't brush your teeth for any reason, *it just doesn't feel right*. As you regularly practise meditation, you eventually find the same: you become nourished by the practice itself, and what may at times have felt difficult to do now feels strange *not* to do. This is the sign that you've created a wonderful, positive way to uplift your health and wellbeing. Of course, at times you'll feel reluctant to practise, such as when you're reluctant to brush your teeth if you're really tired, but on the whole you're now a keen mindfulness meditator.

Your informal practice, which involves being mindfully aware of your day-to-day activities (see Chapter 8), will happen almost naturally if you regularly practise meditation for a set amount of time every day.

Inspiring yourself with extra motivation

Still struggling with the idea of self-discipline? Here are a final few thoughts to help you.

Think of your mind as being like a puppy. When you train a puppy, you need to be kind and gentle at first. If you put a leash on it and drag it hard from one place to another, the puppy won't learn. You'll probably upset it and will never train it well. However, if you let it do whatever it wants, you're also in trouble! The dog will be the master, and will rule the house. The young puppy learns that whatever it feels like doing at the time, it can do, making you feel very tired and frustrated with cleaning up and meeting its never-ending needs and desires. The puppy may end up eating too much and become sick. The middle way is best. You need to guide the puppy to particular actions, and whenever it does them, you reward it. If the puppy does the wrong thing, you don't give it much attention, and eventually it stops.

Nothing beats the real thing

I find that all the time I spend talking, writing or teaching mindfulness makes almost no difference to how mindful I am. The only thing that deepens my mindfulness is regular practice of mindfulness meditation itself; this can be mindful walking, mindful body scan meditation or the mindful sitting meditation. You may spend every waking hour reading, writing, studying and talking about meditation, but hardly ever practise it.

And just as describing a mango isn't the same as tasting one, so talking or reading about mindfulness isn't the same as practising it. Reading about and discussing mindfulness may seem much more comfortable and easy than doing it, but unfortunately it makes no difference to your mind or body. So I recommend you aim at doing 'non-doing' every day, for however long you decide and in whatever form that works for you.

Train your own mind in the same way. When your mind comes up with all sorts of ideas about what you could be doing instead of meditating, just kindly ignore it, without fighting or blocking the thoughts. Give your attention to the inner commitment to meditate, and reward that aspect of mind by meditating. Before long, your puppy mind will be a well-trained and beautiful dog, behaving itself most of the time. You need lots of patience and progress may be slow, but the rewards make the puppy-training programme well worth it!

Each time you practise mindfulness, you increase the chance of meditating again on another day. This is because any new activity you take on, whether physical or mental, creates a new pathway in the brain. It's a bit like creating a new pathway through a forest. At first, walking through all the overgrowth is difficult. You need to push the overhanging branches out of the way and tread on the long grass under your feet. However, if you keep walking on that path, it becomes easier and easier. Soon enough, you don't need to battle any more or think about which way to go next. The path is clear. It's the same with pathways in the brain. In fact, that's what commitment to an action creates in the brain – a pathway to greater mindfulness, awareness and 'aliveness'.

Dealing with resistance to practice

People often ask me, both in person and on social media, how to overcome the resistance to practising mindfulness. They know it's good for them, but for some reason they just can't make themselves sit down and meditate. I think it's a common experience for many people.

Here are some tips I suggest:

- ✔ **Make peace with the resistance.** If you really don't feel like meditating, that's okay. You don't need to set up a battle within yourself! Instead, take a break. Let go of the inner fight to practise. Come back to it when you're ready to do so.

- ✔ **Feel the resistance.** Notice when you feel the resistance in your body. Is the feeling in the pit of your stomach, your chest or somewhere else? Feel the sensation together with your breathing. Now you're already practising some mindfulness without knowing it – sneaky, but cool!

- ✔ **Boost your informal mindfulness practice.** This means just being more conscious of whatever your daily activities are. If you need to walk to the bus stop, really feel the sensations in your feet and the breeze against your skin. If you're drying clothes on the washing line, make an extra effort to notice the fresh scent of the clothes and the stretch in your body as you peg the clothes up. Give your mind a break from your usual recurring thoughts.

The donkey and the well

Once upon a time, a farmer's donkey fell into a well. The farmer tried all sorts of different ways to get the donkey out, to no avail. Eventually and regrettably he gave up. The well needed filling up anyway, so he decided to bury the donkey. He convinced himself that the donkey wouldn't suffer any longer. He began shovelling soil into the well.

At first the donkey was scared and brayed loudly, but then calmed down and was silent. After shovelling for a while, the farmer decided to take a closer look inside, using a torch. The donkey was alive, and closer to the top of the well. Each time the farmer threw mud onto the donkey, he shook it off his back and stepped up onto the soil. Before long the donkey was able to step out of the well and into safety, as if nothing had happened.

The donkey was *motivated* to stay alive. If the donkey had thought, 'Oh no, I have no hope, I'm going to die,' then the donkey would have been buried. With the motivation and commitment to succeed in mindfulness you can come up with simple yet effective and creative solutions to challenges along the way.

Chapter 4

Growing Healthy Attitudes

· ·

In This Chapter

▶ Developing key mindful attitudes

▶ Understanding 'heartfulness'

▶ Dealing with unhelpful attitudes

· ·

> *The greatest discovery of our generation is that human beings can alter their lives by altering their attitudes of mind. As you think, so shall you be.*
>
> *William James*

The three important aspects to mindfulness are intention, attitude and attention (explained fully in Chapter 3). This chapter focuses on attitude.

When it comes to attitude, you have a choice. If you're aware of your outlook, you can begin to choose to change it for the better. Attitude isn't about what happens in your life, how successful you are or even how you feel. You can be feeling the emotion of frustration but think, 'Hey, at least I'm aware of it' or 'This is just a feeling' or 'This is a chance for me to understand the feeling of frustration'. Changing your attitude is difficult but *is* possible. By choosing mindful attitudes towards your moment-to-moment inner and outer experiences, you begin to release self-limiting beliefs and live life with greater fluidity.

Think about singing. What's your attitude towards singing? Maybe you love it and can't wait to jump up on the stage. If you don't care what other people think, or think you're a great singer, then belting out your favourite song isn't a problem. However, if you think you must do it right or worry about what others think, you may be more hesitant to sing and this affects your feelings, mood and how you actually sound.

Knowing How Attitude Affects Outcome

A school once had six different ability groups for maths. Each year, the same maths teachers taught the same ability level in the subject. One year the head teacher decided to experiment. She picked a teacher at random, who turned out to be the teacher of the second from bottom set. The head told the teacher how good she was and that she'd give her the top set for maths next year. The teacher's attitude and expectations for the class totally changed when she received her new class. She knew that the top set should get the top grades as they always had. She taught them accordingly and, sure enough, the pupils achieved straight A grades. The amazing thing was that the class wasn't really the top set at all, but was the second from bottom set. Because the teacher had changed her attitude and expectations for the class, the students rose to the challenge and produced outstanding results. This experiment goes to show the power of attitude.

How does attitude affect the quality of mindfulness meditation? Well, if your attitude is 'Mindfulness is really hard,' then you try very hard to get somewhere. If your attitude is 'Mindfulness is easy' and you then struggle, you may begin to get frustrated. If your attitude is 'I don't know how it'll go. I'm going to give it a good go and see what happens,' you're prepared for whatever arises.

Attitudes are the soil in which your mindfulness practices grow tall and strong. A rich, nutritious soil nourishes the seed of mindfulness and ensures that it grows well. Each time you practise mindfulness, you water the seed, giving it care and attention. However, if that soil deteriorates through unhelpful attitudes, then the young seedling will begin to wither. A plant needs regular watering to grow–; a lack of care and attention results in it perishing.

Discovering Your Attitudes to Mindfulness

Attitudes can become habits – both good and bad. And attitudes, like habits, aren't easy to change. You need to work to improve your attitude. Begin by discovering your current attitudes towards mindfulness, stillness, silence and non-doing. Then, through understanding and effort, you can develop attitudes that are more conducive to a regular mindfulness practice.

Get pen and paper and answer the following ten questions to help you discover what your attitudes towards mindfulness meditation are:

1. What do you hope to get out of practising mindfulness?

2. Why are you practising mindfulness?

3. What experiences do you expect to arrive at through practising mindfulness?

4. How long do you think it'll take before you notice the benefits of mindfulness?

5. What physical sensations do you expect during or after a mindfulness meditation?

6. What are your past experiences of mindfulness? Do you continue to hold onto them or have you let them go?

7. How much effort are you willing to put into the practice? Will you practise mindfulness several times a day, once a day, once a week or whenever you feel like it?

8. When you hear the word 'meditation' or 'mindfulness', what sort of thoughts and feelings arise?

9. How will you know that you're doing your mindfulness practice correctly?

10. What's the best thing about mindfulness?

Now, look at your answers. Do you notice any patterns? Are you very positive about the potential benefits of mindfulness? Are you negative about mindfulness? Or are you indifferent and do you just want to experiment, like being a scientist of your own mind?

Try to be non-judgemental towards your answers. See them as just the way things are. If you can't help being caught up in thinking, 'That's good' or 'Oh, that's a really bad attitude, what's wrong with me?', notice that too. Your mind is simply coming up with judgements.

Developing Helpful Attitudes

This section contains the key foundational attitudes that provide a base from which you can build a strong mindfulness practice. These attitudes help you to handle difficult sensations and emotions, overcome feelings of lethargy and generate energy for taking action. Without these attitudes your practice may become stale and your intention may weaken, along with your power to pay attention in the present moment. Some helpful ways of approaching your practice are developed through experience; others are available right from the start.

Think of these key attitudes like strawberry seeds. If you're hoping to taste the delicious strawberries, you need to plant the seeds and water them regularly. In the same way, you need to water your attitudes regularly, by giving them your mindful attention. Then you can enjoy the fruit of your efforts in the form of a sweet, delicious strawberry. I'm a sucker for strawberries.

Although the attitudes identified in this section seem separate, they feed into and support each other. Any one of these attitudes, pursued and encouraged to grow, inadvertently supports the others.

Understanding acceptance

Acceptance turns out to be one of the most helpful attitudes to bring to mindfulness. Acceptance means perceiving your experience and simply acknowledging it rather than judging it as good or bad. You let go of the battle with your present-moment experience. For some people, the word 'acceptance' is off-putting–; replace it with the word 'acknowledgement', if you prefer.

By acceptance, I don't mean resignation. I don't mean, 'If you think you can't do something, accept it' – that would be giving up rather than accepting. I'm talking about your experience from moment to moment.

For example, when you feel pain, whether it's physical, such as a painful shoulder, or mental, such as depression or anxiety, the natural reaction is to try to avoid feeling the pain. This seems very sensible, because the sensation of physical or mental pain is unpleasant. You ignore it, distract yourself, or perhaps even go so far as turning to recreational drugs or alcohol to numb the discomfort. This avoidance may work in the immediate short term, but before long, avoidance fails in the mental and emotional realm.

By fighting the pain, you still feel the pain, but on top of that, you feel the emotional hurt and struggle with the pain itself. Buddha called this the 'second arrow'. If a warrior is injured by an arrow and unleashes a series of thoughts like, 'Why did this happen to me?' or 'What if I can never walk again?' that's a 'second arrow'. You may inflict this on yourself each time you feel some form of pain or even just a bit of discomfort, rather than accepting what has happened and taking the next step. Avoidance – running away – is an aspect of the 'second arrow' and compounds the suffering. Acceptance means stopping fighting with your moment-to-moment experience. Acceptance removes that second arrow of blame, criticism or denial.

A useful formula to remember is:

Suffering = Pain x Resistance

The more your resist the pain you're experiencing, the more you suffer. The pain is already there. Resisting the pain compounds your difficulties. Acceptance teaches you to let go of the resistance and therefore ease your suffering.

Perhaps you meditate and feel bombarded by thoughts dragging you away again and again. If you don't accept the fact that your mind likes thinking, you become more and more frustrated, upset and annoyed with yourself. You want to focus on your mindfulness practice, but you just can't.

In the above example:

- ✔ **First arrow:** Lots of thoughts entering your mind during meditation.

- ✔ **Second arrow:** Not accepting that thoughts are bound to come up in meditation; criticising yourself for having too many thoughts.

- ✔ **Solution:** Acknowledge and accept that thoughts are part and parcel of mindfulness practice. Let go of your resistance. You can do this by gently saying to yourself, 'Thinking is happening' or 'It's natural to think' or simply labelling it as 'thinking . . . thinking'.

By *acknowledging* the feeling, thought or sensation and going into it, the experience changes. Even with physical pain, try experimenting by actually feeling it. Research has found that the pain reduces.

But remember, you're not acknowledging it to get rid of the feeling. That's not acceptance. You need to try to acknowledge the sensation, feeling or thought *without trying to change it* at all – pure acceptance of it, just as it is.

Maybe even relax into the discomfort. One way to relax into the discomfort is by courageously turning to the sensation of discomfort and simultaneously feeling the sensation of your own breath. With each out-breath, allow yourself to move closer and soften the tension around the discomfort.

If all this acceptance or acknowledgement of your pain seems impossible, just try getting a sense of it and make the tiniest step towards it. The smallest step towards acceptance can set up a chain of events ultimately leading towards transformation. Any tiny amount of acceptance is better than none at all.

Another aspect of acceptance is to come to terms with your current situation. If you're lost, even if you have a map of where you want to get to, you have no hope of getting there *if you don't know where you are to start with*. You need to know and accept where you are. Then you can begin working out how to get to where you want to be. Paradoxically, acceptance is the first step for any radical change. If you don't acknowledge where you are and what's currently happening, you can't move on appropriately from that point.

Here are some ways you can try to cultivate acceptance:

- ✔ Gently state the label of the experience you aren't accepting. For example, if you're not accepting that you're angry, state in your mind, to yourself, 'I'm feeling angry at the moment . . . I'm feeling angry'. In this way, you begin to acknowledge your feeling.

✔ Notice which part of your body feels tense and imagine your breath going into and out of the area of tightness. As you breathe in and out, say to yourself, 'It's okay. It's already here . . . It's already here'. Allow the muscles around the sensation to soften and release if you can.

✔ Consider how much you accept or acknowledge your current thoughts/ feelings/sensation on a scale of 1 to 10. Ask yourself what you need to do to increase your acceptance by 1, and then do it as best you can.

✔ Become really curious about your experience. Consider, 'Where did this feeling come from? Where do I feel it? What's interesting about it?' In this way, the curiosity leads you to a little more acceptance.

In the realm of emotions, the quickest way to get from A to B isn't to try and force yourself to get to B, but to accept A. Wholehearted acceptance leads to change automatically.

Discovering patience

Helen Keller, the American deaf-blind political activist, is quoted as saying: 'We could never learn to be brave and patient if there were only joy in the world.' The quote makes a valid point. If every time you practised mindfulness, you were filled with joy and peace, you wouldn't need that wonderful attitude of patience. The reality is that challenging thoughts and emotions sometimes arise in mindfulness, like in any activity. The important thing is how you meet and welcome those feelings.

Although you can experience the benefits of mindfulness after a short period of time, research shows that the more time you dedicate to cultivating mindfulness, the more effective the result. Mindfulness meditation is a training of the mind and training takes time.

If you're a naturally rather impatient person, mindfulness meditation is the perfect training for you. Patience, like all the attitudes I talk about in this section, is a state you can develop through regular effort. Attitudes are muscles you can train in the gym of the mind.

Here are some ways you can develop your patience:

✔ Whenever you're in any situation where you begin to experience impatience, see this as an opportunity to practise mindfulness of thoughts. This means becoming fascinated by the kind of thoughts that are popping into your head. Are they all true? What effect are the thoughts having on your emotional state? What are the thoughts all about?

- ✔ The next time you're driving and see an amber light, stop safely rather than speeding through it. See how that makes you feel. Repeat this several times and notice if it becomes easier or more difficult to be patient.

- ✔ Rather than frantically choosing the shortest queue at the supermarket checkout, just choose the nearest one. Connect with any feelings of impatience that arise and bring a sense of curiosity to your experience, rather than immediately reacting to your impatience.

When having a conversation with someone, spend more time listening rather than speaking. Let go of your initial urge to speak, and listen more. Listening can take tremendous effort, and is excellent patience training. Each time you practise, you train your brain to become slightly more patient.

Seeing afresh

Seeing afresh is normally referred to as the *beginner's mind*, a term that was first used by the Zen master Suzuki Roshi. He once said: 'In the beginner's mind there are many possibilities, but in the expert's there are few.' What does that mean?

Consider a young child. Children, if they're fortunate enough to be brought up lovingly, are the greatest mindfulness teachers in the world! They're amazed by the simplest thing. Give babies a set of keys, and they stare at them, notice the wide range of colours reflected in them, shake them and listen to the sound – and probably giggle too. Then, of course, they taste the keys!

Children epitomise the beginner's mind. They see things as if for the first time, because they're not filled with ideas, concepts, beliefs, names or thoughts about the right or wrong thing to do. Babies don't intellectualise. They connect with the raw sensory data entering their minds and they love it. Young children are naturally mindful, and that mindfulness is a true joy for them.

You can see life in a similar way. You can cultivate this attitude of the beginner's mind, of seeing things afresh – you just need to make a little effort. Try this exercise:

1. Sit or lie down in a relaxed and comfortable posture and close your eyes.

2. Now imagine you've been blind from birth. You've never experienced colour before. You've heard people talking about it, but you can't even imagine colour. Spend at least five minutes doing this. When you find your mind wandering off into thoughts, gently guide it back to this exercise.

3. When you're ready, gently open your eyes as if you're seeing for the first time. See with the beginner's mind. Enjoy the range of colours and forms in front of you. Notice how your mind automatically names different objects. Bring your attention back to the awareness of the variety of colours, shadows and reflections. You may even begin to notice things you've never noticed before; that's a sign that you're engaging with the beginner's mind and seeing things anew.

4. Continue with this beginner's mind attitude as you go about your activities today, and be with each experience as if for the first time.

When you experience the state of the beginner's mind, you live in a world of fascination, curiosity, creativity, attention and fun. You're continuously discovering and looking out with the eyes of a child. You're in 'don't know' mind. When you think, 'I know what's going to happen' or 'I know what the breath feels like,' you stop looking. You don't know what's going to happen; you just think you do. Each moment is fresh. Each moment is different and unique. Each moment is the only moment you have.

If you're a beginner at mindfulness, you're in an enviable position. You really are in the beginner's mind! However, by the time you practise your second mindfulness meditation, you may begin comparing it with your first one and think, 'It was better last time' or 'Why can't I concentrate now?' or 'This is it. I've got it!'. You start to compare, conceptualise or condemn. When this happens, try to let it go – as much as you can – and bring your attention back to the here and now, as if you're engaging in this for the very first time. I'm not saying that the beginner's mind is an easy attitude, but it's fundamental to sustaining a long-term meditative discipline.

Mindful living is about living life afresh. One cool way to do this is to reduce the amount of planning you do. Leave some days unplanned. That way, you make space for new and exciting things to emerge. Most of the time, life doesn't go to plan anyway – so don't try too hard to stick to a schedule. You can even try letting go of planning your work occasionally. When I give a talk without planning, I don't know what I'll say, and it's more fun both for my audience and me. I'm forced to live in the present and respond to the moment; mindfulness arises spontaneously.

Finding trust

Without a certain degree of trust, mindfulness meditation is challenging. This is because trust helps you to continue believing in the process of mindfulness when you feel that nothing's happening or something 'wrong' is happening. For example, if you're meditating and you suddenly feel bored, you need to trust that this is just another feeling, and that by continuing to practise mindfulness, that feeling may go away or it may not. Or, you may find that by the end of a mindfulness practice, you feel a bit worse than when you started. Without trust, you won't be able to see that this is just a temporary experience which, like all experiences, won't last forever.

Trust takes time to develop in relationships. You can't expect to meet people and immediately trust them. You need to see how they behave, what they say, and how they treat you and others. With time, with patience, trust grows. And with that growing trust, the relationships deepen, mature and become more meaningful. A relationship that lacks in trust has little beauty. With trust comes warmth, friendship and a feeling of connection – you feel at ease and comfortable in a trusting relationship. Your relationship with mindfulness is similar. You may not trust in the process to begin with, but with patience, dedicated and regular practice, you may begin to trust it. The more you trust in its power to heal and restore you, the more you relax into it and allow mindfulness to *happen* to you, in a sense, rather than trying to *do* mindfulness. Mindfulness is an act of non-doing, or being, which arises out of the security of trust.

Here are some ways of building your trust:

- ✔ Decide how long you're going to try meditation for and stick to it. So, if you want to try meditation for four weeks, for 20 minutes a day, just do it. Be prepared to find it harder to practise on some days than others, and begin to trust in the process.

- ✔ If you're scientifically minded, look up all the research on mindfulness and meditation available, in this book or elsewhere. This may help to convince you to stick to the discipline.

- ✔ If you know someone else who regularly practises mindfulness, ask her about her relationship with it. Consider meditating with her to help you.

- ✔ Give mindfulness time. Be patient with it as far as you can, and your trust will naturally grow with time.

- ✔ Try trusting your own experience, in the here and now. What is your intuition trying to tell you?

Cultivating curiosity

Einstein was a master of curiosity. He thought that curiosity was an essential part of a fulfilling life. Einstein is quoted as saying:

> 'The important thing is not to stop questioning. Curiosity has its own reason for existing. One cannot help but be in awe when he contemplates the mysteries of eternity, of life, of the marvellous structure of reality. It is enough if one tries merely to comprehend a little of this mystery every day. Never lose a holy curiosity.'

Curiosity is the basis of all true learning. If you're curious, you want to find out something new: you want to gain some new knowledge. A curious person is fully connected with her senses. If you're curious, you look around intently and earnestly to see something you haven't seen before. You ask lots of questions, both of yourself and others. These can be questions like, 'Why is the sky blue?' or 'Why is that shadow over there faint, whereas this one is much darker?'. Or it may be questions about yourself, like 'I wonder why I feel tired after eating X?' or 'Where do thoughts come from?' or 'What happens to the feeling of frustration if I try to feel it in my body and breathe into it?'.

Bringing curiosity to your mindfulness practice is especially helpful. In fact, with curiosity, mindfulness automatically arises: you naturally begin to pay attention and, with a sense of wonder, to notice what's happening. Take the example of thought: if you're really curious about the types of thoughts that you have over a period of ten minutes, you pay attention and watch thoughts in your mind as best you can. That's mindfulness. If your curiosity is genuine, you'll probably keep watching those thoughts until that curiosity is satisfied.

How can you develop curiosity in mindfulness? I say, by asking questions. Here are some questions you can ask yourself before a mindfulness practice, to get you started:

- ✔ What happens if I practise mindfulness every day for 20 minutes for four weeks, whether I feel like it or not?

- ✔ What occurs if I put more effort into my mindfulness practice? What if I put in less effort?

- ✔ What if I sit or lie down really still, even if I have the urge to move. What happens then?

- ✔ Where in the body do I feel positive emotions? Where do I feel negative ones? What shape and colour do the emotions have, if any?

- ✔ What effect does having a gentle smile while meditating have on my practice?

I could go on and on with thousands of questions to ask. Try to come up with some of your own; your own curiosity is more powerful than anything I give you.

Ask yourself a question and investigate. Feed your curiosity and see what you discover. Allow your curiosity to spread from your mindfulness practice to your day-to-day living. Become curious about your thoughts, emotions and physical sensations rather than just ignoring them or trying to instantly change them.

Experimenting with doing things differently is a great way to fuel your curiosity and increase your mindfulness. For example, today I thought, 'How can I brush my teeth in a different way, just for fun?'. The answer came: stand on one leg. So I brushed my teeth while balancing on one leg. I was surprised at how much more mindful I was. Rather than automatically brushing and letting my mind wander, I was conscious of keeping my balance. You probably think I'm mad – perhaps you're right! But the point I'm trying to make is that if you do things differently that immediately makes life a bit more fun and a bit more mindful too. What can you do differently today?

 Mindfulness is like a laboratory, where you come up with ideas, observe, watch, see what happens and perhaps draw conclusions. Keep asking yourself questions, and keep going in that way. Mindfulness gives you the opportunity to find out more about yourself and the workings of your own mind and heart, and when you understand that, you understand not only yourself, but everyone else, because everyone has essentially the same processes going on. Humans are far more similar than you may think.

Letting go

Imagine I told you to hold a glass of water absolutely still. In fact, imagine I said that I'd give you whatever you wanted if you held the glass of water perfectly still. You'd probably try very hard and the glass might look quite still, but if you or anyone else looked really carefully at the water, you'd notice that it was still moving. I suspect that the harder you tried to hold the glass still, the more you'd shake it as you felt more worried or nervous about being 100 per cent still. The best way for the glass of water to be still would be for you to *let it go* and put it down on a solid surface. Then the water would stop moving.

Nature has many beautiful examples of letting go. Apple trees need to let go of their fruit so that the seeds inside can germinate. Animals need to let go of their young so they can find out how to fend for themselves. Young birds need to let go of any fear they feel when they first jump off a branch to begin to fly. You're always letting go of each breath of air to make room for the next one. This last example shows that you naturally know how to let go all the time, in one sense. Remember this the next time you're struggling to let go.

Letting go is the essence of mindfulness. Thoughts, emotions, ideas, opinions, beliefs, emotions and sensations are all to be observed, explored and then let go. If you're struggling to understand or practise mindfulness, try letting go. Just gently practise as best you can and see what you discover – you'll be on the right track.

How do you let go? Imagine you're holding a tennis ball in your hands, and you're asking me how to let go. Letting go isn't something you do. Letting go is about stopping the doing. To let go of something, you stop holding onto it.

The first step is to realise you're holding onto the object in the first place. If you're walking around holding a tennis ball, you can't let go if you don't know that the ball is in your hands. Once you know that the ball is there and feel the tension in your hands, you automatically let go.

Here's a short mindfulness exercise on the practice of letting go. Have a go and see what arises for you. You can use the accompanying guided audio (MP3 Track 5) if you wish.

1. **Find a comfortable posture.** You don't even need to close your eyes if you don't want to.

2. **Notice, right now, the position of your body.** Can you feel any physical tension in your body? Which parts feel warm and which ones cold? Does the tension have a shape, a colour, a texture? Be aware of what they are. What happens to the tension and tightness as you become aware of them? Do they release or stay there?

3. **Become aware of any emotions that are touching you at the moment.** What happens when you observe them? Get a sense of how strong the emotion is. Don't *try* to let go. Putting effort into letting go just creates more tension. Instead, become aware of it and allow the emotion to take its own course. Let the emotion let go of itself if it wants to. If the feeling lingers on, can you be okay with that and accept it as it is?

4. **At the end of this short exercise, see whether you're willing to let go of anything that you found out** – anything that you're holding onto, trusting that you have within you all that needs to be known.

Developing kindness

Kindness is my religion.

Dalai Lama

This is one of the most important of all attitudes you can bring to your mindfulness practice. Your awareness of your breath, or your body or sounds, or whatever you're paying attention to, can have a quality to it. The quality can be cold, harsh and incisive, or it can be warm, kind, friendly, forgiving, caring, gentle – in other words, loving. By bringing a sense of friendliness to your experience, the experience – whether it's pleasant, unpleasant or neutral – is transformed.

Because kindness is such an important attitude, I go into this in more detail in the next section.

Figure 4-1 is the tree of mindfulness. The growth and development of the tree of mindfulness represents your own inner capacity to be mindful. Watering the roots represents the effort you make to cultivate the mindful attitudes and practise mindfulness. The fruit represent the benefits you naturally gain from the effort you put into being mindful. 'As you sow, so shall you reap' is the essence of mindfulness; this is why the fruit from your own tree of mindfulness is the same as the roots.

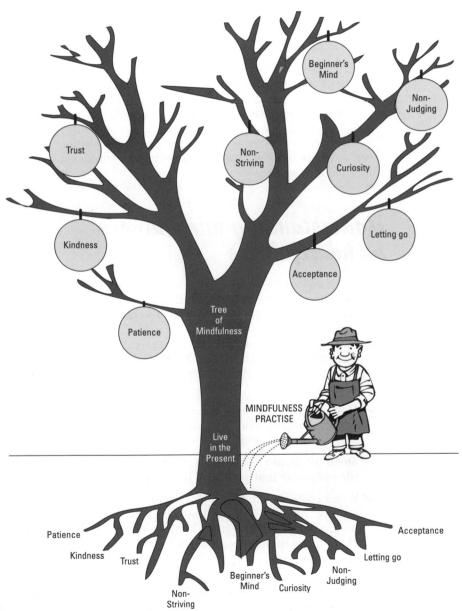

Figure 4-1:
The tree of
mindfulness.

Over time, as you continue to look after the tree of mindfulness within you, the tree strengthens and matures. Your roots grow deep into the earth and your tree stands firmly earthed to the ground, offering shade to those around quite naturally. Mindfulness is firmly established within your being.

Appreciating 'Heartfulness'

With attentiveness, a marksman can shoot an innocent person, a thief can plot a bank robbery, and a drug baron can count his money. But this isn't true mindfulness – mindfulness isn't pure attention alone. In Eastern language, the word for mind and heart is often the same, which is *heartfulness*. Instead of *Mindfulness For Dummies*, this book could just as easily be called *Heartfulness For Dummies*. Heartfulness is giving attention to anything that you can perceive with a sense of warmth, kindliness and friendliness, and thereby avoid self-criticism and blame.

Understanding mindfulness as heartfulness

Here are some ways of specifically generating warmth and friendliness, along with attention. You need to give each of these exercises at least five minutes for best effect. Try to generate an intention rather than a feeling.

- Look at something in front of you in the same way as you may look into the eyes of a beautiful child, or at a flower. Bring a sense of affection to your visual perception, whatever that may be, for a few minutes. Note what happens.

- Listen to your favourite piece of relaxing music. This may be a piece of classical music, New Age music, or perhaps it's the sounds of nature, such as birds singing or the wind rustling through the trees.

- Smell the aroma in the room around you or of the food on your plate, in the same way that you smell the most beautiful scent of a perfume.

- When you next eat, take a few moments to feel your breath. You may find this difficult, because the habit is to dive in and munch, but hold back if you can. Now remember how lucky you are to have food to eat at all. Chew each morsel fully before you tuck into your next helping. Savour the taste.

- Notice the sense of touch as you walk from one place to another. Slow down as much as you can and feel the sensations in the feet. Imagine that your feet are kissing the earth with each step you take. Visualise yourself walking on precious ground, and allow yourself to be fully immersed in the sense of contact.

✔ As you walk around, notice other people and wish them happiness. Think 'May you be happy'. See whether you can make your wish genuine, from your heart.

✔ Listen to any negative thoughts or emotions in yourself. Perhaps you're habitually critical of yourself for having these feelings. Try a radically different approach: befriend your negative thoughts. Bring a sense of warmth and kindness to your anger, jealousy or frustration. Listen to yourself compassionately as you would to a good friend – with care and understanding. What happens?

Developing an Attitude of Gratitude

Gratitude is considered by some as the greatest of all emotions that can be cultivated. Recent studies are beginning to show that gratitude has a unique relationship with wellbeing, and can explain aspects of wellbeing that other personality traits cannot. An attitude of gratitude goes hand in hand with mindfulness.

You're grateful when you're aware of what you *do* have rather than what you don't. The effect of this is an opening of the heart. When you're aware with an open heart, you're in a deeper mindful mode.

Gratitude is a skill that you can develop. If you're bad at tennis or playing the piano, with practice you get better. The same is true of gratitude. Through repeated effort you can develop, strengthen and intensify gratitude. Flex your gratitude muscle by trying this exercise, which is almost guaranteed to make you more grateful:

1. **Think of something you're not grateful for.** Perhaps you're not grateful for your job, a relationship or your place of residence.

2. **Now think of all the things that are good about it.** Give yourself two minutes, and challenge yourself to come up with as many good things as possible. For example, if you're not happy with your job: Does it pay you good money? How much time do you get off? Is there a pension or medical plan with the job? Do you like any of your colleagues? Do you get breaks? Does working make being at home more pleasurable? Think of as many positive aspects for which you're grateful. To supercharge this exercise rather than just thinking about it, write down your answers. Be aware that you may have to overcome some resistance to doing this, especially if you're very ungrateful about the situation.

3. **Try this exercise again for other areas of your life.** See what effect that has on them. Again, remember that the exercise takes some effort, but the rewards make it worthwhile.

4. **Commit to doing this regularly for a week or a month on a daily basis.**
You may find yourself being naturally more grateful for all sorts of other
things too, including meditation.

Letting go through forgiveness

Life has its difficulties. And you're bound to get hurt by others, often wrongly
so. The danger comes when you carry this hurt around with you. If you don't
let the emotional pain go, the next time something hurts you, the suffering
accumulates. Over a period of years, the hurt can feel like you're walking
around carrying a heavy sack everywhere you go. Your shoulders feel tense.
Your face is screwed up. You're tense and uptight.

This harmful state of mind requires forgiveness for you to feel happier.
Being annoyed with someone else hurts you rather than anyone else. You
may admire hearing about others forgiving in situations of hatred, but when
you're called upon to do so yourself, you're stuck. You may find yourself feeling angry, depressed or hateful. Many studies now show that releasing and
letting go of past hurts through forgiveness leads to a longer and happier life.

Forgiveness doesn't mean what the other person did to you was right or
okay. It means you're willing to let that go so you can move on and live a happier life. Forgiveness is an act of kindness towards yourself. And through that
self-kindness, you naturally become a nicer person to be with for others too.

Try this approach to begin to allow yourself to forgive:

- ✔ Understand that hating someone else doesn't actually hurt that person
  at all.

- ✔ List all the beneficial things that have emerged from a situation. Try to
  see the situation from a totally different perspective. Ask a trusted friend
  to help you if you'd like to.

- ✔ Be compassionate with yourself. If you've been ruminating over a problem for some time, perhaps now's the time to let it go. You don't deserve
  all this hurt you're carrying around with you.

- ✔ Understand that the story you're telling yourself is just that: a story.
  This pain and hurt may be repeating itself in your mind through a story.
  Try letting go of the story, or seeing the story from another person's per-
  spective. Something may shift that will help you forgive.

- ✔ Wish the person well. If someone has hurt you, counteract that with
  some loving-kindness meditation. Wish the person well, just as you may
  wish yourself or a friend well. Use the loving-kindness meditations in
  Chapter 6 to help you.

An alternative practice is to do a forgiveness meditation. You can choose to listen to the guided audio (MP3 Track 4) that comes with this book. The steps are:

1. **Sit in a comfortable and relaxed position.** Let your eyes close, if that feels comfortable, and allow your breath to find a natural rhythm.

2. **Imagine or feel the breath going into your heart.** Become aware of and feel the obstructions you've created in your heart due to a lack of for-giveness, whether for yourself or others. Become mindful of the heart-ache from a lack of forgiveness in your core.

3. **Now you can *ask forgiveness of others*.** Say to yourself: 'Let me become aware of the many ways that knowingly or unknowingly I've caused others pain and suffering though my own fear, pain or anger.' Visualise each person who comes to mind – feel the sorrow and pain they feel due to your words and actions. Now, finally, release this sad-ness, sorrow and heartache by asking for forgiveness. As you imagine or feel each person's presence, say: 'I ask for your forgiveness. Forgive me.' Repeat this slowly as many times as you feel appropriate, speaking from the heart.

4. **Now you can move on to *forgiving yourself*.** You've hurt yourself in many ways through thoughts, words or actions. You may have done this consciously – or unconsciously, without even knowing it. Allow yourself to become mindful of any unkindness you've directed towards yourself. Feel the suffering you've caused yourself and begin to release this by saying: 'For all the ways I have been causing suffering to myself through thoughts, words or actions, consciously or unconsciously, I forgive myself. I forgive myself as far as I can.'

5. **Now you can move on to *forgive other people* who've hurt you.** You've been hurt by many people through their words or actions, knowingly or unknowingly. They've caused you suffering in your being to different degrees. Imagine the ways they've done this. Become aware, feel the pain others have caused you, and allow yourself to let go of this sadness from your heart with the words: 'I've been hurt by others many times, in many ways, due to the pain, sorrow, anger or misunderstanding of others. I've carried this suffering in my being for long enough. As far as I'm ready to, I offer my forgiveness. To those who've hurt me, I forgive you.' Repeat these phrases if you want.

With time and practice, you may feel a shift in your heart and be able to for-give. If the shift doesn't happen, notice how you feel, and be soft and kind with yourself. Let the forgiveness be genuine. Forgiveness takes time, so be patient and practise the meditation regularly. With regular commitment, you'll be able to release yourself from the sorrow you're carrying, through gentle forgiveness.

Tackling Unhelpful Attitudes

Just as you have helpful attitudes to cultivate in your mindfulness practice, you also have unhelpful attitudes that you'd be better off staying away from. For example, if you're a bit of a perfectionist and are worried you're going to fall asleep in your mindfulness practice, you don't need to start panicking, or worrying when you start struggling to stay awake. You just need to become aware of the perfectionist mindset and, as best you can, let the unhelpful approach go.

The most unhelpful thing you can do with mindfulness is not to practise. Once you begin practising regularly, in no matter how small a way, you may begin to discover which attitudes to nurture in your meditation and which are unhelpful.

Avoiding quick-fix solutions

If you want a quick fix for all your problems, you've come to the wrong place. *Mindfulness is simple but not easy.* Mindfulness is a powerful process that takes time, and a certain type of effort, energy and discipline. You can find quick fixes in the domain of television advertising, billboards and the Internet. I know these temptations are great, and marketing companies spend billions to work out how to convince you to part with your hard-earned cash. Unfortunately, however, in my limited experience of instant happiness, that form of happiness is just that: instantly present and instantly gone.

What you can do is integrate mindfulness practices into your life in short bursts. You don't have to sit for hours and hours in the lotus posture. One minute of mindful attention on your breath on a daily basis can begin to shift something within you. The more you put in, the more you get out. Five minutes is better than one minute. You need to decide what's right for you: trust in yourself to make a decision and stick to that choice for a period of time.

Mindfulness meditation is not about how long you can sit still for. If that was the case, roosting chickens would be Zen masters. What really matters is the quality of your intention, attention and attitude.

Overcoming perfectionism

'I'll meditate as soon as I've sorted my life out.' 'I'll do the course when things are totally settled.' 'I'll practise mindfulness when I have no more problems in my life.' These excuses are common and, on the whole, unconstructive.

Sometimes you do need to allow major events in your life to settle before you work on a new skill like mindfulness. However, you can't wait for life to become perfect. You don't have time to waste. If you've found a way to systematically and thoroughly create a meaningful way of producing further health and wellbeing in your life, why not take the first step? Yes, you may get it wrong and make mistakes, but imperfection, mistakes and stumbles are an integrated part of the process of finding out about anything. No child ever began to walk without falling. No driver ever learns to drive without stalling. Take the first step today.

Finding out from failure

Failures are finger posts on the road to achievement.

CS Lewis

There's no such thing as a bad mindfulness practice. There's no failure in meditation. If mindfulness was about success and failure, it'd be like any other activity in life. But mindfulness is different – that's the beauty of it. I list here some experiences that people *think* made them fail at being mindful, and reasons why they aren't 'failures':

- ✔ **'I couldn't concentrate. My mind was all over the place.'** You can't concentrate continuously. Sooner or later your mind goes into thoughts, dreams, ideas or problems. The nature of the mind is to wander off. Lack of concentration is an integral part of mindfulness. Expect your mind to wander and be pleased when you've noticed, then gently bring your attention back.

- ✔ **'I couldn't sit still.'** Your body is designed to move. If sitting really isn't for you, remember you can do mindfulness while you move. Try walking meditation (Chapter 6), exercises that integrate awareness, like yoga or tai chi, or any other action you choose, in a mindful and therefore meditative way. You're cultivating awareness, not a motionless body.

- ✔ **'I felt bored, tired, frustrated, angry, annoyed, jealous, excited or empty.'** You're going to feel a variety of emotions in your mindfulness practice, just as you do in your everyday life. The difference is, instead of reacting to them automatically, you've got the valuable opportunity to watch them rise and fall. In the long run, these emotions will probably calm down a bit, but in the meantime you need simply to be aware of them – if you can, enjoy the show!

- ✔ **'I had the experience of X (replace X with *any* negative experience), which I didn't like.'** People have both pleasant and unpleasant experiences in mindfulness meditation. The experience may be anything from deep sadness to feeling you're disappearing, or your arms may feel as if they're floating up. My theory is that your mind is releasing knots within your psyche out into your conscious mind, and freeing you from your own conditioning. This is part and parcel of the process – let the process unfold by itself if you feel you can. If you find the feeling coming up is a difficult one, try saying to yourself: 'This too will pass.'

If you're struggling a lot in your mindfulness practice, you're probably holding onto a desire for something. Maybe you desire to get rid of tension, a feeling of irritation, your mind wandering, or boredom. Maybe you're trying to *get* peace of mind, focus or relaxation. Make peace with your mindfulness practice. Let go of your desire to get anything out of the practice. Then, paradoxically, you'll find the practice far more enjoyable and peaceful.

If you find yourself becoming very concerned or frightened in your mindfulness practice, and if the feelings are ongoing, you may need professional support for what's coming up for you. Get in touch with your doctor or suitable therapist.

Love is a powerful attitude

Once there was a little girl who was ill. She needed a blood transfusion, but had a rare blood type. The doctors searched for a blood match but to no avail. They then tested her younger, six-year-old, brother, and fortunately he was a match. The doctors and his mother explained to the boy that they needed his blood so that they could give it to his sister to help her get better. The boy looked concerned and said that he needed to think about it, which surprised

them. After some time, he returned and agreed. The doctors laid the brother down on a bed next to his sister, and began transferring some blood. Before long, his sister began to get better. Then, suddenly, the boy called the doctor over and whispered in his ear, 'How long do I have left to live?' The boy thought that by giving blood, he'd die, which of course he wouldn't. That was why he took some time to decide before saying yes to giving his blood to his sister.

Chapter 5

Humans Being Versus Humans Doing

*H*uman beings love doing stuff. You go to work, have hobbies, socialise, and become an adept multi-tasker trying to fit everything into the day. But what about the *being* in human being?

Every day, in everything you do, your mind switches between *doing* mode and *being* mode. This doesn't mean that you switch between, say, typing an email and staring into space. Instead, it means *being* in the moment as you're *doing* a task. One mode of mind isn't better than the other. They're both helpful in different ways. However, using the wrong mode of mind for a particular situation can cause difficulties.

In this chapter, I explain how spending some of your time just *being* has huge and far-reaching advantages. I also tell you how to 'just be it'.

Delving into the Doing Mode of Mind

You know the feeling. You've got to get the kids ready, drop them off at school, pay the gas bill, pop that letter in the post, renew the car insurance, and make sure that you call your sister to see if she's feeling better. You're exhausted just thinking about everything! But you know you have to do it all. Your mind is in *doing* mode.

Doing mode is a highly developed quality in humans. You can think and conceptualise how you want things to be, and then work methodically in order to achieve them. That's part of the reason why people have been able to design computers and land on the moon – the products of doing mode.

Doing mode is certainly not a bad thing. If you want to get the shopping done, you need some doing mode! However, sometimes doing mode goes too far, and you start doing more and more without taking a break. That can certainly be draining.

The hallmarks of the doing mode of mind are:

- ✔ **You're aware of how things *are*, and how they *should* be.** For example, if you need to renew your home insurance, you're aware that you currently haven't renewed the insurance, and that you need to at some point soon.

- ✔ **You set a goal to fix things.** If you're in doing mode, you're setting goals for the way things should be. This problem-solving happens all the time without you being conscious of it. In the home insurance example, your goal may be to call several insurance companies or visit several websites to find the right deal for you.

- ✔ **You try harder and harder to achieve your goal.** In doing mode, you feel driven. You know what you want and you try hard to get it. Doing mode is all about getting to the destination rather than considering anything else. So if an insurance company puts you on hold for too long, you begin to feel tense and frustrated. In this driven state of mind, you don't come up with creative solutions such as calling a different company or just trying at a quieter time.

- ✔ **Most of your actions happen automatically.** You're not really aware when you're in doing mode. You're completing tasks on automatic pilot. Thoughts pop into your head, emotions emerge, and you act on them largely unconsciously. If the person you're speaking to on the telephone is rude, you may automatically react, making you both feel bad, rather than considering that the phone operator may have had a really long and bad day too.

- ✔ **You're not in the present moment.** When engaged in doing mode, you're not connected with your senses, in the now. You're thinking about how things should be in the future, or replaying events from the past. You're lost in your head rather than focused in the moment. While you're placed on hold on the telephone, your mind may wander into anxious thoughts about tomorrow's meeting rather than you just taking the chance to have a break and look at the sky or gaze at the beautiful tree through the window.

Doing mode isn't just the mode you're in when you're doing stuff. Even when you're sitting on the sofa, your mind can be spinning. You're in doing mode. Trying to run away from negative emotions or towards pleasant ones is also part of doing mode's speciality.

Doing mode is most unhelpful when applied to emotional difficulties. Trying to get rid of or suppress emotions may seem to work in the very short term, but before long the emotions rise up again. Being mode is a more helpful state of mind for understanding and finding out about emotions, particularly negative ones. See the later section 'Dealing with emotions using being mode'.

Cruising on auto pilot

Aeroplanes have a button called automatic pilot. When pilots push that button, they don't have to consciously control the aircraft – the plane flies by itself. People can also run on auto pilot when they're in doing mode, although I haven't found the button for it yet! You may have had the experience when going to fetch something from another room. You walk down the stairs and into the room and . . . your mind's gone blank! You wandered off somewhere internally and forgot what you wanted. Or you're driving somewhere different and end up unconsciously driving to work. Oops! That's human auto pilot in action.

Auto pilot has some advantages, which is why it evolved in humans. Once something has become automatic, you don't need to consciously think about it again, and can give your attention to something else. Auto pilot also saves some energy. Imagine if you had to think about every movement of your body when you were driving or walking – activities that involve hundreds of muscles; thinking in this way would be very tiring. In fact, you say someone has learnt something properly if he can do it automatically without thinking about it.

The problems of auto pilot are that:

✏ **You can get trapped in auto pilot.** You can spend your whole life in doing mode. With everything happening automatically, you have a lack of connection with the beauty of life. The blue sky, the green trees, the flight of a bird, the eyes of a child, become just ordinary or you don't even notice them. This kind of living leads to a sense of dissatisfaction.

✏ **You don't have a choice.** Auto pilot is particularly dangerous in the field of thoughts and emotions. You may be thinking 'I'm useless,' 'I'm unlovable,' or 'I can't do that' automatically without even noticing it. Thoughts have a huge effect on emotions, especially if you believe the thoughts to be true. Automatic negative thoughts lead to unhelpful and difficult emotions. All you notice is that you're suddenly really low, or angry, or tired. However, if you're conscious of these negative thoughts, you have a choice as to whether you believe them or not.

Embracing the Being Mode of Mind

Society values people achieving goals. You see people in the papers who have record amounts of money, or who've climbed the highest mountain. How many times has someone made the headlines for living in the moment?!

People are very familiar with and almost comforted by the doing mode of mind. To stop doing so much, whether physically or mentally, isn't easy. Doing feels attractive and exciting. However, people are beginning to realise that too much doing is a problem. In fact, a whole philosophy has arisen and lots of books have been written all about how you can slow down.

The hungry tigers

The classic story of the hungry tigers points towards a different way of living.

One day a man was walking through a forest when a tiger spotted him and chased after him. The man ran out of the forest as fast as he could to escape the hungry beast. Eventually he stumbled and fell off the edge of a cliff. As he fell he managed to catch a vine, but continued to dangle precariously over the high drop. The tiger continued to watch him from above. Another pack of hungry tigers paced below the man. Then a mouse popped out of a crevice in the cliff. The mouse started gnawing the vine the man was clinging to. Suddenly, the man saw a beautiful plump strawberry glistening in the light. He plucked it and popped it into his mouth. How wonderful it tasted!

You can interpret this story in many ways. I like to think of the tiger above as worries about the past, and the high drop to the tigers below as concerns about the future. The suggestion is to come to your senses – enjoy the strawberry of the present moment, and engage in being mode! The story also offers hope: no matter how bad your past or future appears to be, you may be able to take some pleasure through connecting with your senses in the here and now.

On the surface, the realm of *being* appears lifeless and boring. In actual fact, this couldn't be farther from the truth. Being mode is a nourishing and uplifting state of mind that's always available to you, in the midst of busy activity. You can be trading in the stock market or teaching young children maths – if you're conscious of your physical, emotional, and psychological state of mind – you're in being mode. In some ways, being mode isn't easy to cultivate, yet the rewards of accessing this inner resource far outweigh any difficulties in reaching it.

Here are some of the qualities of the being mode of mind:

- **You connect with the present moment.** When you're in being mode, you're mindful of sight, sound, smell, taste or touch. Or you're consciously aware of your thoughts or emotions, without being too caught up by them. You're not intentionally getting lost in regrets about the past or concerns about the future.

- **You acknowledge and allow things to be as they are.** You're less goal-oriented. You have less of a burning desire for situations to change. You accept how things are before moving to change anything. Being mode doesn't mean resignation, it means active acceptance of the way things are at the moment. If you're lost but you have a map, the only way of getting anywhere is to know where you are to start with. Being mode is about acknowledging where you are.

✔ **You're open to pleasant, unpleasant, and neutral emotions.** You're willing to open up to painful and unpleasant sensations or emotions without trying to run away from them. You understand that avoiding an emotion just locks you into the feeling more tightly.

The being mode of mind is what mindfulness endeavours to cultivate. Being mode is about allowing things to be as they are already. When you stop trying to change things, paradoxically they change by themselves. As Carl Jung said: 'We cannot change anything until we accept it.'

Accepting a situation or emotion just to make it go away doesn't really work, and misses an important point. For example, say you're feeling a bit sad. If you acknowledge it with a secret desire that the sadness will go away, you haven't fully accepted it yet. Instead, accept an emotion wholeheartedly if you can – emotions are here to teach us something. Listen to your emotions and see what they have to say.

Combining Being and Doing

Think of your mind as like the ocean. The waves rise and fall, but the still, deep waters are always there underneath.

You're tossed and turned in the waves when you're on the surface in doing mode. The waves aren't bad – they're just part of the ocean. Going farther down, the waves of doing rest on the still waters of being, as shown in Figure 5-1. Being is your sense of who you are. Being is characterised as a state of acceptance, a willingness to be with whatever is. Being is tranquil, still, and grounding.

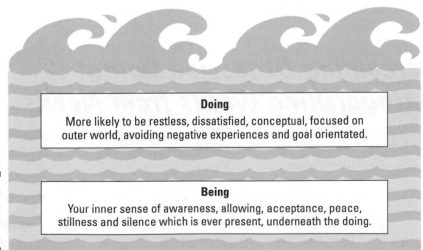

Doing
More likely to be restless, dissatisfied, conceptual, focused on outer world, avoiding negative experiences and goal orientated.

Being
Your inner sense of awareness, allowing, acceptance, peace, stillness and silence which is ever present, underneath the doing.

Figure 5-1:
The ocean
of doing and
being.

Experience itself is neither doing nor being mode. You determine the mode by how you react or respond to the experience. Doing is getting actively involved in the experience in order to change it in some way. Being is simply seeing it as it is. That lack of fixing can result in a sense of calmness even when things are tricky.

Switching from doing to being doesn't require years of mindfulness training. It can happen in a moment. Imagine walking to work and worrying about all the things that you need to get done, and planning how you'll tackle the next project with the manager away on holiday. Suddenly you notice the fiery red leaves on a tree. You're amazed at the beauty of it. That simple connection with the sense of sight is an example of being mode. The mode of mind changes by shifting the focus of attention to the present moment. You're no longer on automatic pilot with all its planning, judging, criticising, and praising. You're in the present moment.

Even something as seemingly mundane as feeling your feet in contact with the ground as you walk is a move towards being mode, too. You can also notice the beauty of a tree, the sounds of birds chirping or the gentle sun on the back of your neck. Changing modes may not seem easy at first, especially when you're preoccupied by thoughts, but it gets easier through practice. You don't have to rush through life.

The key to a mindful way of living is to integrate both doing and being modes of mind into your life. Become aware of which mode you're operating in and make an appropriate choice about which is most helpful for the situation. You need to know where you are on the map before you can move on. Doing mode is important. You need to plan what you're going to do today, what food to buy, how to give feedback to a colleague, and how best to respond when your children start arguing. These activities make you human. However, as a human *being*, you need to integrate a being mode of mind into your doing in order to be fully awake to your life.

Overcoming Obsessive Doing: Distinguishing Wants from Needs

One of the most common addictions people have is work. What started as a 9 a.m. to 5 p.m. job can easily become a 5 a.m. to 9 p.m. job. Naturally, you need to work and earn enough cash to pay the bills. However, before you know it, you're trying to earn a bit more than you actually need. And then your neighbour gets that new car, and you're tempted to do the same. So you do, but it's a touch out of your budget. You go for that promotion, but you need to put in lots more hours – it's a slippery slope to more and more doing.

If working long hours is what you want, you're fine, but if it's too much for you, or the long hours are having a negative impact on your relationships, consider looking into a different way of living.

You're excessively doing when your balance is tipped towards your wants rather than your needs. You need to keep a balance between what you want out of life and what you actually need. I define *wants* as desires that aren't really essential to your life, but that you seem to chase after, like an even bigger house or wanting absolutely everyone to like you. *Needs* are your basic necessities such as food, shelter, clothing, and a sense of security.

Here are some suggestions for reducing your wants and so helping you to have more time to access being mode:

- ✔ Make a list of all the things you need to do today. Then prioritise. Ensure that you put mindfulness on the list too. That goes at the top!

- ✔ Put some things on your to-do list that aren't urgent but are fun, like reading you favourite novel or taking the kids to the cinema. Let's throw an ice-cream in here too! Non-urgent activities give you a chance to have a breather from energy-draining doing mode.

- ✔ Think about people you know who rarely rush from place to place. Ask them how they get everything done, or just spend more time with them. Hang out with those with a mindful disposition, and hopefully their mindfulness will rub off onto you.

- ✔ Simplify your life. Remember who and what's most important in your life, and let go of the rest. As American writer and naturalist Henry David Thoreau said: 'Life is frittered away by detail. Simplify, simplify.'

- ✔ Switch television channels when adverts come on. Adverts are designed to ignite dissatisfaction in you, making you want more, more, more. Or if you're feeling really mindful, just copy me and get rid of the television altogether. Why watch television when you can meditate or mindfully hang out with friends!

- ✔ Invoke the being mode of mind whenever you're doing things. Connecting with your breath or the senses is a helpful way of accomplishing this.

Being in the Zone: The Psychology of Flow

Have you ever noticed that when you're eating your favourite food, you forget all your worries and problems? The experience is so lovely that the sense of who you are, what you do, where you come from, and whatever the plan is for tomorrow all vanish for a moment. In fact, most pleasures that you engage in result in you letting go of the sense of 'you' with all your problems and issues.

Imagine skiing downhill at high speed. You sense the wind whooshing past you, feel the cool mountain breeze, and enjoy the deep blue colour of the sky. You're *in the zone*, in the moment, at one with all around you. When you're in the zone, you let go of doing mode and come into being mode – the present moment.

This 'in the zone' state of mind is called *flow* by psychologist Mihaly Csíkszentmihályi. But what's flow got to do with the being mode of mind? Surely being in the zone is always about doing? Not quite. Practising mindfulness helps to generate flow experiences directly. Everything you do, you can do in the moment, giving you a deeper sense of aliveness.

Here's what you experience when you're in a state of flow:

- ✔ You feel at one with the world.
- ✔ You let go of your sense of being an individual and any worries and problems.
- ✔ You're completely focused.
- ✔ You feel very satisfied with what you're doing.
- ✔ You're happy, although you don't really notice it at the time because you're so engrossed in whatever you're doing.

Understanding the factors of mindful flow

Csíkszentmihályi found some key factors that accompany an experience of flow. I've adapted them here so you can generate what I call a mindful flow experience. As long as you do a task mindfully, it's potentially going to be a flow experience.

Here are some of key factors of mindful flow and how you can generate them using mindfulness:

- ✔ **Attention.** Flow experiences need attention. Mindfulness is all about attention, and mindfulness increases your level of attention with practice. Through regular mindfulness practice, your brain becomes better at paying attention to whatever you choose to focus on, making a flow experience far more likely. When driving, you simply pay attention to your surroundings rather than letting your mind wander off.
- ✔ **Direct and immediate feedback.** Flow needs direct feedback as to how you're doing. When you're practising mindfulness, you're getting immediate feedback because you know at any time if you're paying attention

or if your mind has wandered off for the last few minutes. So, if driving, you notice when your mind has drifted into dreaming about what's for dinner tonight, and you bring your attention gently back to the here and now.

✔ **Sufficiently challenging task.** Mindfulness is an active process of repeatedly rebalancing to come back to the present moment while the mind – doing what minds do – wants to pull you away into other thoughts. To drive in a mindful way from work to home would be a suitable challenge for anyone, potentially creating a flow experience.

✔ **Sense of personal control.** When you're mindful of your thoughts and feelings that are arising, you've created a choice. You don't have to react to your thoughts or do what they tell you to do. This generates a sense of control as you become aware of the choices you have. If, while you're driving, someone cuts in front of you, you've got the choice to either react and feel annoyed, or practise letting it go. Even if you do react, you can notice how you react and what effect the reaction has on your thoughts and feelings. Eventually, mindfulness goes beyond trying to control – you discover the flow experience is accessed through letting go rather than controlling your attention.

✔ **Intrinsically rewarding.** As you carry out a task, you're doing it for the sake of itself. If you're driving your car to get home as fast as possible to have your cup of tea, you're not going to be in a flow experience. If you drive to simply enjoy each moment of the journey, that's different. You can feel the warmth of the sunshine on your arms, appreciate the colour of the sky while sitting in traffic, and marvel at the miracle of the human body's ability to do such a complex task effortlessly. You're in a flow experience.

 Normally, mindfulness would make you a safer driver rather than a more dangerous one. However, begin by being mindful of safer tasks like washing dishes or going for a walk before you attempt mindfulness of driving, just so you get used to being mindful. Don't use mindfulness of driving if you find the experience distracting.

Discovering your flow experiences

Everyone's had flow experiences. By knowing when you've been in flow, you can encourage more opportunities to experience it in the future. The following are some typical activities that people often find themselves flowing in. You may even find something here to try yourself:

✔ **Reading or writing.** When you're fully engaged in a good book full of fascinating insights or a challenging storyline, you're in flow. You forget about everything else and time flies by. When writing in flow, words simply pop into your head and onto your page with effortless ease. You stop criticising what you're creating, and enjoy seeing the report or book pouring out of you. I've discovered how to do this myself by writing whatever words arise into my awareness first, and avoiding all self-judgement. Then I go back and edit the writing later on. In this way, the writing seems to flow naturally. This is an example of mindful writing.

- ✔ **Art or hobbies (such as drawing, painting, dancing, singing, or playing music).** Most artistic endeavours involve flow. You're directly connected with your senses, and people often describe themselves as being 'at one with the music'. If you're forced to do a particular hobby, it may or may not be a flow experience, because the intrinsic motivation isn't there.

- ✔ **Exercise (walking, running, cycling, swimming, and so on).** Some people love exercise so much that they get addicted to it. The rush of adrenaline, the full focus in the present moment, and the feeling of exhil-aration make for a flow experience.

- ✔ **Work.** Perhaps surprisingly, you can be in flow at work. Research has found that people are happier at work than they are in their leisure time. Work encourages you to do something with a focused attention, and often involves interaction with others. You need to give something of yourself. This can set the stage for flow. In contrast, watching television at home can drain your energy, especially if you're watching unchalleng-ing programmes.

- ✔ **Anything done mindfully.** Remember, anything that you do with a mind-ful awareness is going to generate a flow state of mind, from making love to making a cup of tea. Just let go of your judgement, be fully present as best you can, and see whether you can enjoy the experience.

Encouraging a Being Mode of Mind

Generally speaking, most people spend too much time in doing mode and not enough in being mode. Doing mode results in chasing after goals that may not be what you're really interested in. Being mode offers a rest – a chance to let go of the usual, habitual patterns of the mind and drop into the awareness that's always there.

You can be in being mode even though you're doing something. Being mode doesn't necessarily mean that you're doing nothing. You can be busy working hard in the garden, and yet if your attention is right in the moment, and you're connecting directly with the senses, you can be in being mode.

Here are ten ways of switching from doing mode to being mode:

- ✔ When walking from place to place, take the opportunity to feel your feet on the floor, see the range of different colours in front of you, and listen to the variety of different sounds. (Move to Chapter 6 to discover the art of mindful walking.)

✔ When moving from one activity to another, take a moment to rest. Feel three complete in-breaths and out-breaths.

✔ Establish a regular meditation routine using formal mindfulness meditation practices (for more on this, head to Chapter 6).

✔ Use the three-minute mini meditation several times a day (see Chapter 7). Whenever you catch yourself becoming excessively tense or emotional, use the mini meditation to begin moving towards being mode and opening up to the challenging experience, rather than reacting to try to avoid or get rid of the experience.

✔ Avoid multi-tasking whenever you can. Doing one thing at a time with your full and undivided attention can engage being mode. Doing too many things at the same time encourages your mind to spin.

✔ Find time to do a hobby or sport. These activities tend to involve connecting with the senses, which immediately brings you into being mode. Painting, listening to music, or playing an instrument, dancing, singing, walking in the park, and many more activities all offer a chance to be with the senses.

✔ When taking a bath or shower, use the time to feel the warmth of the water and the contact of the water with your skin. Allow all your senses to be involved in the experience; enjoy the sound of the water and breathe in the scent of your favourite soap or body wash.

✔ When you're eating, pause before your meal to take a few conscious breaths. Then eat the meal with your full attention. Check out Chapter 6 for ways to munch mindfully.

✔ Treat yourself to a day of mindfulness once in a while. Wake up slowly, feel your breath frequently, and connect with your senses and with other significant people around you as much as you can. Chapter 8 sets out some suggestions for having a mindful day.

Dealing with emotions using being mode

Using doing mode in the area of thoughts and emotions is like using the wrong remote control to change the channel on your television. No matter how hard you push the buttons, the channel isn't going to change – and pushing the buttons harder just makes you more tired and breaks the remote control. You're using the wrong tool for the job.

Say you're feeling sad today. Doing mode may feel the emotion and use the problem-solving, goal-oriented mind to try to fight it, asking, 'Why am I sad? How can I escape from it? What shall I do now? Why does this always happen to me? Let me try watching television. Oh, I feel worse. What if this feeling never goes away? What if I feel depressed again?'

Doing mode sets thoughts spinning in your head, which just makes you feel worse. Your focus is on getting rid of the feeling instead of feeling the emotion. The more you fight the emotion, the stronger it seems to get. So, what's the solution?

Next time you have an uncomfortable feeling like sadness, anger, frustration or jealousy, try this exercise to get into being mode:

1. **Set your intention.** Let your intention be to feel the emotion and its effects as best you can with a gentle curiosity. You're not doing so as a clever way to get rid of it. You're just giving yourself space to learn from the emotion rather than running away.

All emotions, no matter how strong, have a beginning and an end.

2. **Feel the emotion.** Feel the emotion with care, kindness, and acceptance, as best you can. Open up to it. Notice where the emotion manifests itself in your body. Breathe into that part of your body and stay with it. Allow the emotion to be as it is. You don't need to fight or run away. Be with the experience.

3. **De-centre from the emotion.** Notice that you can be aware of the emotion without being the emotion itself – create a space between yourself and the feeling. This is an important aspect of mindfulness. As you observe the feeling, you're separate from it in the sense that you're free from it. You're watching it. It's like sitting on a riverbank as the water rushes by rather than being in the river itself. As you watch the water (emotion) pass by, you're not in the river itself. Every now and then, you may feel like you've been sucked into the river and washed downstream. As soon as you feel this, simply step back out of the river again. Figure 5-2 illustrates this idea.

4. **Breathe.** Now simply feel your breath. Be with each in-breath and each out-breath. Notice how each breath is unique, different, and vital for your health and wellbeing. Then continue with whatever you need to do in a mindful way.

Finding time to just be

Are you a busy bee? Do you have too much to do to have time to be? One of the attractive things about mindfulness is that you don't have a fixed amount of time that you're 'supposed' to practise for. Your daily practice can be meditating for one minute or one hour – it's up to you. The other great thing about mindfulness is that you can simply be mindful of your normal everyday routine and in that way build up your awareness and *being* mode. That takes no time at all; in fact, it can save time because you're more focused on your activities.

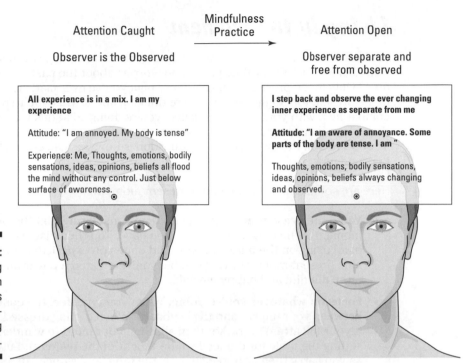

Attention Caught

Mindfulness Practice →

Attention Open

Observer is the Observed

Observer separate and free from observed

All experience is in a mix. I am my experience

Attitude: "I am annoyed. My body is tense"

Experience: Me, Thoughts, emotions, bodily sensations, ideas, opinions, beliefs all flood the mind without any control. Just below surface of awareness.

I step back and observe the ever changing inner experience as separate from me

Attitude: "I am aware of annoyance. Some parts of the body are tense. I am "

Thoughts, emotions, bodily sensations, ideas, opinions, beliefs always changing and observed.

Figure 5-2: Stepping back from thoughts and emotions using mindfulness.

These mindful practices require almost no time at all:

✔ When waiting in a queue, rather than killing time, engage your awareness. Time is too precious to be killed. Notice the colours and sounds around you. Or challenge yourself to see whether you can maintain the awareness of your feet on the floor for ten full breaths.

✔ When you stop at a red traffic light, you have a choice. You can let yourself get frustrated and impatient, or you can do traffic light meditation! Close your eyes and nourish yourself with three mindful breaths – very refreshing!

✔ The next time the phone rings, let it ring three times. Use that time to breathe and smile. Telesales companies know that you can 'hear the smile' on the phone and ask employees to smile when they're on a call. You're in a more patient and happy state of mind when you speak.

✔ Change your routine. If you normally drive to work, try walking or cycling for part of it. Speak to different friends or colleagues. Take up a new hobby. When you change your habits, you engage different pathways in the brain. You instinctively wake up to the moment and just be.

Living in the moment

You're always in the present moment. You've never been in any other moment. Don't believe me? Every time your mind worries about the past, when does it do it? Only in the present moment. Every plan you've ever made is only made in the present too. Right now, as you're thinking about what you're reading and comparing it with your past experience, you're doing so in this moment, now. Your plans for tomorrow can only be thought about now. Now is all you're ever in. So what's all the fuss about? The question is how you can connect with the here and now.

Here are some tips for living in the present moment:

- ✔ **Value the present moment.** Spend time considering that the present moment is the *only* moment that you have. You then discover the value of focusing on the here and now. And once you experience how enjoyable present-moment living can be, you've created a powerful shift into a more mindful and happy lifestyle.

- ✔ **Focus on whatever you're doing.** When you type, feel the contact between your fingers and the keyboard. When getting dressed, try giving it your full attention rather than allowing your mind to wander. When setting the table for dinner, feel the weight of the plates and utensils as you carry them. Appreciate how the table looks once you have set it. Enjoy doing tasks to the best of your ability. Living in the present is trickier than it sounds, but each time you try, you get a little better at it. Slowly but surely, you start really living in the moment.

- ✔ **Reduce activities that draw you out of the moment.** I found that watching too much television sent my mind spinning, so I got rid of it. For you, you may need to reduce the time you spend on social media or surfing websites. Or it may be as simple as not lying in bed in the morning for too long, allowing youself to worry unnecessarily about the day. Nothing's wrong with any of these activities, but they don't encourage moment-by-moment living. They capture your attention and lead to a passive state of mind. Switching from channel to channel while slumped on the sofa drains your energy much faster than an activity done with a gentle awareness.

- ✔ **Establish a daily mindfulness practice.** Doing so strengthens your ability to stay in the present rather than being drawn into the past or pulled into the future. The strength of your daily habit extends into your everyday life, without you even trying. You hear the sound of that bird in the tree, or find yourself listening intently to your colleague in an effortless way. Now mindfulness becomes fun.

- ✔ **Look deeply.** Consider and reflect on all the people and things that come together in each moment. For example, you're reading this book. The book's paper came from trees which needed sunshine and rain, soil and nutrients. The book was edited, marketed, printed, transported, distributed, and sold by people. It also required the invention of the printing press, language, and more. You were taught English by someone to enable you to understand the words. This awareness of all that's come together and been provided for you to enjoy naturally creates gratitude and present-moment awareness. This is called *looking deeply*. You're connecting in the moment, and also seeing the bigger picture of how things have come together in an interconnected way. Looking deeply isn't thinking about your experience, but seeing your experience in a different way. You can try it in any situation – it transforms your perspective, and perspective transforms experience.

If you want to let go of your baggage from the past and future, try this meditation. I discovered it from a mindfulness teacher and monk called Ajahn Brahm. This present-moment meditation is also available as an MP3 (Track 6), so you can plug in your headphones and enjoy being guided. To let go of the weight of the past and future:

1. **Find a nice comfortable position to sit or lie in.** Be kind to yourself, and ensure you're in a relaxed posture, loosening any tight clothing, removing any glasses you're wearing and slipping off your shoes if you wish.

2. **Take your time to take a few deep, smooth breaths.** Let each in-breath represent nourishment and energy. Let each out-breath signify letting go.

3. **Gently close your eyes. Imagine you're holding two heavy shopping bags. Imagine how heavy they feel.** Feel the strain on your fingers and how much effort it takes to hold both bags. Their weight is pulling you down. The strain makes you feel tired and tense.

4. **Let the bag in one hand represent your past.** Imagine the bag is labelled 'past'. The bag contains all your regrets and mistakes. All your successes and failures. Past relationships. The choices you've made and the sorrows you've felt. You may even be able to visualise all your past experiences contained within this heavy bag. Holding this bag all day is tiring.

5. **Imagine that you decide it's time to let go of the 'past' bag.** You want to put the bag down and have a rest. So imagine slowly lowering the bag to the ground. Eventually the bag makes contact with the ground, and as it does so, immediately you begin to feel a release. Eventually your whole bag, representing all your past, is down on the ground. You smile as you let go completely. Imagine your hand opening and imagine yourself feeling so much better. You're liberated from carrying your past around with you.

6. **In your other hand, you're holding a heavy bag signifying your future.** Imagine the word 'future' written on the bag. The bag contains all your hopes, dreams, and plans. And also all your anxieties and worries. All your concerns and fears about what may or may not happen. Holding this hefty burden is no joke. The bag slows you down. But now you know how to put this bag, which is full of your future, down.

7. **Imagine that you slowly lower the 'future' bag until the bottom of the bag starts to make contact with the ground.** You begin to feel a relief. As you continue to lower the bag, all the weight is transferred to the earth. You feel an immense burden lifted. Your hand is now free, and you completely let go of your worries about the future.

8. **Imagine yourself standing with a bag representing your past on the floor on one side, and a bag representing your future on the floor on the other side.** Because you're standing between the past and future, where are you? You're in the best place to be: the present moment. Give yourself the go-ahead to feel free. The bags are perfectly safe on the ground. Rest in the joy of being in the present moment. Rejoice in the childlike innocence of the here and now – timelessness.

9. **Spend as much time as you want to in this experience of the present moment. And any time you feel you're carrying too much weight from the past or future, practise this meditation and put the weights down again.**

Part III
Practising Mindfulness

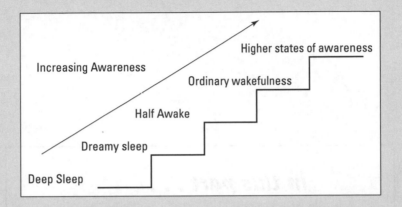

Increasing Awareness

Higher states of awareness

Ordinary wakefulness

Half Awake

Dreamy sleep

Deep Sleep

In this part . . .

✔ Explore the delights of practising mindfulness at any time of the day.

✔ Find out how to design a mindfulness routine that is right for you.

✔ Discover how to avoid the common pitfalls in the mindfulness game.

Chapter 6

Getting Into Formal Mindfulness Meditation Practice

. . . .

In This Chapter

▶ Trying eating, walking and body scan mindfulness meditation practices

▶ Breathing and walking in a mindful way

▶ Understanding and overcoming pitfalls

. . . .

*M*editation is like diving to the bottom of the ocean, where the water is still. The waves (thoughts) are at the surface, but you're watching them from a deeper, more restful depth. To submerge to that peaceful depth takes time. Extended meditations in the formal mindfulness meditation practices in this chapter offer the diving equipment for you to safely reach those tranquil places.

Formal practice is mindfulness meditation you specifically make time for in your day – it doesn't mean you need to put on a suit or a posh dress though! You decide when and for how long you're going to meditate, and you do it. A formal mindfulness routine lies at the heart of a mindful way of living. Without such a routine, you may struggle to be mindful in your daily life. This chapter explores some formal mindfulness practices for you to do while lying down, sitting or walking.

Preparing Your Body and Mind for Mindfulness Meditation

Here are some useful pointers on preparing yourself to practise mindful meditation:

✔ You can practise the meditation any time and anywhere that suits you. For more help on deciding when and where you'll practise, see Chapter 9.

✔ Avoid meditating immediately after a big meal or when you're feeling very hungry; your stomach may then become the object of your attention rather than anything else.

✔ Try and find conditions conducive for meditation: ideally, , somewhere that is not too noisy, with the right temperature for you and soft or natural lighting. Wear clothing that's loose and comfortable. None of these conditions are essential – it's possible to meditate anytime and anywhere – but if you're a beginner, these environmental factors help.

✔ You can be in any posture that feels comfortable for you for mindfulness meditation. If you're interested in advice on specific sitting postures, see further on in this chapter.

✔ Experiment by gently smiling when you meditate. This is a simple and powerful secret to help you enjoy meditation. Think of smiling as the most important posture in meditation. A cute little grin on your face sends a signal to your mind to be friendly towards yourself. You let go of being too serious or trying too hard; meditation can then become a joyful non-activity.

Savouring Mindful Eating Meditation

Starting with mindful eating meditation demonstrates the simplicity of meditation. Mindfulness meditation isn't about sitting cross-legged for hours on end; it's about the awareness you bring to each present moment. Mindfulness is about living with an open and curious awareness. Anything done with mindful awareness is meditation, including eating, driving, walking, talking and much more.

Try the following exercise, which is available as an audio track (Track 7):

1. **Place a small piece of fruit in your hand.** Imagine you dropped in from outer space and have never seen or tasted this fruit before. Spend a few minutes looking at the colour and texture. Explore the creases and folds of its skin, how it catches the light as you rotate it, and how much varying detail it contains. Observe the skill in your fingers to be able to delicately hold and rotate the fruit precisely and at will.

2. **Bring the fruit towards your nose.** Feel the sensations in your arm as you bring the fruit towards your nose. As you breathe, notice whether the fruit has a scent, and the quality of it. Notice how you feel if the fruit doesn't have a scent. Spend a few minutes doing this.

3. **Hold the fruit to your ear.** Squeeze the fruit gently between your thumb and finger and listen to the sound it produces, if any. Perhaps it makes a quiet sound or no sound at all. When you've done this, bring your arm back down.

4. **Feel the texture of the fruit.** Close your eyes to tune in to the sense of touch more deeply. Feel the shape of the object and its weight. Gently squeeze the fruit and observe whether you can get a sense of its juice.

5. **Bring the fruit towards your mouth.** Are you salivating? If so, your body has already begun the first stage of digestion. Touch the fruit gently onto your upper and lower lips to see what sensations you can detect. Place the fruit inside your mouth, on your tongue. Do you have a sense of relief now, or frustration? Feel the weight of the fruit on your tongue. Move the fruit around your mouth, noticing how skilled your tongue is at doing this. Place the fruit between two teeth and slowly bring your teeth together. Observe the phenomenon of tasting and eating. Spot the range of experiences unfolding, including a change in taste and the fluxing consistency of the fruit as it slowly breaks up and dissolves. Be aware of yourself chewing and how you automatically start to swallow. Stay with the experience until you've finished eating.

6. **Notice the aftertaste in your mouth when you've finished eating the fruit.**

Now, reflect on these questions:

✔ How do you feel having done that exercise?

✔ What effect will this process have on your experience of eating?

✔ What did you notice and find out?

There's no correct experience in this mindful eating meditation. Different people have different experiences. You probably found it wasn't your normal experience of eating. The first thing to discover about all mindful meditations is that *whatever your experience is, it is your experience and it is correct and valid.*

By connecting with the senses, you move from automatic pilot mode to a mindful mode. (Refer to Chapter 5 for more about mental modes.) In other words, rather than eating while doing something else and not even noticing the taste, you deliberately turn your attention to the whole process of eating.

You may have found the taste of the fruit to be more vivid and intense than usual. Perhaps you noticed things about this fruit that you hadn't noticed before. Mindfulness reveals new things and transforms the experience itself, making for a deeper experience. If this is true of eating something ordinary like a piece of fruit, consider what effect mindfulness may have on the rest of your experiences in life!

You may have noticed that you were thinking during the exercise, and perhaps you felt you couldn't do the mindful eating properly because of thinking.

Don't worry: you're pretty much *always* thinking, and it's not going to stop any time soon. What you can do is begin to become aware that it's happening and see what effect that has.

Relaxing with Mindful Breathing Meditation

If you're keen to try a short, simple, ten-minute sitting mindfulness meditation, this one's for you. This meditation focuses your attention on the breath and enables you to gently guide yourself back to your breathing when your attention wanders away.

This meditation is available as an audio track (Track 8) and shows you how to practise ten minutes of mindful breathing:

1. **Find a comfortable posture.** You can be sitting up in a chair, cross-legged on the floor or even lying down (see the later section 'Finding a posture that's right for you'). Close your eyes if you want to. And hold a charming little smile on your face if you can.

   This is an opportunity to be with whatever your experience is from moment to moment. This is a time for you. You don't need to achieve anything. You don't need to try too hard. You simply need to be with things as they are, as best you can, from moment to moment. Relax any obvious physical tensions if you can.

2. **Become aware of the sensations of breathing.** Feel your breath going in and out of your nostrils, or passing through the back of your throat, or feel your chest or belly rising and falling. As soon as you've found a place where you can feel your breath comfortably, endeavour to keep your attention there.

   Before long, your mind will take you away into thoughts, ideas, dreams, fantasies and plans. That's perfectly normal and absolutely fine. Just as soon as you notice that it's happened, gently smile again and guide your attention back to your breath. Try not to criticise yourself each time your mind wanders away. Instead, celebrate that you're back in the here and now. Understand that it's all part of the mindfulness process. If you find yourself criticising yourself or getting frustrated, say to yourself, 'It's okay . . . it's okay . . . gently come back to the breath.'

3. **Continue to stay with the meditation, without trying to control the depth or speed of your breathing.** If the breath changes, that's fine. If the breath stays the same, that's fine too. Everything's fine!

4. **After ten minutes, gently open your eyes.**

A cure for breathing boredom

A meditation student went up to her teacher and said that she was bored of feeling the breath. Could a different technique make breathing more interesting? The teacher replied, 'Yes. Close your mouth and breathe with your nose. Then take your left arm and with the thumb block your left nostril. With your index finger block the other nostril. You can no longer breathe. In less than a minute, you'll enjoy your breathing more than anything else in the whole world. Try it for just 30 seconds and you'll find it hard to think about anything else but breathing.'

Remember how important your breathing is, and try not to take it for granted. Breathing is special.

All the timings I suggest in this book are for guidance only. You can be flexible and reduce or increase the time you meditate depending on your circumstances. I suggest you decide, before each sitting, for how long you're going to practise meditating and then stick to your decision. You can use an alarm with a gentle ring, or perhaps a countdown timer on your phone to indicate when you've finished. This avoids having to keep opening your eyes to check whether you need to bring the mindful meditation to a close.

If that was one of the first times you've practised meditation, you're starting a journey. The meditation may have felt fine or awful. That doesn't matter. What matters is your willingness to accept whatever arises and keep practising. Starting meditation is a bit like going to the gym for the first time in months: the experience can be unpleasant to begin with! Keep practising and try not to judge it as a good or bad meditation – there's no such thing. And remember, there's nothing to be frightened about in meditation either: if you feel too uncomfortable, you can simply open your eyes and stop the meditation.

Engaging in Mindful Movement

Moving and stretching in a slow and mindful way is a wonderful preparation for more extended meditation exercises. Movement can also be a deep formal meditation in itself, if you approach it with full awareness.

When practising mindful movement, tune in to the sensations of your breath as you move and hold different postures. Become aware of thoughts and emotions that arise, notice them, and shift your awareness back to the body. Be mindful when a stretch is slightly out of your comfort zone and begins to feel uncomfortable. Explore what being at this edge of your comfort zone feels like. Notice whether you habitually drive yourself through the pain, or whether you always avoid the discomfort completely. Be curious about your relationship with movement and stretching, and bring a playful attitude to your experience.

Practising mindful movement has many benefits. You can:

✔ **Explore limits and discomfort.** When you stretch, you eventually reach a limit beyond which the discomfort becomes too intense (the *edge*). Mindfulness offers the opportunity to explore your mind's reactions as you approach your edge. Do you try to push beyond it, often causing injury, or do you stay too far away, avoiding the slightest discomfort? By approaching the edge with a mindful awareness, you open up to uncomfortable physical sensations rather than avoiding them.

You can transfer this skill of mindful awareness to your experience of difficult thoughts and emotions, encouraging you to stay with them and acknowledge them, and see what effect mindfulness has on them.

✔ **Tune in to the sensations in your body and tune out of the usual wandering mind.** By focusing in on the range of feelings and sensations in your body, you bring yourself into the present moment. Mindful movement shows you a way of coming into the here and now. Most of the other formal meditation practices involve being still; you may find movement an easier door into mindful practice.

✔ **Discover how to be mindful while your body is in motion.** You can transfer this discovery into your daily life and become more mindful of all the movement you do, such as walking, cooking, cleaning, and getting dressed. You're training your mind to be mindful in your day-to-day activities.

✔ **Practise being kind to your body.** Mindful movement and stretching is an opportunity to relate to your physical sensations with a spirit of friendliness. Allow physical sensations to soften by feeling them with a sense of warmth and affection rather than resistance or avoidance.

✔ **Gain an understanding about life through movement practice.** When trying to balance in a yoga posture, notice how your body isn't stiff or still but continuously moving and correcting to maintain your balance. Sometimes you lose your balance and have to start again. In the same way, living a life of balance requires continuous correction, and sometimes you get it wrong. You just need to start again.

Consider other lessons about life you can take from doing a sequence of mindful yoga or any other mindful movement. Think about how you cope with the more challenging poses, or how you may compare yourself with others, or how you compete with yourself.

Breathing into different parts of your body

In mindfulness practice, I often mention 'breathing into' your toes or fingers or your discomfort. What does that mean? Your lungs don't extend into your toes! Here's how you breathe into a particular part of the body:

1. Feel the sensations in the particular part of the body you're working on.

2. As you breathe in, imagine your breath going from your nose up or down into that part of your body or experience.

3. When you breathe out, sense your breath going out of that part of the body and back

out of your nose. Allow the sensations in that part of the body to gently soften as you do this.

If this technique doesn't work for you, try feeling the part of the body you're working on at the same time as feeling your breathing. Or try gently smiling as you feel that difficult sensation. Over time, this idea of breathing into your experience may naturally begin to make some sense. If it doesn't, don't worry. Trying different mindfulness tools allows you to find which ones work for you.

Trying Out the Body Scan Meditation

The body scan is a wonderful mindfulness practice to start your journey into contemplative practices. You normally do the body scan lying down, so you get a sense of letting go straight away.

Practising the body scan

Set aside at least half an hour for the body scan. Find a time when and a place where you won't be disturbed, and somewhere you feel comfortable and secure. Turn off any phones you have.

This is a time totally set aside for you, and for you to be with yourself. A time for renewal, rest, and healing. A time to nourish your health and well-being. Remember that mindfulness is about being with things as they are, moment to moment, as they unfold in the present. So, let go of ideas about self-improvement and personal development. Let go of your tendency for wanting things to be different from how they are, and allow them to be exactly as they are. Give yourself the space to be as you are. You don't even need to try to relax. Relaxation may happen or it may not. Relaxation isn't the aim of the body scan. If anything, the aim is to be aware of your experience, whatever it may be. Do whatever feels right for you.

The body scan practice is very safe. However, if the body scan brings up feelings that you can't cope with, stop and get advice from a mindfulness teacher or professional therapist. However, if you can, open up to the feelings and sensations and move in close; by giving these feelings the chance to speak to you, you may find that they dissipate in their own time.

Follow these steps, which are available as an audio track (Track 9):

1. **Loosen any tight clothing, especially around your waist or neck.** You may like to remove your shoes.

2. **Lie down on your bed or a mat with your arms by your sides, palms facing up, and legs gently apart.** If you feel uncomfortable, place a pillow under your knees or just raise your knees. Experiment with your position; you may even prefer to sit up. You can place a blanket over yourself, because your body temperature can drop when you're still for an extended time. Hold a slight, gentle smile on your face for the duration of this practice. This helps to remind you to be kind to yourself and not to take any experience too seriously.

3. **Begin by feeling the weight of your body on the mat, bed, or chair.** Notice the points of contact between that and your body. Each time you breathe out, allow yourself to sink a little deeper into the mat, bed, or chair.

4. **Become aware of the sensations of your breath.** You may feel the breath going in and out of your nostrils, or passing through the back of your throat, or feel the chest or belly rising and falling. Be aware of your breath wherever it feels most predominant and comfortable for you. Continue for a few minutes.

5. **When you're ready, move your awareness down the left leg, past the knee and ankle and right down into the big toe of your left foot.** Notice the sensations in your big toe with a sense of curiosity. Is your big toe warm or cold? Can you feel the contact of your socks, or the movement of air? Now expand your awareness to your little toe, and then all the toes in between. What do they feel like? If you can't feel any sensation, that's okay. Just be aware of lack of sensation.

6. **As you breathe, imagine the breath going down your body and into your toes. As you breathe out, imagine the breath going back up your body and out of your nose.** Use this strategy of breathing into and out of each part to which you're paying attention (see the nearby sidebar 'Breathing into different parts of your body').

7. **Expand your awareness to the sole of your foot.** Focus on the ball and heel of the foot. The weight of the heel. The sides and upper part of the foot. The ankle. Breathe into the whole of the left foot. Then, when you're ready, let go of the left foot.

8. **Repeat this process of gentle, kind, curious accepting awareness with the lower part of the left leg, the knee, and the upper part of the left leg.** Notice how your left leg may now feel different to your right leg.

9. **Gently shift your awareness around and down the right leg, to the toes in your right foot.** Move your awareness up the right leg in the same way as before. Then let it go.

10. **Become aware of your pelvis, hips, buttocks, and all the delicate organs around here.** Breathe into them and imagine you're filling them with nourishing oxygen.

11. **Move up to the lower torso, the lower abdomen, and lower back.** Notice the movement of the lower abdomen as you breathe in and out. Notice any emotions you feel here. See whether you can explore and accept your feelings as they are.

12. **Bring your attention to your chest and upper back.** Feel your rib cage rising and falling as you breathe in and out. Be mindful of your heart beating, if you can. Be grateful that all these vital organs are currently functioning to keep you alive and conscious. Be mindful of any emotions arising from your heart area. Allow space for your emotions to express themselves.

13. **Go to both arms together, beginning with the fingertips and moving up to the shoulders.** Breathe into and out of each body part before you move to the next one, if that feels helpful.

14. **Focus on your neck. Then move your mindful attention to your jaw, noticing whether it's clenched. Feel your lips, inside your mouth, your cheeks, your nose, your eyelids and eyes, your temples, your forehead (checking whether it's frowning), your eyes, the back of your head, and finally the top of your head.** Take your time to be with each part of your head in a mindful way, feeling and opening up to the physical sensations with curiosity and warmth.

15. **Imagine a space in the top of your head and soles of your feet. Imagine your breath sweeping up and down your body as you breathe in and out. Feel the breath sweeping up and down your body, and get a sense of each cell in your body being nourished with energy and oxygen.** Continue this for a few minutes.

16. **Now let go of all effort to practise mindfulness. Get a sense of your whole body. Feel yourself as complete, just as you are. At peace, just as you are.** Remember this sense of being is always available to you when you need it. Rest in this stillness.

17. **Acknowledge the time you've taken to nourish your body and mind. Come out of this meditation gently, being aware of the transition into whatever you need to do next.** Endeavour to bring this mindful awareness to whatever activity you engage in next.

Appreciating the benefits of the body scan meditation

The body scan meditation has many benefits:

✔ **Getting in touch with your body.** You spend most of your time in your head, constantly thinking, thinking, thinking. By practising the body scan, you're connecting with your own body and disconnecting from your mind with all its ideas, opinions, beliefs, judgements, dreams, and desires. Thinking is a wonderful and precious aspect of being human, but by connecting with the sensations in the body, you tune in to the intelligence and wisdom of the body. Hearing what the body has to say is fascinating if you listen carefully and give your body the space to express itself. The body scan helps you acknowledge that understanding and insight comes not only from the thinking brain but from the whole body, a supremely intelligent system from which you can discover so much.

✔ **Letting go of doing mode and coming into being mode.** As you lie down to do the body scan, you can completely let go physically. Your mind can follow on from this and also begin to let go of thinking on automatic pilot. Through the body scan, you begin to move from the autopilot doing mode of mind into the being mode of mind, which is about allowing things to be just as they are (see Chapter 5 for more).

✔ **Training your attention.** The body scan alternates between a wide and a narrow focus of attention – from focusing on your little toe all the way through to the entire body. The body scan trains your mind to be able to move from detailed attention to a wider and more spacious awareness from one moment to the next. In other words, you're more able to zoom in and out of an experience – a skill you can use outside of meditation.

✔ **Releasing emotions stored in the body.** Stressful events experienced from childhood, such as divorce or extreme discipline, cause great fear and can get locked and stored in the body as physical tension, an absence of sensation, or as a dysfunctional part of the body that causes, for example, problems with digestion. The body scan helps to release that stored-up emotion and tension. Some clients have had years of physical ailments relieved through the regular practice of the body scan meditation.

✔ **Using the body as an emotional gauge.** Practising the body scan and becoming increasingly aware of your body enables you to become more sensitive to how your body reacts in different situations throughout the day. If you become stressed or nervous about something, you may be able to notice this earlier through the body, and so be able to make an informed choice as to what to do next. Without that awareness, you don't have a choice and face the possibility of unnecessarily spiralling down into unhelpful emotions and a tense body. For example, if you notice your forehead tightening up or your shoulders tensing in a meeting, you can do something about it rather than letting the tension unconsciously build and build.

Diaphragmatic breathing

Diaphragmatic or *belly breathing*, rather than just chest breathing, is the type of breathing that takes place when you're relaxed and calm. You can see it in babies and young children when they breathe. Their bellies come out as they breathe in, and go back in when they breathe out. This belly breathing is caused by a deep, relaxed breath in which the diaphragm goes up and down, pushing the stomach in and out. When you practise diaphragmatic breathing, you nourish your body with greater levels of oxygen, and the breathing is easier for the body. Many people find it therapeutic, and yoga emphasises it too. Try taking a few belly breaths before you start your meditation to help lead yourself into a more focused state of mind.

Here's how to do diaphragmatic breathing (see Figure 6-1):

1. **Loosen any tight clothing, especially around your waist.**

2. **Get into a comfortable position, sitting or lying down.**

3. **Place one hand on your chest and the other on your belly.**

4. **As you breathe in and out, allow the hand on your belly to gently rise up and down while keeping the hand on your chest relatively still.**

Diaphragmatic breathing may take some practice at first, but in time it becomes easy and natural. Practise as often as you want, and it soon becomes a healthy habit.

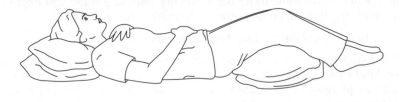

Figure 6-1:
An example of how to encourage diaphragmatic breathing.

Overcoming body scan obstacles

The body scan seems easy on the surface. All you need to do is lie down, turn on the audio MP3, and guide your awareness through your body. In reality you're doing a lot more than that. If you've spent your life ignoring your body, trying a different approach takes both courage and determination. Problems may arise. Perhaps:

- You felt more pain in your body than you normally do.
- You wanted to stop the body scan.
- You couldn't concentrate.
- You fell asleep.
- You became more anxious, depressed, or frustrated than when you started.
- You couldn't do the body scan.
- You didn't like the body scan.
- You couldn't stop crying.
- You couldn't see the point of the body scan.

All these are common experiences. Of course, experiences of pleasure and peace occur too! Remember the following sentence when you begin to struggle with the body scan and other long meditations:

You may not always like it – you just need to keep at it.

You may be struggling with your mindfulness meditation because you're seeking a particular outcome. Maybe you want your mind to shut up, or the pain to go away, or you want to get rid of your restlessness. Try letting go of these desires. The fewer desires you have, the more you're likely to enjoy the mindfulness practices. Make peace with whatever you're experiencing in the moment by becoming aware of it with friendliness. Look at the experience like you look at a little kitten, or a baby, or a really good friend: with affection, as best you can.

Enjoying Sitting Meditation

Sitting meditation is simply being mindful in a sitting position. In this section I share some common sitting postures and guide you through seated practice. Once you establish yourself in the practice, you can adapt it in any way that suits you.

Try sitting meditation after a couple of weeks' practising the body scan every day (explained in the previous section). The body scan helps you begin to get accustomed to paying attention to your breath and your body in an accepting and kindly way. You also begin to understand how easily the mind wanders off, and how to tenderly bring the attention back. The sitting meditation continues to develop your attention, bringing a wider range of present-moment experiences to be mindful of. Although your mind still strays into thoughts, you begin to shift your *relationship* to thoughts, which is a small but fundamental shift.

Finding a posture that's right for you

When it comes to postures in mindfulness practice, I offer all sorts of suggestions in this section. But the key principle is the following:

> *Find a posture that you feel comfortable with.*

If you spend too much energy and experience unnecessary discomfort in a particular posture, you'll either be put off from the mindfulness practices or you'll associate mindfulness with painful experiences. There's no need for this. Mindfulness is about being kind to yourself, so be nice and comfortable when you're finding the right sitting posture for yourself.

When sitting for meditation, you may like to imagine yourself as a mountain: stable, grounded, balanced, dignified, and beautiful. Your outer posture is more likely to be translated in your inner world, bringing clarity and wakefulness.

Sit on a chair or on the floor, in any posture as long as you can sit with your back relatively upright so it doesn't cause too much discomfort over time.

Try lifting your hips several inches above your knees by sitting on a cushion or pillow. This can help to straighten and ease tension from your back.

Sitting on a chair

You may have become accustomed to slouching on chairs. Over time, slouching causes damage to your back. You may habitually lean against the chair with an arched back and crooked neck, which isn't conducive to sitting meditation.

Here's one suggestion for sitting on a chair for meditation. See whether it works for you (see Figure 6-2):

1. **Try putting a couple of magazines, wooden blocks, or perhaps even telephone directories underneath the back two legs of the chair.** By giving your chair a slight tilt forwards, you help to make your back straight naturally, without much effort.

2. **Place your feet flat on the floor, or on a cushion on the floor if the chair's too high.** Your knees need to be at more than about 90 degrees so that your hips are above your knees.

3. **Position your hands on your knees face down or face up, or place your hands in each other.** If your hands are facing up, you may find it comfortable to allow your thumbs to gently touch each other. Some people also like to allow their hands to rest on a small cushion on their legs to prevent the shoulders dragging downwards.

4. **Imagine that your head is a helium-filled balloon. Allow your head to lift naturally and gently, and straighten your spine without straining.** No need to create excessive tension or discomfort. Tuck in your chin slightly.

5. **Lean forwards and backwards a few times until you find the middle balance point; at this position, your head neither falls back nor forwards but is naturally balanced on the neck and shoulders. Then lean to the left and right to find the point of balance again. Now relax any extra tension in the body.** If that feels good for you, you're ready to meditate! If not, take your time to adjust your body to find the right posture for yourself.

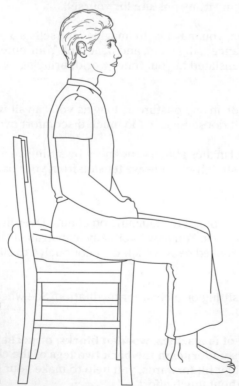

Figure 6-2:
Sitting on
a chair for
meditation.

Sitting on the floor

You can also do seated meditation sitting in the more traditional posture on the floor. Some people find sitting on the floor more grounding and stable. However, sitting in the most comfortable posture for you is more important than anything else.

On the floor, you can do the *kneeling posture*, shown in Figure 6-3, in which you support your buttocks using a meditation stool or a cushion. If you use a meditation stool, ensure that you have a cushion for it too, or you may find it uncomfortable.

It's important to find a stool or cushion at the right height for yourself. Too high, and your back will feel strained and uncomfortable. Too low, and you're more likely to slump and feel sleepy.

The instructions for the kneeling posture are:

1. **Begin by shaking your legs and rotating your ankles to prepare yourself for the posture.**

2. **Kneel on a carpet or mat on the floor.**

3. **Raise your buttocks up and place the kneeling stool between your lower legs and your buttocks.**

4. **Gently sit back down on the kneeling stool.** Place a cushion on top of the kneeling stool if you haven't already done so, to make the posture more comfortable for yourself.

5. **Shift your body around slightly to ensure you're in a posture that feels balanced and stable.** You don't need to be overly rigid in your posture.

The other position is the *Burmese posture*. This simply involves sitting on a cushion and placing both lower legs on the floor, one folded in front of the other (shown in Figure 6-4).

The Burmese posture instructions are:

1. **Shake your legs, rotate your ankles and have a stretch, however feels right for you.** This helps to prepare your body to sit.

2. **Place a mat or soft blanket on the ground. On top of that, place a firm cushion, or several soft cushions on top of each other.**

3. **Sit down by placing your buttocks on the cushion. Allow your knees to touch the ground.** If your knees don't touch the ground, either use more cushions or try one of the other postures suggested in this section.

4. **Allow the heel of your left foot to be close to or to gently touch the inside thigh of your right leg. Allow the right leg to be in front of the left leg, with the heel pointing towards your lower left leg.** If your legs aren't that supple, adjust as necessary, always ensuring you're comfortable.

5. **Invite your back to be quite straight but relaxed too. Gently rock back and forth to find the point where your head is balanced on your neck and shoulders. Tuck your chin in slightly, so the back of your neck isn't straining.**

6. **Place your hand on your knees, facing down or facing up with thumb and first finger gently touching. Alternatively, place a small cushion in your lap and place your hands on the cushion in any way that feels right for you.** I find that the cushion helps to prevent my shoulders being dragged forwards and down.

7. **Meditate to your heart's content.**

You'll find it more comfortable to sit on a firm meditation cushion, often called a *zafu*. Ordinary cushions on their own are too soft. The zafu helps to raise your hips above your knees, making the sitting position more stable. Alternatively, use lots of small cushions or fold a large cushion to give yourself better support. Find a position you're happy with.

Figure 6-3:
Kneeling position with a meditation stool.

Figure 6-4:
The
Burmese
position.

Practising sitting meditation

The mindful sitting practice I describe here comprises several stages. To begin with, I recommend that you just do the first stage – mindfulness of breath – daily. Then, after about a week, you can expand the meditation to include mindfulness of breath and body, and so on.

This book includes MP3 audio tracks that you can download for each stage of this sitting meditation. You can listen to them separately, or back to back for the full guided sitting meditation.

If you find the sitting posture too uncomfortable, you can do this mindfulness exercise lying down, or in any other posture that feels right for you. Go with what you prefer rather than forcing yourself to do what I suggest. This mindfulness exercise is available as an audio track (Tracks 10-14):

Practising mindfulness of breath (Track 10)

1. **Find a comfortable upright sitting posture on the floor or in a chair.**

2. **Remember that the intention of this practice to be aware of whatever you're focusing on, in a non-judgemental, kind, accepting and curious way.** This is a time set aside entirely for you, a time to be aware and awake to your experience as best you can, from moment to moment, non-judgementally. Hold a soft, gentle smile on your face.

3. **Become aware of the feeling of your breath.** Allow your attention to rest wherever the sensations of your breath are most predominant. This may be in or around the nostrils, as the cool air enters in and the warmer air leaves the nose. Or perhaps you notice it most in your chest as the rib cage rises and falls. Or maybe you feel it most easily and comfortably in the area of your belly, the lower abdomen. You may feel your belly move gently outwards as you breathe in, and back in as you let go and breathe out. As soon as you've found a place where you can feel the breath, simply rest your attention there for each in-breath and each out-breath. You don't need to change the pace or depth of your breathing, and you don't even need to think about it – you simply need to feel each breath.

4. **As you rest your attention on the breath, before long your mind will wander off. That's absolutely natural and nothing to worry about. As soon as you notice it's gone off, realise that you're already back! The fact that you've become aware that your mind has been wandering is a moment of wakefulness. Now, simply label your thought quietly in your own mind. You can label it 'thinking, thinking' or if you want to be more specific: 'worrying, worrying' or 'planning, planning'. This helps to frame the thought. Then gently, kindly, without criticism or judgement, guide your attention back to wherever you were feeling the breath.** Your mind may wander off a thousand times, or for long periods of time. Each time, softly, lightly and smoothly direct the attention back to the breath, if you can.

5. **Continue this for about ten minutes, or longer if you want to.**

At this point, you can stop or carry on to the next stage, which is mindfulness of both breath and body:

Practising mindfulness of breath and body (Track 11)

6. **Expand your awareness from a focused attention on the breath, to a more wide and spacious awareness of the body as a whole.** Become aware of the whole body sitting in a stable, balanced and grounded presence, like a mountain. The feeling of breathing is part of the body, so get a sense of the whole body breathing.

7. **When the mind wanders off into thoughts, ideas, dreams, or worries, gently label it and then guide the attention back to a sense of the body as a whole, breathing as in Step 4.**

8. **Remember that the whole body breathes all the time, through the skin. Get a sense of this whole-body breathing.**

9. **Continue this open, wide, curious, kind, and accepting awareness for about ten minutes – or longer if you feel like it. If certain parts of your body become uncomfortable, choose to breathe into that discomfort,**

and note the effect of that, or slowly and mindfully shift your bodily position to relieve the discomfort. Whatever you choose, doing it mindfully is the important bit.

At this point, you can stop or carry on to mindfulness of sounds.

Practising mindfulness of sounds (Track 12)

10. **Let go of mindfulness of breath and body and become aware of sounds.** Begin by noticing the sounds of your body, the sounds in the room you're in, the sounds in the building, and finally the furthest sounds outside. Let the sounds permeate into you rather than straining to grasp them. Listen without effort: let it happen by itself. Listen without labelling the sound, as best you can. For example, if you hear the sound of a plane passing, or a door closing, or a bird singing, listen to the actual sound itself – its tone, pitch, and volume – rather than thinking, 'Oh, that's a plane.'

11. **As soon as you notice your thoughts taking over, label the thought and tenderly escort the attention back to listening.**

12. **Continue listening for ten minutes or so.**

At this point, you can stop or carry on to mindfulness of thoughts and feelings.

Practising mindfulness of thoughts and feelings (Track 13)

13. **When you're ready, turn your attention from the external experience of sound to your inner thoughts.** Thoughts can be in the form of sounds you can hear or in the form of images you can see. Watch or listen to thoughts in the same way you were mindful of sounds: without judgement or criticism, and with acceptance and openness.

14. **Watch thoughts arise and pass away like clouds in the sky.** Neither force thoughts to arise nor push them away. As best you can, create a distance, a space, between yourself and your thoughts. Notice what effect this has, if any. If the thoughts suddenly disappear, see whether you can be okay with that too.

15. **Imagine that you're sitting on the bank of a river, as another way of watching thoughts. As you sit there, leaves float on the surface and continuously drift by. Place each thought that you have onto each leaf that passes you.** Continue to sit and observe your thoughts passing by.

16. **As soon as you notice your attention get stuck in a train of thought, calmly take a step back from your thoughts and watch them once again from a distance, as best you can.** (Every so often, your attention may get stuck in a train of thought; your mind just works that way.) If you criticise yourself for your mind wandering, observe that as just a thought too.

17. **Now try turning towards emotions. Notice whatever emotions arise, and whether they're positive or negative. As far as you can, open up to the emotion and feel it.** Notice where that emotion manifests itself in your body. Is it new or familiar? Is it just one emotion or several layers? Do you feel like running away from the emotion, or staying with it? Breathe into the feeling as you continue to watch it. Observe your emotion in a curious, friendly way, like a young child looking at a new toy.

18. **Continue to practise for ten minutes or so.** These subtle activities take time to develop. Just do your best and accept however you feel they've gone, whether you were successful at focusing or not.

At this point, you can stop or carry on to *choiceless awareness*, which is simply an open awareness of whatever arises in your consciousness: sounds, thoughts, the sensations in your body, feelings, or the breath. Here's how:

Practising choiceless awareness (Track 14)

19. **Just be aware of whatever arises, in an expansive, receptive, and welcoming way.** Put the welcome mat out for your experience. Notice whatever predominates most in your awareness and let it go again.

20. **If you find your mind wandering (and it's particularly easy to get swept up and away into thoughts when practising this), come back to mindfulness of breath to ground yourself, before trying again.** Become curious about what's happening for you, rather than trying to change anything.

21. **Practise for about ten minutes, then begin to bring the sitting meditation to a close.** Gently congratulate yourself for having taken the time to nourish your health and wellbeing in this practice, for having taken time out of doing mode to explore the inner landscape of being mode, and allow this sense of awareness to permeate whatever activities you engage in today.

Overcoming sitting meditation obstacles

One of the most common problems with sitting meditation is posture. After sitting for some time, the back, knees, or other parts of the body start to ache. When this happens, you have two choices:

✔ **Observe both the discomfort as well as your mind's reaction to it, while continuing to sit still.** I recommend this if the discomfort doesn't hurt too much. Mindfulness is about welcoming experiences, even if they feel unpleasant at first. What does the discomfort feel like exactly?

What's its precise location? What do you think about it? Because all experience is in a state of flux and change, you may find that even your feeling of physical discomfort changes.

✔ By you discovering how to stay with these sensations, your meditation skills flow into your everyday life. You can manage other difficult emotions and challenging problems in the same welcoming, curious, and accepting way, rather than fighting them. Your body and mind are one, so by sitting still, your mind has a chance to stabilise and focus too.

✔ **Mindfully move the position of your body.** If your bodily discomfort is overwhelming, you can, of course, move your body. That's a lovely act of kindness to yourself. Try not to react quickly to the discomfort. Instead, shift your position slowly and mindfully. In this way, you enfold your shift of position into the practice. You're responding instead of reacting, which is what mindfulness is about. Responding involves a deliberate choice by you: you feel the sensation and make a conscious decision about what to do next. Reacting is automatic, lacks control, and bypasses an intentional decision by you. By you becoming more skilful in responding to your own experience in meditation, your ability spills out into everyday life: when someone frustrates you, you can respond while remaining in control of yourself rather than reacting in an out-of-control way.

Besides arising from the posture, frustration can arise from the practice itself. You're so used to judging all your experiences that you judge your meditation too. But mindfulness means non-judgemental awareness. *Bad meditation doesn't exist – there's no such thing.* Sometimes you can concentrate and focus your mind, and other times it's totally wild. Meditation is like that. Trust in the process, even if it feels as if you're not improving. Mindfulness works at a level both above and below the conscious mind, so on the surface it may seem as though you're not getting anywhere. Don't worry: each meditation is a step forwards, because you've actually practised.

Stepping Out with Walking Meditations

Walking meditation is meditation in which the process of walking is used as a focus. The ability to walk is a privilege, and walking is a miraculous process that you can feel grateful for.

Imagine being able to walk to work in a mindful, calm, and relaxed way, arriving at your destination refreshed and energised. You can walk in a stress-free way with walking meditation. My students often say that walking meditation is one of their favourite practices. The walking gives them time out from an over-occupied mind. Meditative walking is also a good way of preparing for the other, more physically static, meditations.

Examining your walking habits

You probably rarely just walk. You may walk and talk, walk and think, walk and plan, or walk and worry. Walking is so easy that you do other things at the same time. You probably walk on automatic pilot most of the time. However, you can get into negative habit patterns and end up spending all your time planning when you walk, and rarely just enjoying the walking itself.

When you walk, you're normally trying to get somewhere. That makes sense, I know. In walking meditation, you're not trying to get anywhere. You can let go of the destination and enjoy the journey, which is what all meditations are about.

Practising formal walking meditation

In this section I describe a formal walking meditation, which means you make special time and space to practise the exercise. You can equally introduce an awareness of your walking in an informal way, when going about your daily activities. You don't have to slow down the pace at which you walk for that.

To practise formal walking meditation, sometimes called mindful walking, try the following steps, available as an audio track (Track 15):

1. **Decide for how long you're going to practise.** I suggest ten minutes the first time, but whatever you feel comfortable with. Also choose where to practise. The first time you try it, practise walking *very* slowly, so a quiet room at home may be best.

2. **Stand upright with stability.** Gently lean to the left and right, forwards and backwards, to find a central, balanced standing posture. Let your knees unlock slightly, and soften any unnecessary tension in your face. Allow your arms to hang naturally by your sides. Ensure that your body's grounded, like a tree – firmly rooted to the ground with dignity and poise.

3. **Become aware of your breath.** Come into contact with the flow of each inhalation and exhalation. Enjoy breathing. Maintain a beautiful little grin on your face for the duration of this practice, if you can.

4. **Now slowly lean onto your left foot and notice how your sensations change. Then slowly shift your weight onto your right foot. Again perceive how the sensations fluctuate from moment to moment.**

5. **When you're ready, gradually shift most of your weight onto your left foot, so almost no weight is on the right foot. Slowly take your right heel off the ground. Pause for a moment here. Notice the sense of anticipation about something as basic as taking a step. Now lift your right foot off the ground and place it heel first in front of you. Become aware of the weight of your body shifting from the left to the**

right foot. Continue gradually to place the rest of the right foot flat and firmly on the ground. Notice the weight continue to shift from left to right.

6. **Continue to walk in this very slow, mindful way for as long as you want.** When you finish, take some time to reflect on your experience.

Trying alternative walking meditations

Here are a couple of other ways of practising walking meditation that you can use while moving at your own pace:

✔ **Walking body scan.** In this walking meditation, you gradually move your awareness up your body as you walk, from your feet all the way to the top of your head.

1. **Begin by walking as you normally do.**

2. **Now focus on the sensations in your feet.** Notice how the weight shifts from one foot to the other.

3. **Continue to move your mindful attention up your body.** Feel your lower legs as you walk, then your upper legs, noticing their movement.

4. **Now observe the movement and sensations in the area of the hips and pelvis.**

5. **Continue to scan your awareness to the lower and then upper torso, then your arms, as they naturally swing to help you keep balance.**

6. **Observe the sensation in your shoulders, your neck, your face, and then the whole of your head.**

7. **Now get a sense of the body as a whole as you continue to stroll, together with the physical sensation of the breath. Continue this for as long as you wish.**

✔ **Walking with happiness.** This practice is recommended by world-famous mindfulness teacher Thich Nhat Hanh. This mindfulness exercise is about generating positive feelings as you walk. Try the following as an experiment. Have fun with it:

1. **Find a place to walk by yourself or with a friend.** Try to find a beautiful place to walk if possible.

2. **Remember that the purpose of walking meditation is to be in the present moment, letting go of your anxieties and worries.** Just enjoy the present moment.

3. **Walk as if you're the happiest person on earth.** Smile – you're alive! Acknowledge that you're very fortunate if you're able to walk.

4. **As you walk in this way, imagine you're printing peace and joy with every step you take.** Walk as if you're kissing the earth with each step you take. Know that you're taking care of the earth by walking in this way.

5. **Notice how many steps you take when you breathe in, and how many you take when you breathe out.** If you take three steps with each in-breath, in your mind say 'in – in – in' as you breathe in. And if you take four steps as you breathe out, say 'out – out – out – out'. Doing so helps you to become aware of your breathing. You don't need to control your breathing or walking; let it be slow and natural.

6. **Every now and then, when you see a beautiful tree, flower, lake, children playing, or anything else you like, stop and look at it.** Continue to follow your breathing as you do this.

7. **Imagine a flower blooming under each step you take.** Allow each step to refresh your body and mind. Realise that life can only be lived in the present moment. Enjoy your walking.

Overcoming walking meditation obstacles

Walking meditation doesn't create as many issues as the other meditations. However, here are a couple that often crop up, with ideas to solve them:

✔ **You can't balance when walking very slowly.** Walking straight at a very slow pace is surprisingly tricky. If you think that you may fall over, use a wall to support yourself. Additionally, gaze at a spot in front of you and keep your eyes fixed there as you walk forwards. As you practise, your balance improves.

✔ **Your mind keeps wandering off.** Walking meditation is like all other mindfulness practices. The mind becomes distracted. Gently guide your attention back to the feeling of the feet on the floor, or of the breath. No self-criticism or blaming is required.

Generating Compassion: Metta Meditations

Metta is a Buddhist term meaning loving kindness or friendliness. Metta meditation is designed to generate a sense of compassion both for yourself and towards others. All mindfulness meditations make use of an affectionate awareness, but metta meditations are specifically designed to deepen this skill and direct it in specific ways.

Meeting the Olympic meditators

Metta meditation is a skill you can develop in the same way as you can become skilful at tennis or driving: brain scans of experienced meditators have proved it. Renowned brain scientist Professor Richard Davidson and his team of neuroscientists at the University of Wisconsin–Madison in the USA have shown that short-term meditators can become more compassionate through metta-type meditations. Long-term meditators – so-called 'Olympic meditators' – who've spent over 10,000 hours meditating (not all at the same time!), have among the highest levels of wellbeing and compassion ever recorded in brain scans! In brain scan experiments, these expert meditators stepped out of uncomfortable and noisy scientific experiments after hours of testing with a smile on their faces – a reaction not seen before by scientists. The scientists proved that a sense of compassion is the most positive of positive emotions and is extremely powerful and healing for both body and mind.

Many religious traditions and ancient cultures emphasise the need to love and care for yourself and those around you. When you're feeling particularly harsh and self-critical, metta meditation can act as an antidote and generate feelings of friendliness and affection. The reason metta meditation works is due to an important aspect of human beings: you can't feel both hatred and friendliness at the same time: by nourishing one, you displace the other. Metta meditation is a gentle way of healing your inner mind and heart from all its pain and suffering.

If you're new to meditation, try some of the other meditations in this book first. When you've had some experience of those meditations, you're ready to try the metta meditation. Take your time with it: work through the practice slowly and regularly, and you're sure to reap the benefits.

Practising loving kindness meditation

Here's a guided metta meditation. Work through it slowly, taking it step by step. If you don't have the time or the patience to do all the stages, do as many as you feel comfortable with. Be gentle with yourself, right from the beginning. This meditation is available as an audio track (Track 16):

1. **You can practise loving kindness in a seated or lying down position. You can even practise it while walking.** What's most important isn't the position you adopt, but the intention of kindness and friendliness you bring to the process. Make yourself warm and at ease. Gently close your eyes or keep them half open, looking comfortably downwards.

2. **Begin by feeling your breath.** Notice the breath sensation wherever it feels most predominant for you. This awareness helps create a connection between your body and mind. Continue to feel your breath for a few minutes.

3. **When you're ready, see whether certain phrases arise from your heart for what you most deeply desire for yourself in a long-lasting way, and ultimately for all beings.** Phrases like:

   May I be well. May I be happy. May I be healthy. May I be free from suffering.

4. **Softly repeat the phrases again and again.** Allow them to sink into your heart. Allow the words to generate a feeling of kindness towards yourself. If that doesn't happen, don't worry about it: your intention is more important than the feeling. Just continue to repeat the phrases lightly. Let the phrases resonate.

5. **Now bring to mind someone you care about: a good friend or person who inspires you.** Picture the person in your mind's eye and inwardly say the same phrases to her. Don't worry if you can't create the image clearly. The intention works by itself. Use phrases like:

   May you be well. May you be happy. May you be healthy. May you be free from suffering.

   Send loving kindness to the person using these words.

6. **When you're ready, choose a neutral person: someone you see daily but don't have any particular positive or negative feelings towards.** Perhaps someone you walk past every morning or buy coffee from. Again send a sense of loving kindness using your phrases:

   May you be well. May you be happy. May you be healthy. May you be free from suffering.

7. **Now choose a person you don't get on with too well.** Perhaps someone you've been having difficulties with recently. Say the same phrases again, from the mind and heart. This may be more challenging.

8. **Now bring all four people to mind: yourself, your friend, your neutral person, and your difficult person.** Visualise them or feel their presence. Try to send an equal amount of loving kindness to them all by saying:

   May we be well. May we be happy. May we be healthy. May we be free from suffering.

9. **Finally, expand your sense of loving kindness outwards, towards all living beings.** Plants, animals of the land, air, and sea. The whole universe. Send this sense of friendliness, care, loving kindness, and compassion in all directions from your heart:

   May all be well. May all be happy. May all be healthy. May all be free from suffering.

If the metta phrases I suggest don't work for you, then here are other suggestions. Choose two or three and use them as your metta phrases. Or you can be creative and come up with your own, too:

- *May I be at peace with myself and all other beings.*

- *May I accept myself just as I am.*

- *May I find forgiveness for the inevitable hurt peopole bring to one another.*

- *May I live in peace and harmony with all beings.*

- *May I love myself completely just as I am now no matter what happens.*

- *May I be free from the suffering of fear and anger.*

- *May I love myself unconditionally.*

Metta meditation can be a profoundly healing practice. Be patient with yourself and practise it slowly and lovingly. Let the phrases come from your heart and see what happens.

Once you become experienced at this meditation, you can even practise it while walking. However, remember to keep your eyes open, or you may mindfully bump into something!

Overcoming metta meditation obstacles

You may experience a few specific problems with metta meditation. Some common issues, with suggestions for overcoming them, include:

- **You can't think of a specific person.** If you can't think of a suitable friend, or neutral person, or someone you're having difficulties with, don't worry. You can miss that step for now, or just choose anyone. The intention of loving kindness is more important than the specific person you choose.

- **You say the phrases but don't feel anything.** This is perfectly normal, especially when you start. Imagine the phrases coming out of your chest or heart, rather than your head, if you can. Again, the feeling isn't as important as your attitude of friendliness in the practice. The feelings may come in the future, or may not – you don't need to worry about that.

- **Your mind keeps wandering off.** This is simply the nature of mind, and happens in all meditations. As always, as soon as you notice, kindly and gently bring your attention back to the practice. Each time you bring it back, you're strengthening your mind to pay attention.

✔ **You have great trouble with the difficult person.** If you have a strong aversion to bringing a sense of kindness to the difficult person, try remembering that she's a human being, just like you. She too has her challenges in life, which may be why she behaves in the way she does. And she, too, ultimately wants to be happy and peaceful, although it may not seem that way on the outside. If these thoughts don't help either, try focusing on someone less difficult to begin with. Be patient with yourself: this isn't an easy process, but it's certainly worth the effort.

✔ **You feel very emotional.** Feeling emotional is a very common reaction. You may not be used to generating feelings in this way, and it can unlock deep-seated emotions. If you can, try to continue with the practice. If your emotions become overwhelming, try just the first phase, sending metta towards yourself, for the whole meditation. Doing just one phase for a whole meditation is perfectly fine. Alternatively, stop the practice and come back to it later, when it feels more appropriate.

Chapter 7

Using Mindfulness for Yourself and Others

In This Chapter

▶ Discovering a short mindful exercise you can use anywhere

▶ Finding mindful ways of taking care of yourself

▶ Applying mindfulness in relationships

You require a lot of looking after. You need to eat a balanced diet and exercise regularly to maintain optimum health and wellbeing. You need to have the right amount of work and rest in your life. And you need to challenge yourself intellectually, to keep your mind healthy. You need to socialise and also save some time just for yourself. Achieving all this perfectly is impossible, but how can you strive to take care of yourself in a light-hearted way, without becoming overly uptight and stressed?

Mindfulness can help you look after both yourself and others. Being aware of your thoughts, emotions and body, as well as the things and people around you, is the starting point. This awareness enables you to become sensitive to your own needs and those of others around you, therefore encouraging you to meet everyone's needs as far as possible.

A caring, accepting awareness is the key to healthy living. Mindfulness is a wonderful way to develop greater awareness. This chapter details suggestions for looking after yourself and others through mindfulness.

Using a Mini Mindful Exercise

You don't need to practise mindfulness meditation for hours and hours to reap its benefits. Short and frequent meditations are an effective way of developing mindfulness in your everyday life.

Tree, rope or wall? Describing an elephant

Six blind people were asked to determine what an elephant looks like. Each of them was guided to the elephant and felt a different part. One felt a leg and said that the elephant was like a pillar. One felt the trunk and said that the elephant was like the branches of a tree. One felt the tail and said that the elephant was like a rope. Another felt the ear and said that the elephant felt like a fan. The one who felt the belly thought the elephant felt like a wall. And the one who felt the tusk said that the elephant was like a solid pipe. Then they all started arguing, insisting that they were right about the nature of the elephant. A wise person happened to be passing (they always do in these stories) and said that they were all right to a certain extent. If they felt other parts of the elephant they would get a different perspective.

The moral of the story? Mindfulness enables you to see both your outer and inner experience fully, shifting your perspective and helping you to resolve inner and outer conflicts. You begin to understand how other people can be restricted by their views because that's all they know – they're just feeling one part of the elephant. This insight can result in greater compassion and understanding.

Introducing the breathing space

When you've had a busy day, you probably enjoy stopping for a nice hot cup of tea or coffee, or another favourite beverage. The drink offers more than just liquid for the body. The break gives you a chance to relax and unwind a bit. The three-minute mini meditation, called the *breathing space* (illustrated in Figure 7-1 and 7-2), is a bit like a tea break, but beyond relaxation, the breathing space enables you to check what's going on in your body, mind, and heart – not getting rid of feelings or thoughts, but looking at them from a clearer perspective.

Practising the breathing space

You can practise the breathing space at almost any time and anywhere. The meditation is made up of three distinct stages, which I call A, B, and C to help you to remember what to practise at each stage. The exercise doesn't have to last exactly three minutes: you can make it longer or shorter depending on where you are and how much time you have. If you only have time to feel three breaths, that's okay; doing so can still have a profound effect. Follow these steps, which are available as an audio track (Track 17):

1. **Sit upright with a sense of dignity, but don't strain your back and neck.** If you can't sit upright, try standing; even lying down on your back or curling up is acceptable. Sitting upright is helpful, because it sends a positive message to the brain – you're doing something different.

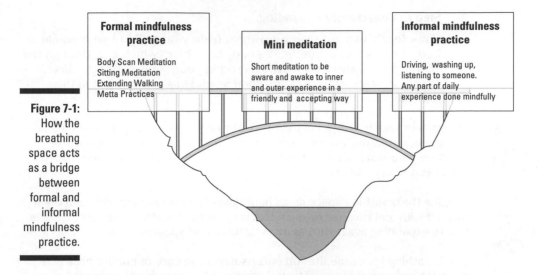

Figure 7-1: How the breathing space acts as a bridge between formal and informal mindfulness practice.

Formal mindfulness practice

Body Scan Meditation
Sitting Meditation
Extending Walking
Metta Practices

Mini meditation

Short meditation to be aware and awake to inner and outer experience in a friendly and accepting way

Informal mindfulness practice

Driving, washing up, listening to someone. Any part of daily experience done mindfully

2. **Practise step A below for about a minute or so, then move on to B for a minute, ending with C also for a minute – or however long you can manage:**

   Step A: Awareness:

   Reflect on the following questions, pausing for a few seconds between each one:

   i. **What bodily sensations am I aware of at the moment?** Feel your posture, become aware of any aches or pains, or any pleasant sensations. Just accept them as they are, as far as you can.

   ii. **What emotions am I aware of at the moment?** Notice the feelings in your heart or belly area or wherever you can feel emotion.

   iii. **What thoughts am I aware of, passing through my mind at the moment?** Become aware of your thoughts, and the space between yourself and your thoughts. If you can, simply observe your thoughts rather than becoming caught up in them.

   Step B: Breathing:

   Focus your attention in your belly area – the lower abdomen. As best you can, feel the whole of your in-breath and the whole of each out-breath. You don't need to change the rate of your breathing – just become mindful of it in a warm, curious and friendly way. Notice how each breath is slightly different. If your mind wanders away, gently and kindly guide your attention back to your breath. Appreciate how precious each breath is.

Step C: Consciously expanding:

Consciously expand your awareness from your belly to your whole body. Get a sense of your entire body breathing (which it is, through the skin). As our awareness heightens within your body, notice its effect. Accept yourself as perfect and complete just as you are, just in this moment, as much as you can.

Experiment with having a very gentle smile on your face as you do the breathing space, no matter how you feel. Notice whether doing so has a positive effect on your state of mind. If it does, use this approach every time. You don't even need to say 'cheese'!

Imagine the breathing space as an hourglass. The attention is wide and open to start with and then narrows and focuses on the breath in the second stage, before expanding again with more awareness and spaciousness.

The breathing space meditation encapsulates the core of mindfulness in a succinct and portable way. The full effects of the breathing space are:

- ✔ **You move into a restful 'being' mode of mind.** Your mind can be in one of two very different states of mind: *doing* mode or *being* mode. Doing mode is energetic and all about carrying out actions and changing things. Being mode is a soothing state of mind where you acknowledge things as they are. (For lots more on being and doing mode, refer to Chapter 5.)

- ✔ **Your self-awareness increases.** You become more aware of how your body feels, the thoughts going through your mind, and the emotion or need of the moment. You may notice that your shoulders are hunched or your jaw is clenched. You may have thoughts whizzing through your head that you hadn't even realised were there. Or perhaps you're feeling sad, or are thirsty or tired. If you listen to these messages, you can take appropriate action. Without self-awareness, you can't tackle them.

- ✔ **Your self-compassion increases.** You allow yourself the space to be kinder to yourself, rather than self-critical or overly demanding. If you've had a tough day, the breathing space offers you time to let go of your concerns, forgive your mistakes and come back into the present moment. And with greater self-compassion, you're better able to be compassionate and understanding of others too.

- ✔ **You create more opportunities to make choices.** You make choices all the time. At the moment, you've chosen to read this book and this page. Later on you may choose to go for a walk, call a friend, or cook dinner. If your partner snaps at you, your reaction is a choice to a certain extent too. By practising the breathing space, you stand back from your experiences and see the bigger picture of the situation you're in. When a difficulty arises, you can make a decision from your whole wealth of knowledge and experience, rather than just having a fleeting reaction. The breathing space can help you make wiser decisions.

✔ **You switch off automatic pilot.** Have you ever eaten a whole meal and realised that you didn't actually taste it? You were most likely on automatic pilot. You're so used to eating, you can do it while thinking about other things. The breathing space helps to connect you with your senses so that you're alive to the moment.

Try this thought experiment. Without looking, remember whether your wrist watch has roman numerals or normal numbers on it. If you're not sure, or get it wrong, it's a small indication of how you're operating on automatic pilot. You've looked at your watch hundreds of times, but not really looked carefully. (I explain more about automatic pilot in Chapter 5.)

✔ **You become an observer of your experience rather than feeling trapped by it.** In your normal everyday experience, no distance exists between you and your thoughts or emotions. They just arise and you act on them almost without noticing. One of the key outcomes of the breathing space is the creation of a space between you and your inner world. Your thoughts and emotions can be in complete turmoil, but you simply observe and are free from them, like watching a film at the cinema. This seemingly small shift in viewpoint has huge implications, which I explore in Chapter 5.

✔ **You see things from a different perspective.** Have you ever taken a comment too personally? I certainly have. Someone is critical about a piece of work I've done, and I immediately react or at least feel a surge of emotion in the pit of my stomach. But you have other ways of reacting. Was the other person stressed out? Are you making a big deal about nothing? The pause offered by the breathing space can help you see things in another way.

✔ **You walk the bridge between formal and informal practice.** Formal practice is where you carve out a chunk of time in the day to practise meditation. Informal practice is being mindful of your normal everyday activities. The breathing space is a very useful way of bridging the gap between these two important aspects of mindfulness. The breathing space is both a formal practice because you're making some time to carry it out, and informal because you integrate it into your day-to-day activities.

✔ **You create a space for new ideas to arise.** By stopping your normal everyday activities to practise the breathing space, you create room in your mind for other things to pop in. If your mind is cluttered, you can't think clearly. The breathing space may be just what the doctor ordered to allow an intelligent insight or creative idea to pop into your mind.

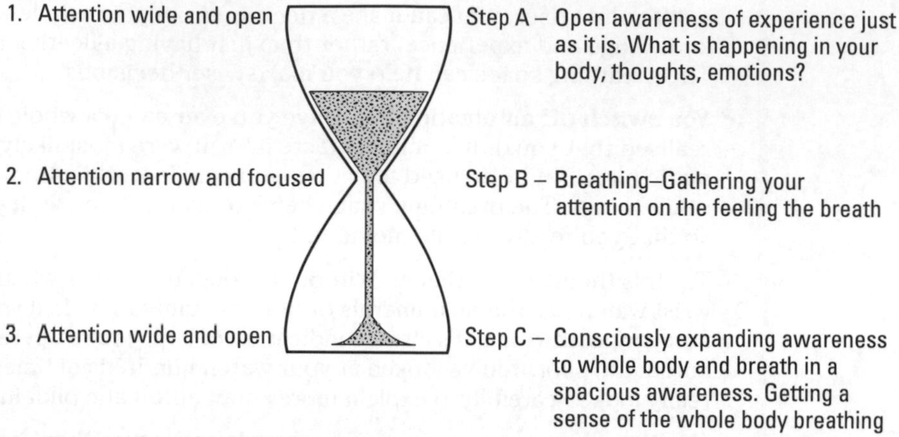

1. Attention wide and open

Step A – Open awareness of experience just as it is. What is happening in your body, thoughts, emotions?

2. Attention narrow and focused

Step B – Breathing–Gathering your attention on the feeling the breath

3. Attention wide and open

Step C – Consciously expanding awareness to whole body and breath in a spacious awareness. Getting a sense of the whole body breathing

Figure 7-2: The three-minute breathing space meditation progresses like an hourglass.

Using the breathing space between activities

Aim to practise the breathing space three times a day. Here are some suggested times for practising the breathing space:

- **Before or after meal times.** Some people pray with their family before eating a meal to be together with gratitude and give thanks for the food. Doing a breathing space before or after a meal gives you a set time to practise and reminds you to appreciate your meal too. If you can't manage three minutes, just feel three breaths before diving in.

- **Between activities.** Resting between your daily activities, even for just a few moments, is very nourishing. Feeling your breath and renewing yourself is very pleasant. Research has found that just three mindful breaths can change your body's physiology, lowering blood pressure and reducing muscle tension.

- **On waking up or before going to bed.** A short meditation before you jump out of bed can be a wholesome experience. You can stay lying in bed and enjoy your breathing. Or you can sit up and do the breathing space. Meditating in this way helps to put you in a good frame of mind and sets you up for meeting life afresh. Practising the breathing space before going to bed can calm your mind and encourage a deeper and more restful sleep.

- **When a difficult thought or emotion arises.** The breathing space meditation is particularly helpful when you're experiencing challenging thoughts or emotions. By becoming aware of the nature of your thoughts, and listening to them with a sense of kindness and curiosity, you change your relationship to them. A mindful relationship to thoughts and emotions results in a totally different experience.

Using Mindfulness to Look After Yourself

Have you ever heard the safety announcements on a plane? In the event of an emergency, cabin crew advise you to put your own oxygen mask on first, before you help put one on anyone else, even your own child. The reason is obvious. If you can't breathe yourself, how can you possibly help anyone else? Looking after yourself isn't just necessary in emergencies. In normal everyday life, you need to look after your own needs. If you don't, not only do you suffer, but so do all the people who interact or depend on you. Taking care of yourself isn't selfish: it's the best way to be of optimal service to others. Eating, sleeping, exercising, and meditating regularly are all ways of looking after yourself and hence others.

Exercising mindfully

You can practise mindfulness and do physical exercise at the same time. In fact, Jon Kabat-Zinn, one of the key founders of mindfulness in the West, trained the USA men's Olympic rowing team in 1984. A couple of the men won gold – not bad for a bunch of meditators! And in the more recent 2012 Olympics in London, several athletes claimed that meditation helped them to reach peak performance and achieve their gold medals.

Regular exercise is beneficial for both body and mind, as confirmed by thousands of research studies. If you already exercise on a regular basis, you know the advantages. If not, and your doctor is happy with you exercising, you can begin by simply walking. Walking is an aerobic exercise and a great way to practise mindfulness. (See Chapter 6 for a walking meditation.) Then, if you want to, you can build up to whatever type of more strenuous exercise you fancy. Approach each new exercise with a mindful attitude: be curious of what will happen, stay with uncomfortable sensations for a while, explore the edge between comfort and discomfort, and look around you.

Whatever exercise you choose, allow yourself to enjoy the experience. Find simply physical activities that make you smile rather than frown, and you're much more likely to stick with the discipline.

To start you off, here are a few typical physical exercises and ideas for how to suffuse them with mindfulness.

Mindful running

Leave the portable music player and headphones at home. Try running outside rather than at the gym – your senses have more to connect with outside. Begin by taking ten mindful breaths as you walk along. Become aware of your body as a whole. Build up from normal walking to walking fast to running. Notice how quickly your breathing rate changes, and focus on your breathing whenever your mind wanders away from the present moment. Feel your heart beating and the rhythm of your feet bouncing on the ground. Notice whether you're tensing up any parts of your body unnecessarily. Enjoy the wind against your face and the warmth of your body. Observe what sort of thoughts pop up when you're running, without being judgemental of them. If running begins to be painful, explore whether you need to keep going or slow down. If you're a regular runner, you may want to stay on the edge a little bit longer; if you're new to it, slow down and build up more gradually. At the end of your run, notice how you feel. Try doing a mini meditation (described in the first section of this chapter) and notice its effect. Keep observing the effects of your run over the next few hours.

Mindful swimming

Begin with some mindful breathing as you approach the pool. Notice the effect of the water on your body as you enter. What sort of thoughts arise? As you begin to swim, feel the contact between your arms and legs and the water. What does the water feel like? Be grateful that you can swim and have access to the water. Allow yourself to get into the rhythm of swimming. Become aware of your heartbeat, breath rate, and the muscles in your body. When you've finished, observe how your body and mind feel.

Mindful cycling

Begin with some mindful breathing as you sit on your bike. Feel the weight of your body, the contact between your hands and the handlebars, and your foot on the pedal. As you begin cycling, listen to the sound of the wind. Notice how your leg muscles work together rapidly as you move. Switch between focusing on a specific part of your body like the hands or face to a wide and spacious awareness of your body as a whole. Let go of wherever you're heading and come back to the here and now. As you get off your bike, perceive the sensations in your body. Scan through your body and detect how you feel after that exercise.

Preparing for sleep with mindfulness

Sleep, essential to your wellbeing, is one of the first things to improve when people do a course in mindfulness. People sleep better, and their sleep is deeper. Studies found similar results from people who suffered from insomnia who did an eight-week course in MBSR (mindfulness-based stress reduction).

Sleep is about completely letting go of the world. Falling asleep isn't something you *do* – it's about *non-doing*. In that sense sleep is similar to mindfulness. If you're *trying* to sleep, you're putting in a certain effort, which is the opposite of letting go.

Here are some tips for preparing to sleep using mindfulness:

✔ **Stick to a regular time to go to bed and to wake up.** Waking up very early one day and very late the next confuses your body clock and may cause difficulties in sleeping.

✔ **Avoid over-stimulating yourself by watching television or being on the computer before bed.** The light from the screen tricks your brain into believing it's still daytime, and then it takes longer for you to fall asleep.

✔ **Try doing some formal mindfulness practice like a sitting meditation or the body scan (refer to Chapter 6) before going to bed.**

✔ **Try doing some yoga or gentle stretching before going to bed.** I've noticed cats naturally stretch before curling up on the sofa for a snooze. This may help you to relax and your muscles unwind. Try purring while you're stretching, too – maybe that's the secret to their relaxed way of life!

✔ **Do some mindful walking indoors before bed.** Take five or ten minutes to walk a few steps and feel all the sensations in your body as you do so. The slower, the better.

✔ **When you lie in bed, feel your in-breath and out-breath.** Rather than trying to sleep, just be with your breathing. Count your out-breaths from one to ten. Each time you breathe out, say the number to yourself. Every time your mind wanders off, begin again at one.

✔ **If you're lying in bed worrying, perhaps even about getting to sleep, accept your worries.** Challenging or fighting thoughts just makes them more powerful. Note them, and gently come back to the feeling of the breath.

If you seem to be sleeping less than usual, try not to worry about it too much. In fact, worrying about how little sleep you're getting becomes a vicious circle. Many people sleep far less than eight hours a day, and most people have bad nights once in a while. Not being able to sleep doesn't mean something is wrong with you, and lack of sleep isn't the worst thing for your health. A regular mindfulness practice will probably help you in the long run.

Looking at a mindful work–life balance

Work–life balance means balancing work and career ambitions on the one side, and home, family, leisure and spiritual pursuits on the other. Working too much can have a negative impact on other important areas. By keeping things in balance, you're able to get your work done quicker and your relationship quality tends to improve.

With the advent of mobile technology, or a demanding career, work may be taking over your free time. And sometimes you may struggle to see how you can re-dress this imbalance. The mindful reflection below may help.

Try this little reflection to help reflect on and improve your work–life balance:

1. Sit in a comfortable upright posture, with a sense of dignity and stability.

2. Become aware of your body as a whole, with all its various changing sensations.

3. Guide your attention to the ebb and flow of your breath. Allow your mind to settle on the feeling of the breath.

4. Observe the balance of the breath. Notice how your in-breath naturally stops when it needs to, as does the out-breath. You don't need to do anything – it just happens. Enjoy the flow of the breath.

5. When you're ready, reflect on this question for a few minutes:

   What can I do to find a wiser and healthier balance in my life?

6. Go back to the sensations of the breathing. See what ideas arise. No need to force any ideas. Just reflect on the question gently, and see what happens. You may get a new thought, image or perhaps a feeling.

7. When you're ready, bring the meditation to a close and jot down any ideas that may have arisen.

Refer to *Work/Life Balance For Dummies* by Katherine Lockett and Jeni Mumford (Wiley) for more on this topic.

Using Mindfulness in Relationships

Humans are social animals. People's brains are wired that way. Research into positive psychology, the new science of wellbeing, shows that healthy relationships affect happiness more than anything else does. Psychologists have found that wellbeing isn't so much about the quantity of relationships but the quality. You can directly develop and enhance the quality of your relationships through mindfulness.

Starting with your relationship with yourself

Trees need to withstand powerful storms, and the only way they can do that is by having deep roots for stability. With shallow roots, the tree can't really stand upright. The deeper and stronger the roots, the bigger and more plentiful are the branches that the tree can produce. In the same way, you need to nourish your relationship with yourself to effectively branch out to relate to others in a meaningful and fulfilling way.

Here are some tips to help you begin building a better relationship with yourself by using a mindful attitude:

✔ **Set the intention.** Begin with a clear intention to begin to love and care for yourself. You're not being selfish by looking after yourself; you're watering your own roots, so you can help others when the time is right. You're opening the door to a brighter future that you truly deserve as a human being.

✔ **Understand that no one's perfect.** You may have high expectations of yourself. Try to let them go, just a tiny bit. Try to accept at least one aspect of yourself that you don't like, if you can. The smallest of steps make a huge difference. Just as a snowball starts small and gradually grows as you roll it through the snow, so a little bit of kindness and acceptance of the way things are can start off a positive chain reaction to improve things for you.

✔ **Step back from self-criticism.** As you practise mindfulness, you become more aware of your thoughts. You may be surprised to hear a harsh, self-critical inner voice berating you. Take a step back from that voice if you can, and know that *you're not your thoughts*. When you begin to see this, the thoughts lose their sting and power. (The sitting meditation in Chapter 6 explores this.)

✔ **Be kind to yourself.** Take note of your positive qualities, no matter how small and insignificant they seem, and acknowledge them. Maybe you're polite, or a particular part of your body is attractive. Or perhaps you're generous or a good listener. Whatever your positive qualities are, notice them rather than looking for the negative aspects of yourself or what you can't do. Being kind to yourself isn't easy, but through mindfulness and by taking a step-by-step approach, it's definitely possible.

✔ **Forgive yourself.** Remember that you're not perfect. You make mistakes, and so do I. Making mistakes makes us human. By understanding that you can't be perfect in what you do, and can't get everything right, you're more able to forgive yourself and move on. Ultimately, you can learn only through making mistakes: if you did everything correctly, you'd have little to discover about yourself. Give yourself permission to forgive yourself.

✔ **Be grateful.** Develop an attitude of gratitude. Try being grateful for all that you do have, and all that you can do. Can you see, hear, smell, taste, and touch? Can you think, feel, walk, and run? Do you have access to food, shelter, and clothing? Use mindfulness to become more aware of what you have. Every evening before going to bed, write down three things that you're grateful for, even if they're really small and insignificant. Writing gratitude statements each evening has been proven to be beneficial for many people. Try this for a month, and continue if you find the exercise helps you in any way.

✔ **Practise metta/loving kindness meditation.** This is probably the most effective and powerful way of developing a deeper, kinder, and more fulfilling relationship with yourself. Refer to Chapter 6 for the stages of the metta practice.

Dealing with arguments in romantic relationships: A mindful way to greater peace

Arguments are often the cause of many difficult interactions with others, especially in romantic relationships. Romantic relationships can be both deeply satisfying and deeply painful. And they're most difficult when disagreements arise. Sometimes (or often) those disagreements turn into arguments. Here's a typical scenario:

> **A**: Why do you keep leaving your clothes lying on the floor in the bedroom? It looks so messy!
>
> **B**: Why are you so picky! Relax, will you. It's not a big deal. You're always nagging about everything.
>
> **A**: Me, nagging! Who's been doing all the cooking today? And all I ask is for you to pick up a few clothes, and that's too much effort. You're so childish.
>
> **B**: Childish! Listen to yourself shouting about some clothes . . .

And so on. Your higher brain function becomes unavailable when you get into an argumentative state of mind. The frustration and emotional reactivity build with each sentence that each person says.

So, how on earth can mindfulness help when these small things start to escalate into a full-blown argument and a negative atmosphere? Mindfulness creates a mental and emotional inner space – some space between the moment when you feel your irritation rising and your decision to speak. In that space, you have time to make a choice about what to say.

If your partner accuses you of leaving clothes on the floor, you notice yourself getting defensive. But in that extra space you have, you can also think about your partner: he's had a long day, is tired and has a bit of a short fuse. From that understanding, you're able to say a few kind words or offer a little hug or massage. The situation begins to defuse itself.

That all-important few seconds between your emotional experience and your choice of words is created through mindfulness practice. As you become adept in mindfulness, you become less automatically reactive. You're conscious of what's happening within you and can make these better decisions.

Here's how to deal with potential arguments:

1. **Notice the emotion rising up in your body when your partner says something that hurts you.**

2. **Become aware of where you feel the emotion in your body and take a few breaths. Be as kind and friendly to yourself as you can.** Say to yourself, 'This emotion is difficult for me to feel right now . . . Let me gently breathe with it.'

3. **Choose the words you respond with wisely from your more mindful state of mind.** Perhaps begin with agreeing with part of your partner's statement. Soften your tone of voice. Let your partner know how you feel, if you can. And avoid making accusations – doing so will just feed the argument.

4. **As you begin to calm down, try to be more and more mindful.** Keep feeling your breathing. Or be conscious of your bodily sensations or other emotions. Gently smile if you can. This approach will make you less reactive and more likely to shift the conversation into more positive territory.

Engaging in deep listening

Deep or mindful listening occurs when you listen with more than your ears. Deep listening involves listening with your mind and heart – your whole being. You're giving completely when you engage in deep listening. You let go of all your thoughts, ideas, opinions, and beliefs and just listen.

 Deep listening is healing. By healing, I mean that the person being listened to can feel a great sense of release and let go of frustrations, anxieties, or sadness. Through deep listening, true communication occurs: people want to be listened to more than anything else.

Mindfulness and me

Before I discovered the art of mindfulness and meditation, I was a bit of a perfectionist. I worked very hard to get the top marks at school, and when I went to university I continued the habit. I was being too hard on myself. I searched for ways of reducing the stress and eventually found meditation. I was very reluctant and sceptical at first: I spent a year deciding whether to learn it though a course. Meditation and mindfulness seemed too mystical and spiritual for my scientific mind. In the end I gave it a go and haven't looked back since! As I practise, it changes my relationship with myself. I don't feel the driving need to be absolutely brilliant in the work I do, which for some may sound like a bad thing. For me, that means I have more time for myself. I'm a bit kinder towards myself. I'm on a journey and certainly haven't 'got there' (I don't think that I or anyone can be perfect in that sense). More recently, I've discovered not to take mindfulness too seriously. Mindfulness isn't a religion or philosophy, but a creative way of living that each person uses in his own way. By having a light-hearted approach, I'm more relaxed about my own thoughts, words, and actions, and I allow life to unfold in a more natural way. If I remember to be mindful, that's great, but if I forget or have a lapse, that's human and not a problem at all.

Deep listening comes from an inner calm. If your mind is wild, it's very difficult for you to listen properly. If your mind is in turmoil, go away to listen to your breathing or even to your own thoughts. By doing so, you give your thoughts space to arise out of the unconscious, and you thereby release them.

Here's how to listen to someone deeply and mindfully:

- Stop doing anything else. Set your intention to listen deeply.
- Look the person in the eye when he speaks and gently smile, if appropriate.
- Put aside all your own concerns and worries.
- Listen to what the person is saying and how he's saying it.
- Listen with your whole being – your mind and heart, not just your head.
- Observe posture and tone of voice as part of the listening process.
- Notice the automatic thoughts popping into your head as you listen. Do your best to let them go and come back to listening.
- Ask questions if necessary, but keep them genuine and open rather than trying to change the subject. Let your questions gently deepen the conversation.
- Let go of judgement as far as you can. Judging is thinking rather than deep listening.
- Let go of trying to solve the problem or giving the person the answer.

When you give the other person the space and time to speak without judging, he begins to listen to himself. What he's saying becomes very clear to him. Then, quite often, the solution arises naturally. He knows himself far better than you do. By jumping straight into solutions, you only reduce the opportunity that person has to communicate with you. So, when listening, simply listen.

Arguing with monks

Researchers wanted to see the effect of an argument and confrontation on an experienced meditator. They chose a monk who had extensive meditative practice behind him. The researchers found the most confrontational university professor to argue with the monk. They measured the men's blood pressure and heart rates during the conversation. The professor's heart beat started off very high, but the monk's stayed calm. As the conversation went on, the professor became calmer and calmer (but still didn't want to stop talking!). In this way, if you remain peaceful and calm, having established a mindfulness routine, you can spread a sense of wellbeing quite naturally as you talk to others. Your relationships flourish in this way.

Being aware of expectations

Think about the last time someone annoyed you. What were your expectations of that person? What did you want him to say or do? If you have excessively high expectations in your relationships, you're going to find yourself frustrated.

Expectations are ideals created in your mind. The expectations are like rules. I expect you to behave; or to be quiet; or to make dinner every evening; or to be funny, not angry or assertive. The list is endless.

I aim to have low rather than high expectations with friends and family. I don't expect any presents on birthdays or any favours to be returned. I don't expect people to turn up to meetings on time or to return phone calls. This way, I'm not often disappointed. In fact, I'm pleasantly surprised when a friend does call me, does a favour for me or is kind to me! I feel very fortunate to have lovely friends and family who are supportive and fun to be with. But if I had very high expectations, I'd be setting myself up for disappointment. With reduced expectations, you set the stage for greater gratitude and positivity in your relationships when others do reach out.

If a person doesn't meet your expectations, you may react with anger, sadness, frustration, or jealousy. These emotions are natural to a certain extent, but if you experience them too frequently or too intensely, too much negative emotion harms your health and wellbeing. And just because you have high expectations or react emotionally when your expectations aren't met doesn't mean the other person is going to change, especially if you treat that person with emotional outbursts.

The next time you're about to feel annoyed, angry, or sad about an expectation of yours not being met, try the following mindfulness exercise. The practice helps you to move from an emotional or verbal reaction, to a mindful and balanced response. This is how:

1. **Don't speak yet.** A negative reaction just fuels the fire.

2. **Become aware of your breathing without changing it.** Is it deep or shallow? Is it slow or rapid? If you can't feel it, just count the out-breaths from one to ten. Or just to three if that's all you have time for.

3. **Notice the sensations in your body.** Do you feel the pain of the unfulfilled expectation in your stomach, shoulders, or somewhere else? Does it have a shape or colour?

4. **Imagine or feel the breath going into that part of the body.** Feel it with a sense of kindness and curiosity. Breathe into it and see what happens.

5. **Take a step back.** Become aware of the space between you, the observer, and your thoughts and feelings, which are the observed. See how you're separate and therefore free of them. You're going into observer mode, taking a step back, having a bird's-eye view of the whole situation from a bigger perspective.

6. **If necessary, go back to that person and speak from this wiser and more composed state of mind**. Don't speak unless you're settled and calm. Most of the time, speaking in anger may get what you want in the short term, but in the long term you leave people feeling upset. Play this by ear.

Looking into the mirror of relationships

Relationship is a mirror in which you can see yourself.

J Krishnamurti

All relationships, whether with a partner or work colleague, are a mirror that help you to see your own desires, judgements, expectations, and attachments. Relationships give an insight into your own inner world. What a great learning opportunity! You can think of relationships as an extension of your mindfulness practice. You can observe what's happening, both in yourself and the other person, with a sense of friendly openness, with kindness and curiosity. Try to let go of what you want out of the relationship, just as you do in meditation. Let the relationship simply be as it is, and allow it to unfold moment by moment.

Here are some questions to ask yourself as you observe the mirror of relationships:

- ✔ **Behaviour.** How do you behave in different relationships? What sort of language do you use? What's your tone of voice like? Do you always use the same words or sentences? What happens if you speak less, or more? Notice your body language.

- ✔ **Emotions.** How do you feel in different relationships? Do certain people or topics create fear or anger or sadness? Get in touch with your emotions when you're with other people, and see what the effect is. Try not to judge the emotions as good or bad, right or wrong: just see what they do.

- ✔ **Thoughts.** What sort of thoughts arise in different relationships? What happens if you observe the thoughts as just thoughts and not facts? How are your thoughts affected by how you feel? How do your thoughts affect the relationship?

Being mindful in a relationship is more difficult than it sounds. You can easily find yourself caught up in the moment and your attention is trapped. Through regular mindfulness practice, your awareness gradually increases and becomes easier. Although mindfulness in relationships is challenging, it's very rewarding too.

Working with your emotions

'You make me angry.' 'You're annoying me.' 'You're stressing me out.'

If you find yourself thinking or saying sentences like these, you're not really taking responsibility for your own emotions. You're blaming someone else for the way you feel. This may seem perfectly natural. However, in truth, no one can affect the way you feel. *The way you feel is determined by what you think about the situation.* For example, say I accidentally spill a cup of tea on your work. If you think that I did it on purpose, you may think, 'You damaged my paperwork deliberately, you idiot,' and then feel angry and upset. You blame me for your anger. If you see it as an accident and think that I may be tired, you think, 'It was just an accident – I hope he's okay,' and react with sympathy. The emotion is caused by your thought, not by the person or the situation itself.

Rather than blame the other person for your anger, actually feel the emotion. Notice when it manifests in your body if you can. Observe the effect of breathing into it. Watch it with a sense of care. This transforms your relationship to the anger from hate to curiosity, and thereby transforms the anger from a problem to a learning opportunity.

An easy way to remember and manage your emotions is to use the acronyn ABC:

- ✔ **A:** Activating event
- ✔ **B:** Belief
- ✔ **C:** Consequence

For example:

- ✔ **Activating event:** A colleague doesn't turn up to a meeting.
- ✔ **Belief:** You believe they must always be there on time.
- ✔ **Consequence:** You feel annoyed.

Now go back and change your belief. Think differently, such as: 'People aren't always on time – that's a fact of life. Some people are just always late. Other times, they get held up in traffic or on a slow train.' Now you'll notice that you'll feel less annoyed.

So, be mindful of your beliefs whenever you feel a strong emotional reaction to someone else, and see whether changing the belief, or simply smiling at the belief, helps.

Seeing difficult people as your teachers

Relationships are built on the history between you and the other person, whoever that may be. Whenever you meet another human being, your brain automatically pulls out the memory file on the person, and you relate to him with your previous knowledge of him. This is all very well when you're meeting an old and dearly loved friend, for example, but what about when you need to deal with someone you've had difficulties with in the past? Perhaps you may have had an argument or just don't seem to connect.

When dealing with difficult people, it's worth remembering you have two ways of meeting another human being. The first way is to see your ideas, memories, thoughts, opinions, and beliefs about that person. The other way is to actually see that person as he is, without the judgements and ideas and stories. This is meeting anew, meeting afresh, as if for the first time. Mindfulness is about meeting *all* experience afresh. When you connect with your senses, you're no longer in the realm of ideas, opinions, and beliefs. You're in the field of the present moment. Meeting another human being in that way you can't help but feel a warmth towards him as well as a sense of wonder.

Here are some ways of dealing with difficult relationships:

- ✔ **Take five mindful breaths or carry out a mini meditation (check out Chapter 8) before meeting the other person.** This may help prevent the feeling of anger or frustration becoming overpowering. Simple, yet awesome!

- ✔ **Observe the difference between your own negative image about the person and the person himself.** As best you can, let go of the image and meet the person as he is by connecting with your senses when you meet him.

- ✔ **Understand the following, which Buddha is quoted as saying: 'Remembering a wrong is like carrying a burden on the mind.' Try to forgive whatever has happened in your relationship.** See whether that helps. Buddha usually knows what he's talking about!

- ✔ **See the relationship as a game.** Mindfulness is not to be taken too seriously, and nor are relationships. Often relationships become stagnant because you're both taking things too seriously. Allow yourself to lighten up. See the funny side. Crack a joke. Or smile, at least.

- ✔ **Consider what's the worst that may happen.** That question usually helps to put things back in perspective. You may be overestimating how bad the other person is, or the worst that he can realistically do to you.

- ✔ **Become curious about the kind of thoughts that arise in your head when you meet the difficult person.** Are the thoughts part of a familiar pattern? Can you see them as merely thoughts rather than facts? Where did you get these ideas from? This is an example of mindfulness of thoughts: becoming curious about your thinking patterns and noticing what's happening. You're not trying to fix or change; that happens by itself if you observe the current thought patterns clearly.

Relationships are difficult. Don't be too hard on yourself if things don't work out. You have your own character, and sometimes you just don't connect with another person. Let go of the negatives from the past, as best you can, and follow your instincts. Allow things to unfold in their own natural way as best you can. And if it doesn't work out, it doesn't work out. You have another 6.99 billion people to try your mindful relationship skills on!

Lake meditation: Discovering acceptance

You can try this meditation, which is available as an audio track (Track 18):

This meditation is normally done lying down, but you can do it in any posture that's comfortable for you. Close your eyes softly. Feel your breathing for a few minutes. Now, when you're ready, imagine a beautiful lake. The lake is perfectly still and calm. The surface of the lake is so still it looks like a polished mirror. Majestic mountains are in the background, and the sky is predominantly blue, with a few small, white, fluffy clouds. The sky and mountains are reflected in the lake. Around the sides of this wonderful lake are old, mighty trees, with branches leaning out over the lake. A few birds fly across the lake in the distance. When the wind blows, small ripples and larger waves whip up on the surface, reflecting a dance of glints across the water. You're aware that, as the seasons change, the lake embraces the rain and fallen leaves, and in the winter may freeze on the surface. Deep under the surface, little changes or moves, and the water continues to teem with life. The lake openly accepts whatever is offered to it.

Now, when you're ready, allow yourself to merge and become one with the lake. As you lie or sit, you allow yourself to be the lake itself, if that makes sense to you. You're both the deep, still lake underneath and the ripples on the surface. Just allow yourself to absorb the slightest sense of what this may mean for you. In your compassion, kindness, and gentleness, you're supporting this body of water. As the weather changes, the water becomes muddied and gathers twigs and leaves. Can you softly allow all this to happen and continue to just be the lake? Appreciate how the changing conditions of the lake give it character, charm, and richness. Allow yourself to feel your own tranquillity and serenity underneath the turbulent surface. Is that possible to some extent? Are you able to allow the continual change that persistently unfolds around and in the lake to be part of the natural process of nature, and even embrace the beauty of it in yourself?

If you find it helpful, use this image of the lake to enrich your meditation practice from time to time. Even bringing it to mind as you go about your daily activities helps you to perceive life from a place of acceptance and peacefulness. Evoke the memory of how the lake can be both still, deep, and unmoving underneath, and disturbed at the surface. Recognise the continually fluxing thoughts and feelings of the mind and heart, and identify with the awareness that's both always there and just behind them. See your story, your world, your ideas, thoughts, dreams, opinions, and beliefs as part of that vast awareness, but not all of it. Enjoy the vision of the lake as it effortlessly reflects the sun and sky, birds and bees, plants and animals during the day, and the exquisite pale moon and twinkling stars at night, in the dark, cool sky — ever present, always changing, and yet always the same.

Chapter 8

Using Mindfulness in Your Daily Life

Mindfulness is portable: you can be mindful anywhere and everywhere, not only on the meditation cushion or yoga mat. You can engage in a mindful state of mind while giving a presentation, feeding the cat, or hugging a friend. By cultivating a mindful awareness, you deepen your day-to-day experiences and break free from habitual mental and emotional patterns. You notice that beautiful flower on the side of the road, you become aware and release your tense shoulders when thinking about work, and you give space for your creative solutions to life's challenges. All the small changes you make add up. Your stress levels go down, your depression or anxiety becomes a bit more manageable, and you begin to be more focused. You need to put in some effort to achieve this, but a totally different effort to the kind you're probably used to; you're then bound to change in a positive way. This chapter offers some of the infinite ways of engaging this ancient art of mindfulness in your daily life.

Using Mindfulness at Work

Work. A four-letter word with lots of negative connotations. Many people dislike work because of the high levels of stress they need to tolerate. A high level of stress isn't a pleasant or healthy experience, so welcome any way of managing that stress with open arms.

In many countries, managing the level of stress that employees face, and taking active steps to reduce stress, is a legal obligation. If you think that you're suffering from work-related stress, you need to consider talking to your manager or other appropriate person about the situation. Poor management standards are linked to unacceptably high levels of stress, and changes need to be made to ensure that stress is kept at reasonable levels, according to the Health and Safety Executive in the UK.

So how can mindfulness help with work?

- ✔ Mindfulness is proven to lower levels of stress, anxiety, and depression.

- ✔ Mindfulness leads to a greater ability to focus, even when under pressure, which then results in higher productivity and efficiency and more creativity.

- ✔ Mindfulness improves the quality of relationships, including those at work.

Mindfulness isn't simply a tool or technique to lower stress levels. Mindfulness is a way of being. Stress reduction is the tip of the iceberg. One business organisation I trained aptly said: 'Mindfulness goes to the heart of what good business is about – deepening relationships, communicating responsibly, and making mindful decisions based on the present facts, not the limits of the past.' When employees understand that giving mindful attention to their work actually improves the power of their brain to focus, their work becomes more meaningful and inspiring.

Beginning the day mindfully

Watching the 100-metre race in the Olympics, you see the athletes jump up and down for a few minutes before the start, but when they prepare themselves in the blocks, they become totally still. They focus their whole being completely, listening for the gunfire to signify the start. They begin in stillness. Be inspired by the athletes: begin your day with an inner stillness, so you can perform at your very best.

Start the day with some mindfulness meditation. You can do a full formal meditation such as a body scan or a sitting meditation (both these meditations are in Chapter 6), or perhaps some yoga or stretching in a slow and mindful way. Alternatively, simply sit up and feel the gentle ebb and flow of your own breath, or listen to the sounds of the birds as they wake up and chirp in the morning. Other alternatives include waking up early and eating your breakfast mindfully (see the mindful eating exercise in Chapter 6), or perhaps tuning in to your sense of smell, sight, and touch fully as you have your morning bath or shower; see what effect that has. That's better than just worrying about your day.

Dropping in with mini meditations

When you arrive at work, you can easily be swept away by it all and forget to be mindful of what you're doing. The telephone rings, you get email after email, and you're called into endless meetings. Whatever your work involves, your attention is sure to be sucked up.

This habitual loss of attention and going from activity to activity without really thinking about what you're doing is called *automatic pilot mode*. You simply need to change to mindful awareness mode. The most effective way of doing this is by one- to three-minute mini meditations, by feeling the sensation of your own breath as it enters and leaves your body. (Head to Chapter 5 for more about changing from automatic pilot.)

The breathing space meditation (a type of mini meditation) consists of three stages. In the first stage you become aware of your thoughts, emotions, and bodily sensations. In the second stage you become aware of your own breathing. And in the third and final stage you expand your awareness to the breath and the body as a whole. For lots more on how to do the breathing space meditation, check out Chapter 7.

When you're at work, give a mini meditation a go:

✔ **When?** You can do a mini meditation at set times or between activities. So when you've finished a certain task or job, you take time to practise a mini meditation before heading to the next task. In this way you increase the likelihood of being calm and centred, rather than flustered, by the time you get to the end of the day or working week. If you don't like the rigidity of planning your mini meditations ahead of time, just practise them whenever the thought crosses your mind and you feel you need to go into mindfulness mode.

Additionally, you can use the meditation to cope with a difficult situation, such as your boss irritating you. One way of coping with the wash of emotion that arises in such situations is to do a three-minute coping (breathing space) meditation (described in full in Chapter 7).

✔ **How?** Use any posture you like, as long as your spine is relaxed and upright. The simplest form of mini meditation is to feel your breathing. If you find that feeling the breath is too difficult, you can say to yourself 'in' as you breathe in, and 'out' as you breathe out. Alternatively, count each out-breath to yourself, going from one to ten. As always, when your mind drifts off, simply guide the attention gently and kindly back, even congratulating yourself for noticing that your mind had wandered off the breath.

✔ **Where?** You can do a mini meditation anywhere you feel comfortable. Usually, meditating is easier with your eyes closed, but that's not so easy at work! You can keep your eyes open and softly gaze at something while you focus your attention inwards. If you work outside, try going for a slow walk for a few minutes, feeling your breathing and noticing the sensations of your feet as they gently make contact with the earth.

You may dearly want to try out the mini meditation at work, but you simply keep forgetting. Well, why not make an appointment with yourself? Perhaps set a reminder to pop up on your computer, or a screen saver with a subtle reminder for yourself. One of my corporate clients popped a card on her desk with a picture of a beautiful flower. Each time she saw the picture, she took three conscious breaths. This helped to calm her and had a transformative effect on the day. Or, try a sticky note or a gentle alarm on your mobile phone – be creative in thinking of ways to remind yourself to be mindful.

Going from reacting to responding

A *reaction* is your almost automatic thought, reply, and behaviour following some sort of stimulus, such as your boss criticising you. A *response* to a situation is a more considered, balanced choice, often creative in reply to the criticism, and leads to solving your problems rather than compounding them.

You don't have to react when someone interrupts you in a meeting, takes away your project, or sends a rude email. Instead, having a balanced, considered response is most helpful for both you and your relationship with colleagues.

For example, say you hand in a piece of work to your manager, and she doesn't even say thank you. Later on you ask what she thinks of your work, and she says it's okay, but nothing special. You spent lots of time and effort to do a superb report, and you feel hurt and annoyed. You *react* by either automatically thinking negative thoughts about your manager and avoiding eye contact with her for the rest of the week, or you lash out with an outburst of accusations and feel extremely tense and frustrated for hours afterwards. Here's how you can turn this into a mindful response.

Begin to feel the sensations of your breath. Notice whether you're breathing in a shallow or rapid way because of your frustration, but try not to judge yourself. Say to yourself, 'in . . . out' as you breathe in and out. Expand your awareness to a sense of your body as a whole. Become mindful of the processes taking place inside you. Feel the burning anger rising from the pit of your stomach up through your chest and throat, or your racing heart and dry mouth when you're nervous. Honour the feeling instead of criticising or blocking the emotion. Notice what happens if you don't react as you normally do or feel like doing. Imagine your breath soothing the feeling. Bring kindness and curiosity to your emotions. This isn't an easy time for you – acknowledging that is an act of self-compassion.

You may discover that the very act of being aware of your reaction changes the flavour of the sensation altogether. Your relationship to the reaction changes an outburst, for example, to a more considered response. Your tone of voice may subtly change from aggressive and demanding to being calmer and inquisitive. The point is not to try and change anything, but just to sit back and watch what's going on for a few moments.

To help you to bring a sense of curiosity when you're about to react to a situation at work, try asking yourself the following questions slowly, one at a time, and giving yourself time for reflection:

- ✔ What feeling am I experiencing at the moment, here at work? How familiar is this feeling? Where do I feel the feeling in my body?

- ✔ What thoughts are passing through my mind at the moment? How judgemental are my thoughts? How understanding are my thoughts? How are my thoughts affecting my actions at work?

- ✔ How does my body feel at the moment? How tired do I feel at work? What effect has the recent level of work had on my body? How much discomfort can I feel at the moment in my body, and where is the source of it?

- ✔ Can I acknowledge my experiences here at work, just as they are? Am I able to respect my own rights as well as responsibilities in the actions I choose? What would be a wise way of responding right now, instead of my usual reaction? If I do react, can I acknowledge that I'm not perfect and make my next decision a more mindful response?

Perhaps you'll go back to your manager and calmly explain why you feel frustrated. You may become angry too, if you feel this is necessary, but without feeling out of control. Perhaps you'll choose not to say anything today, but wait for things to settle before discussing the next step. The idea is for you to be more creative in your *response* to this frustration rather than *reacting* in your usual way, if your usual way is unhelpful and leads to further problems.

The benefits of a considered, balanced response as opposed to an automatic reaction include:

- ✔ Lower blood pressure. (High blood pressure is a cause of heart disease.)

- ✔ Lower levels of stress hormones in your blood stream, leading to a healthier immune system.

- ✔ Improved relationships, because you're less likely to break down communication between colleagues if you're in a calmer state of mind.

- ✔ A greater feeling of being in control, because you're able to choose how you respond to others rather than automatically reacting involuntarily.

You don't sweep your frustration or anger under the carpet. Mindfulness isn't about blocking emotions. You do the opposite: you allow yourself to mindfully feel and sooth the emotions with as much friendliness and kindness as you can muster. Even forcing a smile can help. Mindfulness is the only way I know of effectively overcoming destructive emotions. Expressing out-of-control anger leads to more anger: you just get better at it. Supressing anger leads to outbursts at some other time. Mindfulness is the path to easing your frustration.

Solving problems creatively

Your ideas need room. You need space for new perceptions and novel ways of meeting challenges, in the same way that plants need space to grow, or they begin to wither. For your ideas, the space can be in the form of a walk outside, a three-minute mini meditation, or a cup of tea. Working harder is often not the best solution: working smarter is.

If your job involves dealing with issues and problems, whether that involves people or not, you can train yourself to see the problems differently. By seeing the problems as challenges, you're already changing how you meet this issue. A *challenge* is something you rise to – something energising and fulfilling. A *problem* is something that has to be dealt with – something draining, an irritation.

To meet your challenges in a creative way, find some space and time for yourself. Write down *exactly* what the challenge is; when you're sure what your challenge is, you find it much easier to solve. Try to see the challenge from a different person's perspective. Talk to other people and ask how they'd deal with the issue. Become mindful of your immediate reactive way of dealing with this challenge, and question the validity of it.

Practising mindful working

Mindful working is simply being mindful of whatever you do when you work. Here are some examples of ways of being mindful at work:

- ✔ When typing, notice the sense of touch between your fingers and the keyboard. Notice how quickly your mind converts a thought into an action on keys. Are you striking the keys too hard? Are your shoulders tense; is your face screwing up unnecessarily? How's your posture?

- ✔ Before writing or checking an email, take a breath. Is this really important to do right now? Reflect for a few moments on the key message you need to get across, and remember it's a human being receiving this message – not just a computer. After sending the message, take time to feel your breath and, if you can, enjoy it.

✔ When the telephone rings, let the sound of the ring be a reminder for you to be mindful. Let the telephone ring a few times before answering. Use this time to notice your breath and posture. When you pick it up, speak and listen with mindfulness. Notice both the tone of your own voice and the other person's. If you want to, experiment by gently smiling as you speak and listen, and become aware of the effect that has.

✔ No matter what your work involves, do it with awareness. Awareness helps your actions become clear and efficient. Connect your senses with whatever you're doing. Whenever you notice your mind drifting out of the present moment, just gently bring it back.

✔ Make use of the mini meditations to keep you aware and awake at work. The meditations are like lampposts, lighting wherever you go and making things clear.

Using mindful leadership

If you're a leader in an organisation, responsibility goes with the job. Good leaders need to make effective decisions, manage emotions successfully, and keep their attention on the big picture. In their book *Resonant Leadership* (Harvard Business School Press), Richard Boyatzis and Annie McKee highlight the need for mindfulness in order for leadership to be most effective. They found that the ability to manage your own emotions and the emotions of others, called emotional intelligence, is vitally important for an effective leader, and to achieve this, you need to find a way to renew yourself.

Renewal is a way of optimising your state of mind so you're able to work most effectively. The stress generated through leadership puts your body and mind on high alert and weakens your capacity for focus and creativity. Renewal is a necessary antidote for leadership stress, and one key way science has found to achieve this is through mindfulness.

Neuroscience has shown that optimistic, hopeful people are naturally in an *approach* mode of mind. They *approach* difficulties as challenges and see things in a positive light. Other people have more *avoidant* modes of mind, characterised by *avoiding* difficult situations and denying problems rather than facing up to them. Mindfulness practised for just eight weeks has been shown to move people from unhelpful, *avoidant* modes to more helpful, creative, emotionally intelligent, *approach* modes of mind, leading to a greater sense of meaning and purpose, healthy relationships, and an ability to work and lead effectively.

For example, one of my clients, a CEO of a medium-sized corporation, felt isolated and highly stressed. Through practising tailor-made mindfulness techniques, he began to renew himself, see the business more holistically, take greater time to make critical decisions, and communicate more effectively with his team about the way forwards. He now practises mindfulness on a daily basis for 10 minutes, as well as using other strategies during the day, to create renewal.

Trying single-tasking: Discovering the multi-tasking myth

Everyone does it nowadays: texting as we walk, or checking emails as we speak on the phone. People multi-task to be efficient, but most of the time it actually makes you *less* efficient. And from a mindfulness perspective, your attention becomes hazy rather than centred.

Many studies by top universities show that multi-tasking leads to inefficiency and unnecessary stress. Some reasons to avoid multi-tasking and to mindfully focus on just one task at a time instead are that doing so will help you to:

- ✔ **Live in the moment:** In one hilarious study, researchers asked people who walked across a park whether they noticed a clown on a unicycle. People who were glued to their phones didn't notice it! Others did.

- ✔ **Be efficient:** By switching between two tasks, you take longer. It's quicker to finish one task and then the other. Switching attention takes up time and energy and reduces your capacity to focus. Some experts found a 40 per cent reduction in productivity due to multi-tasking.

- ✔ **Improve relationships:** A study at the University of Essex found that just by having a phone nearby while having a person-to-person conversation had a negative impact. Give your partner your full attention as much as possible. Most people don't realise how much of a positive effect simply giving your partner your mindful awareness has.

- ✔ **De-stress:** A study by the University of California found that when office workers were constantly checking email as they were working, their heart rates were elevated compared with those of people focusing on just one task.

- ✔ **Get creative:** By multi-tasking, you over-challenge your memory resources. There's no space for creativity. A study in Chicago in 2010 found that multi-taskers struggled to find creative solutions to problems they were given.

Finishing by letting go

You may find letting go of your work at the end of the day very difficult. Perhaps you come home and all you can think about is work. You may spend the evening talking angrily about colleagues and bosses, or actually doing more work to try to catch up with what you should've finished during the day. This impacts on the quality and quantity of your sleep, lowering your energy levels for the next day. This unfortunate negative cycle can spin out of control.

Reducing teacher stress

Teaching in schools in considered one of the most stressful jobs in the world. When I was a full-time schoolteacher, almost all my time was taken up in planning lessons and marking books. I worked until the early hours of the morning and turned up the next day in a daze. The books were marked, but I was of no real use to the children; I easily lost patience with them, and made mountains out of molehills. I was 'sweating the small stuff'.

By meditating for 20 minutes or so when I reached home, I was able to let go of all the worries and anxieties of the workplace and allow my evening to be that little bit more enjoyable. I prioritised my time and ensured that I found more time to exercise and socialise. The meditation gently drew me out of the undue stress, as well as helping me to organise my work and life more effectively.

You need to draw a line between work and home, especially if your stress levels are on the increase. Meditating as soon as you get home, or on your way home (see the following section), provides an empowering way of achieving this. You're saying 'enough'. You're taking a stand against the tidal wave of demands on your limited time and energy. You're doing something uplifting for your health and wellbeing, and ultimately for all those around you too. And you're letting go.

To let go at the end of the day most successfully, choose one of the formal mindfulness meditation practices in Chapter 6. Or take up a sport or hobby in which you're absorbed by gentle, focused attention – an activity that enables the energy of your body and mind to settle, and the mindfulness to indirectly calm you.

Using Mindfulness on the Move

I always find it amusing to see people from abroad on the Underground transport system in London, looking at the trains with awe and taking plenty of photos. Other commuters look up, almost in disgust, before burying their heads back in a book or newspaper or checking their phones. When people are on holiday they live in the moment, and the present moment is always exciting. The new environment is a change from their routine. Travelling is another opportunity to bring mindfulness to the moment.

Walking mindfully

Take a moment to consider this question: what do you find miraculous? Perhaps you find the vastness of space amazing; perhaps you find your favourite book or band a wonder. What about walking? Walking is a miracle too.

Scientists have managed to design computers powerful enough to make the Internet work and for man to land on the moon, but no robot in the world can walk anywhere nearly as smoothly as a human being. If you're able to walk, you're lucky indeed. To contemplate the miracle called walking is the beginning of walking meditation.

Normally, in the formal walking meditation (as described in Chapter 6), you aren't trying to get anywhere. You simply walk back and forth slowly, being mindful of each step you take, with gratitude. However, when walking to work or wherever you're going, you have a goal. You're trying to get somewhere. This creates a challenge, because your mind becomes drawn into thinking about when you're going to arrive, what you're going to do when you get there, and whether you're on time. In other words, you're not in the moment. The focus on the goal puts you out of the present moment.

Practise letting the destination go. Be in the moment as you walk. Feel the breeze and enjoy your steps if you can. If you can't enjoy the walk, just feel the sensations in your feet – that's mindfulness. Keep bringing your mind back into the moment, again and again, and, hey presto, you're meditating as you walk.

Driving mindfully

If everyone did mindful driving, the world would be a safer and happier place. Don't worry: it doesn't involve closing your eyes or going into a trance! Try this driving meditation, and feel free to be creative and adapt it as you like. Remember, don't read this book while you're driving: that would be dangerous.

1. **Set your intention by deciding to drive mindfully.** Commit to driving with care and attention. Set your attitude to be patient and kind to others on the road. Leave in plenty of time to get to where you're going, so you can let go of overly focusing on your destination.

2. **Sit in the driver's seat and practise a minute or so of mindful breathing.** Feel your natural breath as it is, and come into the present moment.

3. **Start your car.** Get a sense of the weight and size of the car – a machine with tremendous power, whatever its size, and with the potential to do much damage if you drive irresponsibly, or to be tremendously helpful if you drive with mindful awareness and intelligence. Begin making your way to your destination.

4. **Be alert.** Don't switch on the radio or CD player. Instead, let your awareness be wide and perceptive. Be aware of what other vehicles and people are doing all around you. Let your awareness be gentle, rather than forcing and straining it.

5. **See how smoothly you can drive.** Brake gradually and accelerate without excessive revving. This type of driving is less stressful and more fuel efficient.

6. **Every now and then, briefly check in with your body.** Notice any tension and let it go if you can, or become aware and accept it if you can't. You don't need to struggle or fight with the tension.

7. **Show a healthy courtesy to your fellow drivers.** Driving is all about trusting and co-operating with others.

8. **Stay within the speed limit.** If you can, drive more slowly than you normally do. You'll soon grow to enjoy that pace, and may be safer.

9. **Take advantage of red traffic lights and traffic jams.** This is traffic meditation! These are opportunities to breathe. Look out of the window and notice the sky, the trees, and other people. Let this be a time of rest for you, rather than a time to become anxious and frustrated. Remember that stress isn't caused by the situation but by the attitude you bring to the circumstance. Bring a mindful attitude, just as an experiment, and see what happens. You discover a different way of living altogether.

Travelling mindfully on public transport

If you travel on a bus, train, or plane, you're not in active control of the transport itself, and so can sit back and be mindful. Most people plug themselves into headphones or read, but meditation is another option. Why not exercise your mind while travelling? If commuting is part of your daily routine, you can listen to a guided meditation or just practise by yourself. If you think you'll go deeply into meditation, ensure that you don't miss your stop by setting the alarm on your watch or phone.

The disadvantage of meditating in this way is the distractions. You may find yourself being distracted by sudden braking or the person who keeps snoring right next to you. I suggest that you practise your core meditation in a relatively quiet and relaxed environment, such as your bedroom, and use your meditation while travelling as a secondary meditation. Ultimately there are no distractions in mindfulness: whatever you experience can be the object of your mindful attention.

Here are some specific mindfulness experiments to try out while on the move:

1. **See whether you can be mindful of your breath from one station to the next, just for fun.** Whether you manage or not isn't the issue: this is just an experiment to see what happens. Do you become more mindful or less? What happens if you put more or less effort into trying to be mindful?

2. **Hear the various announcements and other distractions as sounds to be mindful of.** Let the distractions be part of your meditative experience. Listen to the pitch, tone, and volume of the sound, rather than thinking about the sound. Listen as you'd listen to a piece of music.

3. **See whether you can tolerate and even welcome unpleasant events.** For example, if two people are talking loudly to each other, or someone is listening to noisy music, notice your reaction. What particular thought is stirring up emotion in you? Where can you feel the emotion? What happens when you imagine your breath going into and out of that part of your body?

4. **Allow your mindful awareness to spill into your walk to wherever you're going.** As you walk, feel your feet making contact with the ground. Notice how the rate of your breathing changes as you walk. Allow your body to get into the rhythm of the walk, and enjoy the contact of the surrounding air with your skin as you move.

Using Mindfulness in the Home

Not only is doing mindfulness meditation and exercise at home convenient, but it also helps you to enjoy your everyday activities as well. Then, rather than seeing chores as a burden, you may begin to see them as opportunities to enjoy the present moment as it is.

Waking up mindfully

When you wake up, breathe three mindful breaths. Feel the whole of each in-breath and the whole of each out-breath. Try adding a smile to the equation if you like. Think of three things you're grateful for – a loved one, your home, your body, your next meal – anything. Then slowly get up. Enjoy a good stretch. Cats are masters of stretching – imagine you're a cat and feel your muscles elongate having been confined to the warmth of your bed all night. If you want to, do some mindful yoga or tai chi.

Then, if you can, do some formal mindful meditation. You can do five minutes of mindful breathing, a 20-minute sitting meditation, or a body scan meditation – choose what feels right for you.

Doing everyday tasks with awareness

The word 'chore' makes routine housework unpleasant before you've even started. Give your chores a different name to help spice them up, such as dirt-bursting, vacuum-dancing, mopping 'n' bopping, or home sparkling!

The great thing about everyday jobs, including eating, is that they're slow, repetitive physical tasks, which makes them ideal for mindfulness. You're more easily able to be mindful of the task as you do it. Here are a couple of examples to get you started.

Washing dishes

Recently, one of my clients who works from home found mindful dishwashing a transformative experience. She realised that she used to wash dishes to have a break from work, but when washing up she was still thinking about the work. By connecting with the process of dishwashing, she felt calmer and relaxed, renewed and ready to do a bit more creative work.

Have a go:

1. **Be aware of the situation.** Take a moment to look at the dishes. How dirty are they? Notice the stains. See how the dishes are placed. What colour are they? Now move into your body. How does your physical body feel at the moment? Become aware of any emotions you feel – are you annoyed or irritated? Consider what sort of thoughts are running through your mind; perhaps, 'When I finish this, then I can relax,' or 'This is stupid.'

2. **Begin cleaning, slowly to begin with.** Feel the warmth of the water. Notice the bubbles forming and the rainbow reflections in the light. Put slightly less effort into the scrubbing than you may normally, and let the washing-up liquid do the work of cleaning. When the dish looks completely clean, wash the bubbles off and see how clean the plate looks. Allow yourself to see how you've transformed a grimy, mucky plate into a spotless, sparkling one. Now let it go. Place the dish on the side to dry. Be childlike in your sense of wonder as you wash.

3. **Try to wash each dish as if for the first time.** Keep letting go of the idea of finishing the job or of the other things you could be doing.

4. **When you've finished, look at what you've done.** Look at the dishes and how they've been transformed through your mindful awareness and gentle activity. Congratulate yourself on having taken the time to wash the dishes in a mindful way, thereby training your mind at the same time.

All meditation is like mindfully washing dishes. In meditation you're gently cleaning your mind. Each time your attention wanders into other thoughts and ideas, you become aware of the fact and gently step back. Each step you take back from your unruly thoughts is a cleansing process.

Vacuuming

Using the vacuum cleaner, another common activity in many people's lives, is usually done while your mind is thinking about other things – which isn't actually experiencing the process of vacuuming. Try these steps to experience mindfulness while vacuuming:

1. **Begin by noticing the area you want to clean.** What does it look like and how dirty is the floor? Notice any objects that may obstruct your vacuuming. Become mindful of your own physical body, your emotions, and thoughts running through your mind.

2. **Tidy up the area so you can use the vacuum cleaner in one go, without stopping, if you can.** This ensures you have time to get into the rhythm of the activity without stopping and starting, helping you to focus.

3. **Switch the vacuum cleaner on.** Notice the quality of the sound and feel the vibrations in your arm. Begin moving the vacuum cleaner, getting into a calm rhythm if possible, and continue to focus your mindful attention on your senses. Stay in the moment if you can, and when your mind takes your attention away, acknowledge that and come back into the here and now.

4. **When you've finished, switch off and observe how you feel.** How was the process different to how you normally vacuum the floor? Look at what you've done and be proud of your achievement.

Eating mindfully

Regular, daily mindfulness practice is a key aspect of mindful eating. This acts as a foundation from which you can build a mindful-eating lifestyle. The discipline of mindfulness makes you aware of your emotions and thoughts. You begin to notice the kinds of situations, thoughts, and emotions that lead you to eating particular foods.

Here's how to eat a meal mindfully:

1. **Remove distractions.** Turn off the television, radio, and all other electronics. Put aside any newspapers, magazines, and books. All you need is you and your meal.

2. **Carry out three minutes of mindful breathing.** Sit with your back upright but not stiff, and feel the sensations of your breathing. Alternatively, try the three-minute breathing space detailed in Chapter 7.

3. **Become aware of your food.** Notice the range of colours on the plate. Inhale the smell. Remember how fortunate you are to have a meal today and be grateful for what you have.

4. **Observe your body.** Are you salivating? Do you feel hungry? Are you aware of any other emotions? What thoughts are going through your head right now? Can you see them as just thoughts rather than facts?

5. **Now slowly place a morsel of food into your mouth.** Be mindful of the taste, smell, and texture of the food as you chew. Put your cutlery down as you chew. Don't eat the next mouthful until you've fully chewed this one. At what point do you swallow? Have you chewed the food fully?

6. **When you're ready, take the next mouthful in the same way.** As you continue to eat mindfully, be aware of your stomach and the feeling of being full. As soon as you feel you've had enough to eat, stop. Because you've been eating slowly, you may find that you feel full up sooner than usual.

7. **If you feel full but still have the desire to eat more, try doing another three minutes of mindful breathing.** Remember that the thought 'I need to eat' is just a thought. You don't have to obey the thought and eat if that's not the best thing for you.

Try eating in this way once a day for a week or two, and become mindful of the effect it has.

Second hunger: Overcoming problem eating

When you eat, you need to:

- Eat the right amount of food, neither too much nor too little, to maintain a healthy weight.
- Eat the right types of food for you to meet your daily nutritional needs.

However, you may not eat just to meet those needs. In reality you may eat to:

- Avoid feeling bored
- Cope with a sense of anger
- Fill a feeling of emptiness within you
- Satisfy a desire for some taste in particular (such as sweet or fatty food)
- Help you cope with high levels of stress

This 'comfort' eating, or emotional eating as it's sometimes called, tends to operate on an unconscious level, driving your cravings for food.

Emotional eating is like a second hunger, to satisfy the need for psychological wellbeing. Your emotions are eating rather than your stomach. You're using the food to calm your mind. This can lead to an unhealthy eating cycle. You experience a negative emotion, so you eat food to cope with the emotion, which leads to a temporary feeling of satisfaction but, before long, the negative emotion returns.

Mindful eating offers a way of becoming more aware of the inner thoughts and emotions driving your tendency to eat. Through a mindful awareness you begin naturally to untangle this web and begin to discover how to eat in a healthy and conscious way, making the right choices for you.

Additionally, you may like to try these strategies:

- **Hunger reality check**. Before eating, notice whether your hunger is physical or emotional. If you've eaten recently and your tummy isn't rumbling, perhaps you can wait a little longer and see whether the sensation passes.

- **Keep a food diary**. Simply writing down everything you eat for a few weeks is often an eye-opener. You may begin to see patterns emerging.

- **Manage boredom**. Rather than using boredom as a reason to eat, try doing an activity such as mindful walking, or call a friend and be really aware of your conversation.

- **Avoid extreme dieting**. By depriving yourself of certain foods, you may end up fuelling your desire for that food. Instead, treat yourself occasionally and eat the food mindfully. Actually tasting the treat makes it even tastier!

Living Mindfully in the Digital Age

I've got a smart phone, but it's not very smart. My phone sends me text messages just when I'm writing a chapter for a new book. It rings when I'm driving. Its addictive nature beckons me to check Facebook when I'm supposed to be drifting off to sleep.

The digital age has brought huge benefits: from saving lives in emergencies, to sharing information with the world, the advantages are countless. But without mindfulness, living in the digital age can drive you crazy! If you don't turn your phone or computer off from time to time, your attention can be completely hijacked by websites, incoming messages, social media, games and more. Gadgets are so compelling.

If you think that the digital age is getting too much, check out the suggestions in this section to get yourself back in control.

Assessing your level of addiction to technology

Nowadays, people seem to use their phones a lot. A recent survey of over a thousand managers found that:

- Seventy per cent check their phones within an hour of waking up.

- Fifty-six per cent check their phones within an hour of going to sleep.

- Fifty-one per cent check their phones continuously while on holiday.

Although psychologists hesitate to call excessive use of digital devices an addiction, many signs exist: a compulsion to check your phone, withdrawal symptoms when you don't have access to your phone and the harmful effect of excessive phone use on the rest of your life.

Here's a fun quiz I've developed to find out just how addicted you are to your phone:

1. **You're doing some work and a phone rings in another room. Do you:**

   a. Take no notice: it must be someone else's; your phone is normally off.

   b. Ignore it and check it later.

   c. Walk casually to pick it up.

   d. Run to pick up the phone, sometimes tripping over or stubbing your toe in the process, and screaming to anyone nearby to get out of the way.

2. **You're planning a holiday, but the hotel has no Wi-Fi and no phone signal. Will you go?**

   a. Yes, why not?

   b. Oh, I'd love the chance to get a break from my devices. Heaven!

   c. Probably wouldn't go there.

   d. No way! How can I have a vacation without my phone and/or laptop – that doesn't make sense. I need a good phone signal and superfast Internet 24/7.

3. **Where's your phone right now?**

   a. My what? Oh, phone . . . Err, no idea. I'm not sure if I have a phone actually.

   b. Somewhere around here.

   c. In this room.

   d. It's right here – my beautiful, precious phone. Mmmm, I love it!

4. **What do you use your phone for?**

   a. Phone calls, of course. What else is it for?

   b. Calls and texts from time to time. Mainly emergencies.

   c. Call and texts. And picking up emails sometimes too. A few pictures.

   d. Everything. It's my life! Facebook, Twitter, WhatsApp, Instagram, Snapchat, email, texting, photos, video, playing games, fitness, Skype. Oh yes, and sometimes phone calls too!

5. **Do you keep your phone nearby as you sleep?**

   a. No way!

   b. Sometimes. Or just for my alarm clock. Don't really check last thing at night or first thing in the morning.

   c. Quite often. Send the odd text and maybe have a peek at my messages first thing in the morning too.

   d. Every night. I sleep with my phone. It's the last thing I look at before falling asleep and the first thing I see when I wake up. It's my soul mate.

Add up your score: letter a is 1 point, b is 2 points, c is 3 points, and d is four points.

5–10 points: you're not really addicted to your phone at all – you're probably too busy meditating.

11–15 points: you like your phone, but not that much. You're still in control and can live comfortably without it.

16–18 points: you're pretty dependent on your phone for many things. You might like to take a little break from your phone from time to time.

19–20 points: you love your phone. Have you proposed? What if you lose your phone? Or it gets stolen? Make sure you have some moments in the day where you take a break from your device and do some mindful walking or stretching, or sit and meditate away from your phone. If you feel that your phone usage is out of control, try some of the tips in the section below to help you.

Using mindfulness to get back in control

If you've discovered that you're using digital devices to the point that they're having a negative impact on your work or social life, it's time to get back in control.

You can manage overuse of digital devices in many ways. It's not as hard as you may think. In fact, once you start using some of these strategies, you may find that you don't even want to look at your mobile devices.

Here are some techniques that you can try:

✔ **Engage in other activities.** You can participate in a new hobby regularly, such as knitting, gardening or playing an instrument. By paying mindful attention to your hobby and keeping your phones and computers out of the way, you'll develop greater mindfulness. And you can also get on with a few household chores – you'll feel good once they're done. Again, keep your devices switched off and try focusing on the chore – it can be soothing and enjoyable to polish the dining table or clear your desk with full attention and a little smile.

✔ **Make good use of flight mode, or switch your phone off.** When I have an important task to do, I try to remember to keep my phone off or simply in flight mode. That way, I can't be disturbed. The iPhone even has a new mode called 'do not disturb'. This prevents calls and alerts from coming through. So, from 9pm to 8am I set my phone to 'do not disturb' to automatically prevent any more calls or messages coming in.

✔ **Set boundaries.** Just before you go to bed, it's important not to look at screens too much. Television, laptops and phones emit a light which signals to your body that it's still daytime. Then you may have trouble falling asleep and may wake up tired. Also, you may not want to be disturbed at other specific times in the day. For example, when walking through the park keep your phone off and enjoy nature and the people around you. And obviously, when you're with friends or family or eating a meal, switch your phone off or leave it out of the way. If distancing yourself from your phone sounds like a challenge, just try it once and see how that goes. Eventually, it can feel freeing to leave your gadgets behind.

✔ **Switch off notifications.** Does your computer beep each time an email comes through? Does your phone make a noise each time someone chats to you on social media or sends you a message? If so, you can end up with perpetual distraction. Every time you're doing one task, you're distracted by another. The more you keep switching your attention, the less your mindful awareness develops. Turn off as many notifications as you can. This way, you can focus on doing whatever you need to do with awareness.

✔ **Be kind to yourself when you slip up.** Ever had that feeling of frustration when you've spent the last hour or so just surfing the Internet rather than finishing your work? I have. But when you do eventually catch yourself doing this, don't beat yourself up too much. It's okay. Everyone has their downtime and gets distracted. Say to yourself, 'It's okay. Let me take a break from my computer and phone and have a little mindful walk. I'll then come back with a smile and get on with my tasks. Everyone gets too caught up with the barrage of technology nowadays.'

Using technology to enhance mindful awareness

If you're looking for a way to enhance your mindfulness, you may want to avoid technology altogether – and that's understandable. Use of technology can distract your mind. But for you, using digital devices may be part of your everyday life. Switching them off for an extended period may seem impossible to achieve. In such a case, I encourage you to make good use of mindfulness apps, websites and more.

You can download and use apps for mobile devices like phones and tablets. Simply search for 'mindfulness' or 'meditation' in the app stores and you'll find lots of resources – take your pick. New apps come out every week!

If you use social media a lot, following people or organisations that offer mindful images, tweets and more may help you. I offer this service to my followers on Twitter @shamashalidina and Facebook at www.facebook.com/shamashalidina. Free free to say hi to me! *Mindful* magazine also offers 'mindful interrupters' – reminders in your day to let go of mindlessness and bring a kindly awareness to the moment. You can find the mindful interrupters on Twitter: @MindInterrupter.

You can also use software to help you focus mindfully on your work. My favourite free software that helps me to focus and be productive on my computer is called Self Control. It's available free for Apple Mac computers, and there are equivalent software products for Windows PCs.

For example, today I wanted to focus for a couple of hours on writing this article. So I switched on the Self Control program for an hour. Then I had a break and set it for another hour. I decide what I want to block for that hour. So for me, I block all my social media websites and my email. With those two areas blocked, I can mindfully focus on my writing.

Chapter 9

Establishing Your Own Mindfulness Routine

In This Chapter

▶ Discovering a clinically proven eight-week course

▶ Tailoring the practices to meet your needs

▶ Exploring ways to deepen your mindfulness

*L*earning a new language takes time, effort and patience. You need to dedicate yourself and at the same time not expect rapid progress. You try to practise regularly, preferably daily. You can learn the language by using CDs, books, television programmes, videos, websites, or in person through a teacher – whatever way best suits your lifestyle and learning methods. Learning mindfulness has some similarities. You can begin in many different ways, as long as you practise regularly and with a certain commitment and the right attitude and intention. (Refer to Chapters 4 and 5 for more about nurturing your attitudes and intention.) If you find committing yourself to a mindfulness practice difficult, you're not alone; you can try a different approach, adjust your practice method, explore possible barriers and look for support as you discover the language of mindfulness.

Remember that when you learn a language, you can measure your progress – by, say, the number of new words you know. You can't measure progress in mindfulness so easily, if at all, because mindfulness invites you to stop searching for progress. Mindfulness is about being exactly where you are right now and exploring the landscape, enjoying the scenery and being as you are, whatever that means for you. No matter how long you've been practising mindfulness, the present moment is always the same and yet always fresh, new and full of possibilities.

In this chapter I introduce the eight-week mindfulness-based stress reduction course and explore how to choose which element of mindfulness is best for you to practise. I also give you some ideas you can use if you want to take your mindfulness meditation even deeper.

Trying the Evidence-Based Mindfulness Course

Perhaps the most well-proven stress reduction course is an eight-week programme called *mindfulness-based stress reduction* (MBSR), originally developed at the stress reduction clinic at the University of Massachusetts medical school by Jon Kabat-Zinn. The course has been researched many times with thousands of people and has proved to be effective at reducing stress, so the recommended practices are certainly worth a go. If, after the eight weeks, you've felt no change has happened and sense that mindfulness isn't for you, you can drop the practice. If you found the programme helpful, you can go on to develop your own practice, having experienced the range of meditative exercises.

Begin the programme by making a personal commitment to suspend your judgement and follow the recommended practices for eight weeks. After that, decide whether mindfulness is something for you. You can ask others in your life to help support you over the next eight weeks, or at least to give you some space to engage in mindfulness meditations daily for the next couple of months. Keep a journal on hand during the eight weeks to record your progress and any thoughts or emotions that arise.

Making the mind–body connection

The root meaning of the phrase *to heal* is literally 'to make whole'. Mindfulness meditation leads to a sense of being whole and complete, a sense of seeing the perfection of yourself, just the way you are, no matter what may be wrong with you.

One of the key ways modern medicine broke down the wholeness of being human was by splitting up the body and the mind as two distinct, separate entities. Your attitudes, opinions and beliefs weren't thought to affect your physical health. Ample evidence now shows strong links between your inner attitudes and your physical health and wellbeing. In this context,

healing means to make whole the connection between mind and body and to see the mind and body as two parts of the same entity. Through practising mindfulness you see how your mind influences everything from the rate of your breathing to the way you treat your colleagues at work, and how an emotional rollercoaster ride on a Monday may be influencing your flu-like symptoms on Wednesday. This doesn't mean that you're cause yourself to become ill by thinking certain thoughts, but simply that the way your body functions is linked to the level of stress you experience.

Week One: Understanding automatic pilot

You operate on an automatic pilot far more than you may think you do. You may have experienced driving a car for a significant time before realising you were lost in thoughts, worries, or daydreams. This may be okay for a little while, but if your whole life is run automatically, you miss the show. Your mind thinks the same old thoughts, you may react unnecessarily when things don't go your way, and your stress is compounded without you being fully aware of this process. Mindful awareness, as opposed to automatic pilot, allows for the possibility of responding to situations by offering you choice – a freedom from the mechanical, reactive, habitual patterns of your mind. (Refer to Chapter 5 for more about overcoming living on automatic pilot.)

This is the practice for Week One:

✔ Begin the week by engaging in the 'eating a piece of fruit' meditation described in Chapter 6. Record in your journal what effect the exercise has on you. Reflect on the effect of operating on automatic pilot in your daily life. What are you missing out on? What effect is unawareness having on your thoughts, emotions and body, as well as your relationship with yourself, others and the world?

✔ Practise the body scan meditation (explained in Chapter 6) daily, using the MP3 provided with this book. Play the MP3 and follow the guidance as best you can. Each day, note whether you practised and how you found the meditation. Don't worry if you don't enjoy it; persevere with it. Experiment with doing the body scan at different times of the day to see what works best for you.

✔ Choose a routine daily activity to practise mindfully. This can be brushing your teeth, showering, getting dressed, walking or driving to work, speaking with your partner, cooking, cleaning or anything you can think of. Bring a sense of curiosity to your experience. What matters is not what you choose, but your commitment to being aware of what you're doing, as you're doing it.

Week Two: Dealing with barriers

Daily meditation practice can be pretty challenging. Meditation provides the space for a whole range of trapped thoughts and emotions to rise to the surface, often the ones you want to avoid most. The tendency of the mind is to judge experiences as good or bad. The idea of mindfulness is to be aware of these judgements and let them go. The most important thing is to keep practising, no matter what your experience is. And try not to beat yourself up when you don't manage to do the practices. Instead, just gently understand that, as a human being, you're not flawless. Pick yourself up and when you're ready, try again.

The aim of the body scan or any other meditation isn't relaxation, so don't worry if you don't feel super relaxed. The aim is simply to be aware of whatever your experience is, as far as you can. The experience may be unpleasant, and you may feel more tense by the end of the session, but that's still as good a meditation as any other; your mind may just be doing an emotional 'detox' – who knows? Just be patient and try not to judge the experience.

This is the practice for Week Two:

- ✔ Continue to practise the body scan daily using the MP3. You may now know the best time for you to practise meditation, and be able to stick with it. Make a short record in your journal, even just a sentence, of how the experience of the body scan is for you, on a daily basis.

- ✔ Choose another daily routine activity to do with mindfulness, in addition to the one you selected in Week One. Try pausing for a breath or two before starting the activity, and then connect with your senses, noticing the thoughts and emotions playing in your mind.

- ✔ Practise being mindful of your breath for ten minutes a day, by simply sitting comfortably straight and feeling the sensation of your breath. If your mind naturally wanders off, congratulate yourself for noticing and guide your attention kindly back to the breath sensation. Avoid paying attention to self-criticism; if criticism does arise in your awareness, note the negative thought as just another thought and turn your attention back to the breath. See Chapter 6 for how to practise mindfulness of breath in more detail.

- ✔ Start a pleasant events diary and use it to write down your thoughts, feelings and bodily sensations when you experience something pleasant, in as much detail as you can. In this way, you become more aware of how you automatically react to pleasant experiences. See Chapter 13 for details on how to do this.

Week Three: Being mindful in movement

One of the beauties of mindfulness is that you don't have to be sitting still to be mindfully aware. This week is an opportunity to explore mindfulness in movement. This is also an opportunity to reflect on the power of focusing on the breath. The breath can act like an anchor: a place always available, right under your nose, to draw you into the present moment. Being aware of your breath while focusing on something challenging can enable you to see the difficulty from a different angle, softening the tension a little.

Try this practice for Week Three:

✔ On days one, three and five, practise about 30 minutes of mindful walking or stretching. Many people enjoy developing mindfulness through yoga or tai chi and find the approach very powerful. (You can refer to *Yoga For Dummies* by Georg Feuerstein and Larry Payne (Wiley) or *Tai Chi For Dummies* by Therese Iknoian (Wiley) for ways to do this.)

✔ On days two, four and six, practise the body scan using the MP3.

✔ Begin practising the mini meditation called the three-minute breathing space three times a day (explained in Chapter 7). You may be more likely to remember to do the breathing space if you decide at the beginning of the week exactly when you want to practise.

✔ Complete an unpleasant events diary in your journal (see Chapter 13 for details) on a daily basis. This means writing down one thing each day that was unpleasant for you, and the sensations in your body, the thoughts going through your mind at the time, and how you felt emotionally.

Week Four: Staying present

This week, focus on the present moment. Reflect on the quality of this moment now. How does it compare with thinking about the past or the future? What effect does focusing on the here and now have on your thoughts and emotions?

You react to experience in one of three ways:

✔ Attachment to pleasant experiences

✔ Aversion to unpleasant experiences

✔ Indifference to everyday experiences

Holding onto pleasant experiences leads to fear of what happens when you lose them. Aversion to unpleasant experiences leads to stress each time you have a bad time. Going into automatic pilot when facing a neutral event means you miss out on the mystery and wonder of being alive.

This week, focus on your aversion to unpleasant experiences. You, like everyone on the planet, have to face difficulties from time to time. The question is *how* you meet the challenge: do you run away from, suppress, or fight the feelings? Is there another way? However you meet difficulties, by becoming more mindful of the process, your reactions begin very slowly to untangle themselves. You begin to consider the possibility of responding in a way that reduces rather than compounds your stress.

Here's your practice for Week Four:

✔ On days one, three and five, practise 15 minutes of mindful movement – stretching or walking – followed by 15 minutes of mindful breathing.

✔ On days two, four and six, practise the 30-minute guided sitting meditation explained in Chapter 6, using the MP3 provided.

✔ Practise the three-minute breathing space meditation three times a day at times predetermined by you.

✔ Additionally, practise the three-minute breathing space when something unpleasant happens. Write in your journal what effect the meditation has on your experiences.

✔ Become aware of times of stress. How do you react to the stress? Do you create a block, resist or suppress the stress, or shut down? Become aware of what's happening in your body. When you react in a certain way to the stress, what's going on for you? What effect does staying present with a difficulty have on your response? Allow yourself to be deeply curious about your relationship to stress.

Week Five: Embracing acceptance

This week, try allowing things to be as they are, rather than immediately wanting to change them. For example, if someone irritates you, rather than reacting immediately, just stay with the feeling of irritation. Feel it in your body and notice your automatic thoughts. If you feel a headache coming on, observe what happens if you let the pain be just as it is, and watch it rise and fall. What effect does allowing, accepting and acknowledging have on unpleasant and pleasant sensations?

If you want to become more relaxed, the first step is to allow things to be as they are, however they are. If you feel frustrated, the feeling is already there, so rather than getting frustrated about that too, try to begin accepting the frustration. Notice the thoughts, feelings and bodily sensations that go along with the frustration. You can try saying to yourself, 'It's okay; whatever it is, it's okay. It's already here. Let me feel it.'

Acceptance isn't resignation: you're facing up to the difficulty rather than running away. Mindfulness involves accepting awareness and using it as a way to change, not resigning yourself to a situation in which change will never happen.

Try this practice for Week Five:

✔ Practise the guided sitting meditation using the MP3, noticing how you react to thoughts, emotions and bodily sensations. Record any observations in your journal.

✔ Do the three-minute breathing space meditation three times a day. Try to connect it with everyday activities at times such as meal times, after waking up and just before going to sleep.

✔ Practise the three-minute breathing space when you're going through a difficulty. Use the practice to explore your thoughts and feelings rather than trying to get rid of them, if you can.

✔ Explore the difference in responding in a controlled way to more challenging situations, whether they occur during meditation or not, rather than reacting uncontrollably to your experience. Become more aware of your reactions and the thoughts and emotions that drive them.

Week Six: Realising that thoughts are just thoughts

Usually, when you think of something, like 'He hates me' or 'I can't do this,' you accept it as a fact, a reality. You may believe that almost any thought that pops into your awareness is an absolute truth. If your mind habitually pops up negative or unhelpful thoughts, seeing the thoughts and images as facts has stressful consequences. However, you can free yourself of this burden. Switch things around and try seeing thoughts as automatic, conditioned reactions rather than as facts. Question the validity of thoughts and images. Step back from the thoughts, if you can and don't take them to be you, or reality. Just watch them come and go and observe the effect of this.

Thoughts are just thoughts, not facts. Thoughts are mental events. You're not your thoughts.

When you're feeling challenged, read Chapter 13 and see whether you can identify what types of thoughts are taking place.

Practice for Week Six:

✔ Now you can begin to mix and match as you wish. Combine the sitting meditation, the body scan and mindful movement for 30–45 minutes a day. You can split the time into two or three parts, and spread them out through the day. Some days you may choose not to use the MP3.

✔ Practise the three-minute breathing space three times a day, and additionally practise when a difficulty or challenge arises for you. Notice any recurring patterns, notice the effect of mindful breathing on your body, and let the mindfulness spread into whatever you're facing next.

✔ If you can make time, practise a day of silent mindfulness meditation. See the section 'Setting aside a day for mindfulness' later in this chapter for how you can plan and do this mindfulness day.

Week Seven: Taking care of yourself

The activities you choose to do, from moment to moment and from day to day, strongly influence how you feel. By becoming aware of the activities that uplift you and the activities that deplete you, you may be able to adjust the choices you make to best take care of yourself.

Here's your practice for Week Seven:

- ✔ Choose any formal mindfulness meditations you like – such as the body scan, sitting meditation, or a combination of the meditations – and practise them daily, with or without the MP3.

- ✔ Continue to practise the three-minute breathing space three times a day and when a difficulty arises. Try making a wise choice after or during a difficulty.

- ✔ Design a stress warning system in your journal by writing down all the warning signs you have when under excessive stress, like feeling hot or behaving impatiently, and then write down an action plan you can follow to reduce the stress, such as a mini meditation, going for a walk, or talking to a friend. Refer to your action plan when you next feel overly stressed and notice what effect it has.

Week Eight: Reflection and change

Sometimes, when faced with a problem, no matter how hard you try, no matter how much effort you put into solving the problem, you're still stuck with the difficulty. Nothing seems to work. If you keep trying, you may become more and more tired, and perhaps move farther from a solution rather than nearer. In such circumstances, stop trying to solve the issue, and accept the circumstance for now. In this act of kindness to yourself, a solution may or may not arise. However, you're likely to feel less angry, frustrated, stressed, or depressed. The feeling of helplessness arises when you keep trying and no benefit seems to manifest itself. Acceptance is a change in itself.

You may already know the serenity prayer, which seeks:

The serenity to accept the things I cannot change;

The courage to change the things I can; and

The wisdom to know the difference.

In this last week of the course, reflect on how the experience has been for you. What have you found most helpful? What aspects would you like to integrate into your daily practice? Write your thoughts in your journal.

And finally, your practice for Week Eight:

✔ Decide which formal mindfulness practice you want to do for the next week, and carry out your decision as best you can.

✔ At the end of Week Eight, reflect on how the eight weeks of the course went for you, recording your thoughts in your journal. Consider some of these questions to help with your journal entries. How did your level of stress change over the course of the eight weeks? How did you meet difficulties in your life while engaging in this course? How can you adapt the mindfulness practices to integrate them into your life?

✔ Congratulate yourself for reaching this point, no matter how much or how little mindfulness you actually managed to do. The practice of mindfulness on a daily basis isn't an easy one to do: any mindfulness you managed is better than none at all.

Sticking to your decisions

Research has found that the longer you practice mindfulness for each day, the greater the benefit. Experiments have also shown that even short bouts of mindfulness – even a few minutes or a few mindful breaths – have positive effects on your wellbeing.

How long you decide to practise mindfulness for each day depends on your motivation for meditating in the first place. Deciding how long to meditate for depends on:

✔ Your intentions

✔ Your past experience with meditation or prayer

✔ How committed you are to reaping the long-term benefits of meditation

✔ Your level of discipline

The important thing is: *once you've decided how long you're going to meditate, stick to your decision.* This is *very* important for training your mind. If you practise for as long as you feel like and then get up, you're acting on a feeling. You stop being mindful if your mind says so. However, if you've decided to meditate for ten minutes and after five minutes feel like getting up, you still stay put. This makes you experience feelings of restlessness or boredom, frustration or agitation. What's the benefit of this? Well, you're taking a stand. *You* are saying to *your mind,* 'Thank you for your idea, but I'm in charge here. I've decided to sit still for ten minutes and feel the sensations of my breathing to help me to focus and stay calm.' The mind eventually calms down. You're no longer a slave to what your mind throws at you. This is the *freedom* of mindfulness: you're free to choose what you do and how you act, rather than your mind choosing.

Choosing What to Practise for Quick Stress Reduction

How do you decide what you're going to eat for dinner tonight? Your decision probably depends on how hungry you or your family are, who's cooking, the food in the fridge, the day of the week, the meal you ate yesterday, and so on. Many factors come into account. How do you decide which mindfulness meditation to practise today when establishing your own mindfulness routine? I give you some options in this section.

Many people come to mindfulness for stress reduction. Stress has an impact on everyone. If you're alive, you're going to experience stress. The question is, how do you handle the stress?

Trying to get rid of your stress by brute force can just increase it. Imagine you're trying to pull open a door that has a sign saying push. No matter how hard you pull, the door won't open! If you pull hard enough, the door handle may fall off, which won't help. Stress can come from doing, doing, and more doing. You can't use the same frantic approach for stress reduction. Stress reduction requires you to stop constantly doing – or to start non-doing. This is what mindfulness offers.

Try practising the following tips daily over a period of a few weeks, and see what happens:

✔ For quick stress reduction, try the three-minute breathing space meditation (covered in Chapter 7 and on the MP3). This mindfulness exercise cleverly includes a little bit of all the different types of mindfulness meditation in one neat, bite-size package. How cool is that? You don't have to use the MP3 once you've got the hang of it, and you don't even have to close your eyes. If you're at work, you can softly gaze at the bottom of the computer screen, or pop to the lavatory and practise there – why not?! It's quiet (hopefully!), you can lock the door, lower the lid and sit down. Your boss might even wonder why you look so serene every time you step out of the toilet!

✔ Try ten minutes of mindful breathing, using the MP3 track or practising on your own. Ideally, do this meditation in the morning to set yourself up for the day, but if you don't like that, do it any time of the day that suits you, or whenever you feel stressed.

✔ Walking meditation is a wonderful practice to integrate into your day. You're then combining some gentle exercise with mindfulness – a powerful combination for stress reduction. Head to Chapter 6 for the walking meditation.

✔ Spend ten minutes or more stretching your body in a mindful way. Use any stretching movements you prefer. The stimulation of the body as you stretch draws your attention out of your mind and into the physical sensations. If you have time during the day, you can also engage in the odd gentle stretch now and then. Remember, the most important thing is to be aware of the feelings in the body and mind as you stretch, in a kind and gentle way. Keep breathing mindfully as you move – let go of any tendency to hold your breath if you can.

✔ Spend some time seeing a stressful situation from the other person's perspective or just a different perspective, to help you relieve stress.

✔ Before you go to sleep, think of three things you're grateful for. Doing so relieves stress and has a beneficial long-term effect. See Chapter 4 for more on gratitude.

Also, write down all the events in your day that caused you stress. What was going through your mind? What fixed ideas did you have? Do you notice any patterns? Watch out for these patterns the next time you're in a stressful situation, and notice what effect being aware of the repeating pattern has.

Using mindfulness for self-discovery

Many people use mindfulness as a way to *self-discovery*. This is about deepening your own understanding of who you are and your relationship with yourself, others and the wider environment. In meditation, your conceptual mind with its thoughts and ideas stops being the only reference point for you.

You discover the concept of being separate from everything else as you grow up. Babies don't identify with their own bodies. The baby looks in wonder at its own foot just as it may look at a bunch of keys. There's no sense of me and not me. Humans have a deep-seated need to feel part of a bigger whole, whether socially or spiritually. Albert Einstein is attributed with the following striking observation:

> *A human being is a part of the whole, called by us 'Universe', a part limited in time and space. He experiences himself, his thoughts and feelings as something separated from the rest – a kind of optical delusion of his consciousness. This delusion is a kind of prison for us, restricting us to our personal desires and to affection for a few persons nearest to us. Our task must be to free ourselves from this prison by widening our circle of compassion to embrace all living creatures and the whole of nature in its beauty.*

This is the 'task' of mindfulness. You're seeing this 'optical delusion' as Einstein puts it, as the self-limiting thoughts and beliefs about who you are and your place in the world. Through mindfulness comes insight, and you begin to see this prison of separation and, in doing so, are released, even if only momentarily. But each moment of freedom is nourishing and uplifting, and energises and motivates you to keep walking on the journey towards healing, wholeness, health and self-discovery. Remember, you don't need to travel far for this: the present moment is right here, right now.

Going Even Deeper

So, you've established a mindfulness routine. You feel you're ready for the next step. You can progress in your practice by meditating for more extended periods of time. This section offers ways for you to step beyond your routine and find further support in your journey.

Discovering the value of silence

We live in a busy, noisy world. Just today I've spoken to friends and family members. I've exchanged messages with others. I've watched some YouTube videos and even created one!

Among all this noise and busyness, there's little silence. And when you do find yourself in a quiet place, like on a beach or in a forest or meadow, you may be tempted to call a friend or capture the experience with photos. Constantly communicating can become an impulsive habit rather than a choice.

I'd like to invite you to explore something different if you haven't already: being silent. Explore the value of being silent rather than talking or communicating with others for a period of time. This includes not watching television or surfing the net, or even reading. Just get away from the world of language. This can be for a few hours, a full day, or perhaps longer if you attend a retreat.

Most people think being silent is impossible for them. But why not give it a try? You've got nothing to lose and may discover a whole new way of being that you can revisit from time to time.

It's a bit like believing the earth is flat. If you hold that belief, you won't explore. But if you've got the guts to go to the edge to see what happens, you discover a whole new landscape. In the same way, if you believe that being silent won't teach you anything new, you won't try. But if you're willing to give it a go, who knows what beautiful new inner landscapes you may be able to explore?

The benefits of refraining from speaking for some time include:

✔ A chance for the chatty mind to calm down, so that you can see clearly and observe with greater depth and clarity

✔ An opportunity to reflect upon your life and consider what's going well and which direction you want to take in the future

✔ Time to process and let go of any pent-up emotions that you may have knowingly or unknowingly supressed

✔ Greater levels of creativity

✔ A extended period of time to de-stress, heal and find some inner peace

You don't need to force yourself to be silent. Have a go when you feel ready to do so.

Setting aside a day for mindfulness

In this day and age, people work very hard. You're working hard for your employers or your own business, or perhaps you're at home, looking after your parents or children. Even looking after yourself requires time, energy and effort. Mindfulness meditation offers some respite, a chance to stop doing, to stop fulfilling your endless needs and desires to help others or yourself, and to simply *be*. Have you ever treated yourself to a whole day of non-doing? This doesn't mean watching television all day, or just sleeping all day; even when you sleep, your mind can be in overdrive, going from one dream to another. By non-doing, I mean using the time to let go of excessively thinking about the past or worrying about the future – to softly reside in the here and now.

A day of mindfulness is a beautiful gift you can give yourself. The idea is to spend a whole day in mindful awareness, ideally being silent. Here are some instructions on practising this exercise:

1. **The evening before, place a reminder next to your bed and around the house that you're going to spend the day mindfully.** Be clear in your mind that you're going to keep the phone, computer, television and other electronics switched off. Drift off into sleep by feeling your breathing as you lie in bed.

2. **When you wake up on your day of mindfulness, begin the day with some mindful breathing as you lie in bed.** Feel each in-breath and each out-breath mindfully. If you like, smile gently. Spend some time reflecting on what you're grateful for: your home, your relationships, your income, your family, your body, your senses, or whatever you feel you have that perhaps others don't.

3. **Slowly and mindfully step out of bed.** If you have a pleasant view from your window, spend some time looking outside. Enjoy looking at the trees, or grass, or the people walking purposefully to fulfil their needs. Look, if you can, without encouraging judgements and reactions. Your mind is bound to wander off into other thoughts and worries – just gently bring your attention back as soon as you realise.

4. **Practise some formal mindfulness meditation.** You can do the body scan meditation, for example.

5. **Have a bath or shower.** Do this at a leisurely pace. Take your time, even if you feel like rushing for no apparent reason. Feel the sensations of the water on your body – in many places throughout the world people have to walk for hours to collect water, so be grateful for the easy access you have to water.

6. **Take your time making your breakfast.** Connect with your senses and keep bringing your attention into the here and now. Pause for a few moments before you start eating your breakfast. Ensure that you've tasted and fully chewed each mouthful before you start the next one. This is mindful eating.

7. **You may choose to spend the mid-morning going for some walking meditation or doing some mindful yoga or perhaps a little gardening.** Whatever you choose to do, do it with a gentle, kindly awareness. Avoid spending more than a few minutes reading a book or a magazine. The idea is to connect with your senses rather than encourage the mind to think too much.

8. **Spend some time preparing and eating lunch.** Again, allow the process to unfold in a leisurely way. You don't need to rush. If feelings of boredom, restlessness, or frustration arise, see whether you can offer them the space to come to pass – to surface and diminish again. Eat your meal with gratitude and attention; chew each morsel unhurriedly.

9. **Engage in gentle physical activity after lunch, or perhaps have a siesta.** Why not? Connect your senses with another hobby of your choice. Every now and then, practise the breathing space meditation for a few minutes to help bring you into the present moment. You may even choose to do another extended meditative practice, such as a sitting meditation or some mindful yoga or tai chi. Don't be surprised if you begin to find the whole process challenging or emotional. You may not be used to giving yourself so much room to simply be present, and this can allow unprocessed thoughts and emotions to release themselves into your consciousness. Be as kind and patient with yourself as you're able to be.

10. **Continue to allow the day to unfold in this way, eating, resting, walking and practising meditation.** If you can't help cleaning out a cupboard or organising your paperwork, really take your time with the actions, doing things one step at a time.

11. **Having prepared and eaten your evening meal, which is ideally the lightest of the meals you've had during the day, you can rest and relax before going to bed.** Lie in bed and ride on the waves of your own breathing, allowing yourself to doze naturally into a slumber.

Joining a group

Meditation is often spent sitting down with your eyes closed, in silence. Not much banter goes on; nobody's cracking open the beers. So, why on earth would you need to bother joining a mindfulness meditation group? Here are some reasons:

- **By attending a regular group, you commit to practising frequently.** Without such a commitment, you may lose momentum and end up not meditating, even though you really want to and find it valuable.

- **Your meditation is deeper when practising in a group.** Many of my clients say this when they attend a class. You're less likely to fidget unnecessarily when sitting with others; if the body remains relatively still, the mind also calms down. You're also more likely to make a little more effort in your sitting posture, sitting straighter and with dignity. People who are spiritually inclined believe that by meditating together, you create a certain positive energy in the room that generates a favourable atmosphere, intensifying the quality of the meditation.

- **You often end up making friends with people who enjoy meditation.** This can create a 'positive feedback' system within your social circle, because the more time you spend with other fellow meditators, the more you think about mindfulness and remember to practise and the more you're likely to hear about the latest and greatest book, teacher, or retreat. You begin to support each other in other areas of life too, which is always nice.

How do you go about choosing a group? You may be able to find a mindfulness meditation group in your area by searching on the Internet. You don't have to join a mindfulness group, however. You can join any type of meditation group and, through trial and error, find one you feel comfortable with. Most Buddhist organisations practise some form of mindfulness meditation. And increasingly, yoga centers offer mindfulness groups or classes.

If you can't find a group for you, consider setting up one yourself. I know one couple who started a weekly group that grew naturally by itself, just by word of mouth, until they had about 15 regular members. In each session, you just need a period of silence for meditation – perhaps 30 minutes or so – and then a period to explore and share how the practice and week have gone. You may want to read a paragraph of text from a book on mindfulness. After that, I suggest some time simply to socialise over a cup of tea and a few delicious biscuits. In the summer, I organise mindful walks and picnics in parks or by the river – perhaps these are the kind of events you too can set up.

Finding an appropriate retreat

When you've been practising mindfulness for at least a few months, you may be ready to attend a meditation retreat. This is a magnificent opportunity for you to develop your meditation practice and discover more about yourself. Retreats can be any length from one day to several years! I strongly recommend you begin with the one-day retreat, then gradually extend to a weekend, then a week, and if you're very serious in your practice, you can go for even longer.

Retreats cost between £20 and £200 for a day, or £150 and £2,000 for a week, which includes all food and accommodation. Buddhist retreats usually invite an additional donation for the teachers and organisers, who sometimes work voluntarily.

Some of the questions to ask before booking yourself on a meditation retreat include:

- ✔ **Is the retreat in silence?** Silence offers a powerful way of intensifying your meditative discipline, as explained earlier. If you feel that going on a silent retreat is a little too much, especially to begin with, you can try and find a mindfulness holiday, combining meditation with free time to relax and socialise too. Then try a silent retreat at a future date, when you feel ready.

- ✔ **Is the teacher experienced?** In most retreats, the person leading is normally quite experienced, but this is worth checking, especially if you're attending for an extended period.

- ✔ **What's a typical schedule for the day?** Find out the time at which you're expected to wake up, so you know what you're letting yourself in for. And check how much time is spent in the day meditating too. Waking up at 4 a.m. and meditating in two-hour stretches throughout the day may be too much for you, and may put you off meditation altogether. You can find many retreats with far gentler schedules if you look around.

- ✔ **Is it a cult?** If the organisation says things like 'Our way is the best/only way' or 'If you stop following us, you'll derail/die/suffer/never be happy,' then say thank you and walk away. Many wise organisations run meditation retreats but, as with everything, a few suspect ones do too. If the organisation says 'You're free to walk away at any time' or 'Our way is one way of practising meditation, but there are many other ways that you're welcome to investigate if you wish' or 'Ultimately, only you can discover what is the best way for you to meditate, through your own observation and experience,' you're probably with a good organisation. Good luck with the search.

The best way to find a retreat is to get a recommendation. If you don't know who to ask, try searching online. Some are Buddhist, or some other religion, and others are purely secular. Most retreats welcome people of all faiths, or no faith. Even if the retreats aren't in your area, they may lead you to find a suitable retreat within easy reach. Some are silent retreats. Others combine mindfulness with a holiday, so you can do some mindfulness together with a group and have some time to relax and unwind in your own way too, exploring your surroundings – these can be great fun. I taught such a retreat just last month in Morocco, near the Atlas mountains – a real joy. My next project is to offer a mindfulness coaching and art retreat together with an artist in Berlin.

Chapter 10

Dealing with Setbacks and Transcending Distractions

In This Chapter

▶ Dealing with setbacks in mindfulness practice

▶ Overcoming common problems

▶ Transcending distractions

*W*hen you first learnt to walk you must have fallen over hundreds, if not thousands, of times before you could balance on two legs. But you didn't give up. You probably giggled, got up, and tried again. Learning meditation, a powerful way of deepening mindfulness, is a similar process. When you first try to meditate, you're going to fall over (well, not literally I hope, unless you're trying the lesser-known hopping-on-one-leg meditation). But setbacks are part of the process of meditation. The question is how you deal with them. If you see setbacks as learning opportunities rather than failures, you're bound to succeed. Each time a problem occurs, you simply need to get up and try again, with a smile if possible. In the end you may realise that meditation isn't about achieving a certain state of mind, but about meeting each experience in a warm, accepting way. This chapter shows you how.

Everyone accesses mindfulness in their own sweet way. For you, the mindfulness meditations in this book may just not feel right. In such a case, you can cultivate mindfulness through gardening, cooking, running, cleaning or some other way. If meditating really doesn't appeal, consider which daily activity you could do, or already do, in a mindful way, by fully focusing your attention in that moment. Walking your dog in a local park, for example, can be your daily meditation if done consciously and with an open mind. Discover your unique daily mindful moment.

Getting the Most out of Meditation

Mindfulness meditation means setting aside time to intentionally pay attention to a certain aspect of your experience with a kindly acceptance from moment to moment, as best you can. So, for example, you can pay attention to your breathing as it enters and leaves your body, accepting the rate of the breathing just as it is. Mindfulness meditation can also go on to consciously be aware and open to all your experiences from moment-to-moment – you breath, body, sounds, the thought about your shopping list, the feeling of boredom and so on.

Ultimately, *you have nothing to get out of meditation*. I know that sounds pretty crazy, but it's an important point. Meditation isn't a way of *getting* something, because you already have everything you need to be whole and complete. Rather, meditation is about letting go. All the benefits of meditation (which I cover in Chapter 2) are best seen as side effects. Meditation is about being with whatever your experience is, whether pleasant or unpleasant, and seeing what unfolds. Meditating is a bit like doing your favourite hobby. If you like painting, you paint. If you paint for the love of painting rather than looking for an outcome, you paint in an effortless and joyful way. Meditation is like painting: if you spend your time looking for the benefits, you kind of spoil the fun.

Making time

If you're interested in developing the art of meditation, try engaging in some form of meditation every day, called *formal practice*. Whether you choose to meditate for five minutes or one hour is up to you, but making a daily connection with meditation has a profound effect.

Too busy to meditate daily? I know the feeling. Life is full of so many things to do that finding time to practise meditation can be hard. But you find time to brush your teeth, get dressed, and sleep. You find the time for chores, because you have to. You don't feel right if you fail to do these things. Meditation is like that too. Once you get into the rhythm of daily meditation, you don't feel right if you haven't had your daily fix of it. That's when you find the time to meditate.

The great thing about mindfulness is that you can practise it at any time. Right now, you can become aware of the fact that you're reading. You can feel the position of your body as you're reading this sentence. That's mindfulness. When you put this book down and walk somewhere, you can feel the sensations of your feet on the floor, or the tension in your shoulder, or the smile on your face. When you're aware of what you're doing, that's mindfulness.

Practising mindfulness actually saves time. Research has found that meditators work more efficiently than others. Or, you may say that meditation makes time.

Sharpening your tools

Once upon a time there was a woodcutter. He had lots of trees to cut down and was working frantically, puffing and sweating away to complete his work on time. A wise person happened to be passing through (they always do in these stories) and asked, 'Why are you working so hard trying to cut that tree down? Wouldn't it be easier and faster if you took the time to sharpen your axe?' The woodcutter looked up at the wise person and said, 'Can't you see how many trees I need to cut down today? I don't have time to sharpen the axe!'

Our own lives can be a bit like that. If you find the time to meditate, to sharpen the axe of your mind, you can save much time and energy in your life. Yet a common reaction to meditation is, 'I'm too busy!' If you ever have that thought, think about the woodcutter and the time he'd have saved by sharpening his tools.

Rising above boredom and restlessness

Boredom and restlessness are like opposite poles of an energy scale. Boredom is associated with a lack of enthusiasm and connection, whereas restlessness implies energy that's pumping through the body, itching to burst out. Mindfulness is designed to observe both of these states and find a balance between the two.

Boredom

Meditation can sound like the ultimate boring activity. Sit there and do nothing. What could be more boring? Even watching paint dry may sound like a more exciting prospect. Society seems geared up to help you avoid boredom. Television adverts are short and snappy to grab your attention, and mobile phones help to distract you at any moment that a hint of boredom arises. These continual forms of distraction make you bored more quickly and more easily. Meditation is a courageous step against the tide.

If you feel bored during meditation, you're not really being mindful. Boredom generally implies a lack of connection, or that you're thinking about the past or future instead of the present. If you're finding attending to your breathing boring, imagine if your head was plunged into water: you'd suddenly become very interested in breathing! Each breath is unique and different. Noticing feelings of boredom and moving your focus back to your breathing is all part of the process of mindfulness, and quite natural.

Excessive feelings of boredom may indicate that you're forcing yourself into the mindfulness practice. Try easing off your effort and bringing self-kindness to your practice. Feel your breath with a sense of friendliness and warmth. Watch your bodily sensations in the way you watch a puppy or cute little baby. And try practising the loving kindness meditation (kindly head to Chapter 6 for more on this).

The following techniques can help you work with the feelings of boredom during meditation:

- ✔ **Acknowledge the feeling of boredom.** Boredom is the feeling that has arisen, so accept it in this moment.

- ✔ **Notice the thoughts running through your mind.** Perhaps, 'Ohhhh, I can't be bothered!' or 'What's the point of doing this?'.

- ✔ **Get interested in boredom.** Allow yourself to become curious. Where did the boredom come from? Where's it going? Can you feel boredom in certain parts of your body? Notice the desire to sleep or do something else other than continuing to practise.

- ✔ **Connect your attention to the sensations of breathing and see what happens to boredom.**

- ✔ **Take a step back from the emotion of boredom.** If you're aware of the boredom, you're not the boredom itself. Observe the boredom from this stance of a decentred, detached awareness, as if the boredom is separate from you.

Observing boredom can be very interesting. When boredom arises, you see the thoughts and feelings that run through you every time you get bored. These feelings can rule your life without you noticing. As you become aware of them, the feelings begin to loosen and let go. Your mental programmes are shadows, and through the light of mindfulness the programmes lose their apparent reality and disappear, without you doing anything much.

Restlessness

Restlessness is similar to boredom, but is associated with excessive levels of energy, and is a common mental state. You run around all day doing a million and one things and then when you sit down to meditate, your mind's still racing.

Try these two ways of coping with restlessness:

- ✔ **Begin your meditation practice with some mindful movements.** You may choose to do some mindful walking or perhaps mindful yoga (both talked about in Chapter 6). This helps to slowly calm your mind so that you're able to practise some sitting or lying down meditations.

- ✔ **Observe your restlessness without reacting to it.** Feel the restlessness in your body. What's your mind telling you to do? Continue to sit, despite what the mind says. This is a powerful meditation, a routine that gently trains the mind to do what you tell it to do rather than the other way around. You're beginning to take control, rather than your mind being in control. Just because your mind is restless you don't have to run around like a headless chicken doing what it tells you to. The mind can say things like, 'Oh, I can't stand this. I need to get up and do something.' You can watch this show going on in the mind, breathe into it, and guide your attention back to the inhalation and exhalation. You can even answer back in your head, saying words like, 'Thank you mind for your activity. But let's continue to practise mindfulness for a little bit longer. Then we can move around after that.'

Staying awake during mindful meditation

Due to the stresses of life or constant busyness and digital stimulation, you may not be getting enough sleep. Or your sleep may not be of a high quality. In either case, you may find yourself falling asleep rather than 'falling awake' in your mindfulness practice. That's okay. You probably need sleep more than mindfulness anyway. So allow yourself the time to sleep restfully. No need to fight with yourself. Then, once you've caught up on your sleep, mindfulness can start to help you feel more awake in a refreshed and rejuvenated way.

Ultimately, sleep and mindfulness are opposites, as shown in Figure 10-1. When you fall asleep you're at a low level of consciousness – lower than during normal everyday life. Mindfulness is designed to heighten your state of awareness, so that it's greater than it is during your normal daily existence.

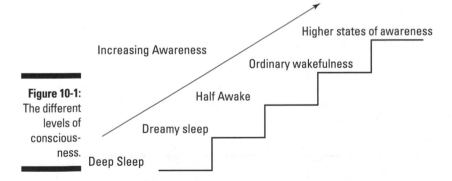

Figure 10-1: The different levels of consciousness.

Sometimes your mind makes you feel sleepy in order to avoid the mindfulness practice. Sleepiness during mindfulness meditation is very common and you're certainly not alone if you experience it. Don't beat yourself up about it. Sometimes, becoming sleepy is a clever trick your mind plays to prevent you from facing up to difficult thoughts or emotions (see the later section 'Getting over difficult emotions'). If you start to feel sleepy, begin to recognise the feeling.

Try these suggestions to cope with or avoid sleepiness:

- **Ensure that you get enough sleep.** If you don't get enough sleep, you're likely to fall asleep in your next meditation.

- **Take a few deep, slow breaths.** Repeat a few times until you feel more awake.

- **Don't eat a big meal before meditating.** If you feel hungry before a meditation, eat a small snack beforehand rather than a three-course meal.

- **Stand up and do some mindful stretching, yoga, tai chi or walking.** Then go back to your sitting or lying-down meditation.

- **Experiment with meditating at different times of day.** Some people feel wide awake in the mornings, others in the afternoon or evening. Find the right time for you.

- **Open your eyes and let some light in.** In some meditation traditions, all meditations are done with eyes half or fully open for the duration of the practice. Experiment to see what works for you. When doing this, continue to focus on your breath, body, sounds, sights, thoughts, or emotions – whatever you've decided to make the focus of your mindful awareness.

- **Become mindful of the state of mind called sleepiness.** This is difficult, but worth a try. Before you feel too sleepy, notice and get curious about how your body, mind, and emotions feel. This can sometimes dissipate the sleepiness and enable you to cope with it next time it happens.

Ironically, one of the first benefits of meditation that many of my students report is better sleep. Through practising mindfulness meditation, people seem to be able to allow difficult thoughts to be released from the brain, enabling the state of sleep to arise more naturally when necessary.

If you do find yourself falling asleep despite your best efforts, don't worry about it too much. I find many of my students overly criticising themselves for falling asleep. If you fall asleep, you fall asleep: you probably needed it. Enjoy the snooze; night-night!

There's a time and a place!

I had a meditation student who, when we meditated together, kept bowing his head and then jolting it up. At the end of the meditation, I asked him if he was feeling sleepy. He said, 'Not at all. When I learnt meditation, my teacher kept doing that, so I thought that was part of the meditation practice and copied him!' His teacher was, of course, falling asleep when teaching this student, and the student innocently imitated him.

Finding a focus

When you sit for meditation, how do you decide what to focus on?

Think of your breathing as your anchor. A ship drops its anchor whenever it needs to stop. By being mindful of a few breaths, you're dropping your anchor. These breaths bring your body and mind together. Breathing can be conscious or unconscious, and focusing on breathing seems to have a wonderful way of creating a state of relaxed awareness. Your breathing also changes with your thoughts and emotions, so by developing a greater awareness of it you can regulate erratic feelings on a daily basis. The simple sensations of your breath as it enters and leaves your body can be like drinking an ice-cool, refreshing drink on a hot, stuffy day. So, don't forget to breathe.

After you feel you've established your attention on breathing, you can go on to focus on bodily sensations, thoughts, feelings, or the different parts of the body, as I describe in Chapter 6.

Re-charging enthusiasm

When you've established yourself in a mindfulness meditation practice, getting into a routine is easy. The habit of practising mindfulness regularly is certainly helpful, but not if you do so in a mechanical way. If you get the feeling that you're doing the same thing every day and keep falling asleep, or you just sit there with no real purpose, then it's time to re-charge your enthusiasm.

Here are some ideas for firing up your enthusiasm:

- **Do a different meditation practice.** Look through this book or refer to the resources in Part III for ideas.

- **Join a meditation group or go on a retreat.** One or other is almost certain to shift something in you. See Chapter 9 for tips on this.

- **Try doing your practice in a different position.** If you normally sit, try lying down or walking. You can even dance, skip or do the can-can and be mindful at the same time.

- **Change the time when you practise meditation.** Usually morning is best, but if you're just too sleepy then, try after work or before lunch, for example.

- **Treat yourself to a day of mindfulness.** Spend the whole day – right from the moment you open your eyes in the morning to the time you go to bed at night – doing nothing in particular, apart from being mindful. Let the day unfold naturally, rather than controlling it too much. Give yourself permission to enjoy the day.

✔ **Get in touch with a mindfulness meditation teacher or try attending a course or workshop.** See whether there's a good teacher in your area, through a Google search. Some readers of this book have attended my live online mindfulness teacher training or coach training; by learning ways of helping others to meditate, they discovered more about their own mindfulness practice too. Get in touch with my team to find out more by emailing info@shamashalidina.com or visiting shamashalidina.com

Practice is important, whether you feel enthusiasm or not. Keep going, and see what benefits you gain from your practice in the long term.

Dealing with Common Distractions

Distractions – whether internal or external – are a part of mindfulness experience in the same way as these words are part of this book. They go hand in hand. If you find yourself frustrated, criticising the distraction, and getting annoyed, feel it, let it be part of the mindfulness practice, and gently guide your attention back to the breathing or the focus of your meditation.

Getting frustrated can be a mind pattern, and watching and noticing the frustration rather than reacting to it may gradually change the pattern. Being distracted during meditation is a very common experience, a part of the learning process. Expect some frustration, and then see how to cope with it rather than trying to run away from it.

Reduce external distractions to a minimum. A few precautions to take are:

✔ Switch off or unplug all your phones.

✔ Turn off all televisions, computers, and pretty much anything electronic.

✔ Ask anyone else in your home to give you some quiet time if possible.

The very effort you make to reduce distractions can have a beneficial effect on your practice. If you still get distracted, remember that everyday events always get in the way of the practice; listen to the sounds and let them become part of the practice rather than blocking them out.

You can manage internal distractions in the following ways:

✔ **Just do it.** If you need to deal with something particularly urgent or important, do it before you start meditating. Your mind can then be at rest during the meditation.

✔ **Take a step back from thoughts.** Watch the stream of thoughts that arise in your mind like clouds that pass across the sky. See the thoughts as separate from you, and note what effect that separation has.

- **Welcome your thoughts for a while.** This is a great approach. Just allow all the thoughts to enter your consciousness. Welcome them. You'll probably find that the more you welcome your distractions, the fewer distractions pop into your head. It's a fun experiment!

- **Be patient.** Remember that it's natural for the mind to think. Label each thought with a word such as 'thinking' or 'planning', and then gently invite the attention back to your breathing.

Handling unusual experiences

Meditation isn't about getting a certain experience, but about experiencing whatever is happening right now. Blissful experiences come and go. Painful experiences come and go. You just need to keep watching without holding onto either. The practice itself does the rest. Meditation is far, far simpler than people think.

Don't think about girls; don't think about girls

One of my favourite mindfulness teachers at the moment is a monk called Ajahn Brahm. Here's a story he often tells to teach the importance of not fighting the distractions in your mind.

When Ajahn Brahm was a young monk, he came across a beautiful, peaceful monastery in Thailand. It was so quiet there. The traffic noise came from one car a week, driving along the nearest road. And there were no sounds of planes flying overhead. It was perfect for meditation.

So Brahm settled into a routine of daily meditation in a nearby cave. The temperature and atmosphere in there couldn't be better. His meditation went well for a few weeks, but then he faced a problem. His mind started thinking about his past girlfriends. Were they still single? Maybe they'd like to meet up again? 'Stop thinking about that!' he ordered his mind. But that didn't work. No matter how hard he tried, his mind kept thinking about girls. And for a monk vowing for a life of chastity, these weren't very 'monkish' thoughts. He wanted to meditate, not think about other stuff. Brahm felt helpless.

Then one day, after asking a statue of Buddha for inspiration, Brahm had an idea: he'd do a deal with his mind! Every day at 3 p.m. he would let his mind think whatever thoughts it wanted to. The rest of the time, his mind had to focus on Brahm's breathing. So he tried that the next day. Unfortunately, that didn't work. All day, from 4 a.m. in the morning to the afternoon, Brahm battled with his mind and couldn't focus on his breathing at all. Finally came the afternoon. Brahm lay down and as he had promised and let his mind think whatever it wanted. He prepared for an hour of 'unmonkish' thoughts. But instead, something amazing happened. For that full hour, he was mindful of every single breath! Wow!

Ajahn Brahm discovered something very important that day about his mind. Never fight with your mind. Make friends with it. By consciously allowing your mind to wander if it wants to, you'll be rewarded with a calmer, gentler, and more mindful mind.

In meditation you may sometimes experience floating (just imaginary; I'm not talking about levitating yet!), flashing lights, flying pigs, or pretty much anything the mind can imagine. Whatever unusual feelings arise, remember that these are just experiences and come back to the focus of the meditation. In mindfulness you don't need to judge or analyse these experiences: simply let them go, as far as you can, and then come back to the senses. If you find yourself really struggling or feeling unwell, gently come out of the meditation and try again later; take things slowly, step by step.

Learning to relax

The word 'relax' originally comes from the Latin word meaning to loosen or open again. Relax is such a common word. 'Just relax,' people say. If only it were so simple. How do you relax during meditation? Essentially by learning to accept the tension you're currently experiencing, rather than fighting with it.

Consider this scenario. You feel tense. Your shoulders are hunched up, and you can't let go. What do you do? Try the following steps if tension arises during your meditation:

1. **Become aware of the tension.** Get a sense of its location in your body.

2. **Notice whether the tension has an associated colour, shape, size, or texture.** Allow yourself to be curious about it rather than trying to get rid of the tension.

3. **Feel right into the centre of the tension and breathe into it.** Feel the tense part of the body as you simultaneously feel your natural breathing. Just be with the tension as it is. Say words like 'softening' in your mind to see what effect that has.

4. **Notice whether you have any feeling or desire to get rid of the tension.** As best you can, let go of that too and see whether you can accept the sense of tension a little bit more than you do already.

5. **Send kindness to that part of your body.** You can do this by gently smiling towards the sensation, or by placing your warm hand on the tension and caring for that part of your body or wishing that part of your body well. Say to yourself words like, 'May you be well, may you soften, may your tension ease.' Showing a sense of affection for this part of your body is probably the best way to ease the tightness in the long run.

Fighting to let go of tension just leads to more stress and tension. That's because trying implies effort, and if the tension doesn't disappear you can end up more frustrated and angry. A warm, gentle acceptance of the feeling is far more effective.

Meditation can lead to very deep relaxation. However, relaxation is not the aim of meditation: meditation is ultimately an aimless activity.

Developing patience

Whenever I'm at a party and I'm asked what I do, I explain that I'm a trainer of mindfulness meditation. One of the comments I often get back is along the lines of, 'Oh, you must be patient. I don't have the patience for teaching anything, let alone meditation.' I don't think patience is something that you have or don't have: you can develop it. You can train your brain to become more patient. And it's a muscle worth building.

Meditation is patience training. To commit to connect with the breath or the senses requires patience. If you feel impatient in your meditation practice but continue to sit there, you're beginning to train the patience muscle. Observe the feeling of discomfort. See whether your impatience stays the same or changes. Just as your muscles hurt when you're training in the gym, sitting through impatience is painful, but gradually the feelings of impatience and discomfort diminish. Keep pumping that iron!

You may be impatient for results if you're a beginner to mindfulness. You've heard of all the benefits of meditation and so you want some. That's fair enough. However, because meditation requires patience, when you begin to practise regularly you'll see that the more impatient you are, the fewer 'results' you get.

Decide how long you're going to practise mindfulness meditation for, and stick to it. Take the meditation moment by moment and see what unfolds. You spend all your life trying to get somewhere and achieve something. Meditation is a special time for you to let go of all that and just be in the moment. As well as requiring patience, meditation develops it.

If you can't cope with being still and feeling your breath for ten minutes, try five minutes. If that's too much, try two minutes. If that's too much, try ten seconds. *Begin with however long you can manage*, and build it up, step by step. The most important thing is to keep at it, practise as regularly as you can, and gradually increase the time you practise for. Eventually, you'll become a super-patient person. Think of those huge bodybuilders who started off skinny but by taking small steps achieved Olympic weightlifting standards. Believe that you can develop patience, and take the next step.

Learning from Negative Experiences

Think back to the first time you met a dog. If your first encounter with a dog was pleasant, you're likely to think that dogs are wonderful. If, as a child, the first thing a dog did was bite you or bark excessively, you probably think dogs are aggressive. Your early experiences have a big impact on your attitudes and ways of coping later in life. By learning to see that a negative experience is just a momentary thing rather than something that lasts forever, you can begin to move forwards.

Meditation is similar. If you happen to get lucky and have a few positive experiences to start with, you'll stick with it. But if you don't, please don't give up. You've only just begun the journey, and you have a lot more to discover. Stay with it and work through any negative experiences you encounter.

Dealing with physical discomfort

In the beginning, sitting meditation will probably be uncomfortable. Learning to cope with that discomfort is an important hurdle to jump in your meditation adventure. When the muscles in your body get used to sitting meditation, the discomfort will probably diminish.

To reduce physical discomfort when meditating, you can try several things:

✔ Sitting on a cushion on the floor:

  • Experiment with using cushions of different sizes.

  • Slowly and mindfully stand up, stretch with awareness, and sit back down.

✔ Sitting on a chair:

  • Try raising the back two legs of the chair using books or wooden blocks, and see whether that helps.

  • You may be sitting at an angle. Gently lean forwards and backwards and to the left and right to find the middle point.

  • Ask a friend to look at your posture to check that you look straight.

  • Ensure that you're sitting with a sense of dignity and uprightness, but not straining too much.

You can always lie down for mindfulness practices. You don't have to sit up if it's too uncomfortable for you. There's no rules here. Do what feels right for you.

Getting over difficult emotions

Many of my clients come to mindfulness with difficult emotions. They suffer from depression, anxiety, or are stressed at work. They're trying to cope with anger, lack of confidence, or are burnt out. Often they feel as if they've been fighting their emotions all their lives and are now just too tired to keep fighting. Mindfulness is the final resort – the answer to coping with their difficulties. What mindfulness asks of people (to stop running away from themselves and to transcend difficulties as they arise in awareness, moment by moment) is both very simple and very challenging. As soon as you get a glimmer of the effect mindfulness has, your trust in the process grows and a new way of living emerges.

The next time you face difficult emotions, whether you're meditating or not, try the following exercise:

1. **Feel the emotion present in the here and now.**

2. **Label the emotion in your mind, and repeat it (perhaps 'fear, fear').**

3. **Notice the desire to get rid of the emotion, and as far as you can, gently be with it.**

4. **Be mindful of where you feel the emotion in your body (most emotions create a physical sensation in the body).**

5. **Observe the thoughts running through the mind.**

6. **Breathe into the emotion, allowing your breathing to help you observe what you're feeling with warmth and friendliness. Say in your mind, 'It's okay. Let me gently be with this feeling. It will pass.'**

7. **Become aware of the effect of this exercise on the emotion for a few moments.**

Try to get a sense of the gentleness of this exercise. Look at the emotion as you would a flower: examine the petals, smell its fragrance, and be tender with it. Think of the emotion as wanting to talk to you, and listen to it. This is the opposite of the normal way people meet emotion, by bottling it up and running away.

If this all sounds too overwhelming, take it step by step. Make the tiniest step you can manage towards the feeling. Don't worry about how small the step is: it's the intention to move towards the difficult emotion rather than run away that counts. A very small step makes a massive difference, because it begins to change the pattern. This is the positive snowball effect of mindfulness.

When you first move towards difficult emotions, they may grow bigger and feel more intense, because you're giving them your attention. This is absolutely normal. Try not to get frightened and run away from these emotions. Give yourself some time, and you'll find that your emotions flux and change and aren't as fixed as you've always believed.

Emotions behave in only three ways when you become mindful of them. The emotion will either grow, stay the same or diminish. That's it. And eventually, all emotions will pass – that's the way they work. Remembering this is a powerful meditation in itself.

Accepting your progress

Mindfulness meditation is a long-term process: the more time and appropriate effort you put in, the more you get out of it. Mindfulness isn't just a set of techniques that you do to see what you get immediately: it's a way of living. Be as patient as you can. Keep practising, little and often, and see what happens. Most of the time your mind may wander all over the place and you may feel you're not achieving anything. This isn't true: just sitting down and making a commitment to practise daily for a certain time has a tremendous effect; you just can't see its effect in the short term.

Think of meditation as planting a seed. You plant the seed in the most nourishing soil you can find, you water it daily, and you allow it to grow in a sunny spot. What happens if you poke around in the soil to see how it's doing? You disturb the progress of course. Germinating a seed takes time. But there's no other way. You just need to regularly water your seed and wait.

Be patient about your progress. You can't see a plant growing if you watch it, even though it's actually growing all the time. Every time you practise meditation you're growing more mindful, although it may seem very difficult to see from day to day. Trust in the process and enjoy watering your seed of mindfulness.

Going beyond unhelpful thoughts

'I can't do meditation' or 'It's not for me' are some comments I heard when I was last at a health and wellbeing conference. These attitudes are unhelpful, because they make you feel as if you can't meditate, no matter what. I believe everyone can learn meditation. 'I can't do meditation' actually means 'I don't like what happens when I look at my mind.'

Some common thoughts with useful antidotes to remember are:

- ✔ **'I can't stop my thoughts.'** Mindfulness meditation isn't about stopping your thoughts. It's about becoming aware of them from a detached perspective.

- ✔ **'I can't sit still.'** How long can you sit still for? A minute? Ten seconds? Take small steps and gradually build up your practice. Alternatively, try the moving meditations detailed in Chapter 6.

- ✔ **'I don't have the patience.'** Meditation is perfect for you! Patience is something you can build up, step by step, too. Start with short meditations and increase them to increase your patience.

- ✔ **'It's not for me.'** How do you know that if you haven't tried meditating? Even if you've tried it once or twice, is that enough? Commit to practising for several weeks or a few months before deciding whether mindfulness meditation is suitable for you.

> ✔ **'This isn't helping me.'** This is a common thought in meditation. If you think this, just make a mental note and gently guide your attention back to your breathing.
>
> ✔ **'This is a waste of time.'** How do you know that for sure? Thousands of scientific studies and millions of practitioners are unlikely to be wrong. Mindfulness meditation is beneficial if you stick to it.

Thoughts of failure have an effect only if you approach meditation with the wrong attitude. With the right attitude, there's no failure, only feedback. By feedback, I mean that if you think your meditation didn't work for some reason, you now know what doesn't work and can adjust your approach next time. Think of when you were a child learning to talk. Imagine how difficult that must have been! You'd never spoken in your life and yet you learnt how to talk at only a few years old. As a young child you didn't know what failure meant, so you kept trying. Most of the time what came out was 'ga-ga' and 'goo-goo', but that was okay. Step by step, before you knew it, you were speaking fluently.

There's no such thing as a good or bad meditation. You sit down to practise meditation – or you don't. It doesn't matter how many thoughts you have or how bad you feel in the meditation. What matters is trying to meditate and making a little effort to cultivate the right attitude.

Finding a Personal Path

The journey of mindfulness is a personal one, although it affects every person you meet, because you interact with them in a mindful way. Many people have walked the path before, but each journey is unique and special. In the end you learn from your own experience and do what feels right for you. If meditation doesn't feel appropriate, you probably won't do it. However, if some quiet, calm voice or feeling underneath all the chatter seems to resonate with the idea of mindfulness, you begin taking steps. You decide in each moment the next course of action that can best deal with setbacks and distractions. These choices shape your personal mindfulness journey.

Approaching difficulties with kindness

When you face a difficulty in life, how do you meet it? How you relate to your difficulty plays a big role in the outcome. Your difficulties offer you a chance to put mindfulness into practice and see these difficulties in a different way. How do you meet problems? You can turn towards them or away from them. Mindfulness is about turning towards them with a sense of kindness rather than avoidance.

Difficulties are like ugly, scary shadows. If you don't look at them properly, they continue to frighten you and make you think they're very real. However, if you look towards them, even though the difficulties scare you, you begin to understand what they are. The more light you shine on them, the more they seem to lose their power. The light is mindfulness or a kindly awareness.

People can be very unkind to themselves through self-criticism, often learnt at a young age. The learnt behavioural pattern of self-criticism can become like an automatic reaction any time you face difficulties or you make mistakes. The question is, how do you change this harsh, critical inner voice that keeps attacking you? The mindful approach is to listen to it. To give it space to say what it wants to say, and to listen, but in a gentle, friendly way, as you may listen to a young child or a piece of beautiful music. This ends up breaking down the repetitive, aggressive tone, and ends up calming and soothing the self-criticism a little. Just a tiny shift in your attitude towards these thoughts makes all the difference in dealing with difficulties.

If a strong memory or worry of a past or present difficulty comes up in your practice of meditation, try taking the following steps:

1. **Become aware of the fact that something challenging has come up for you that keeps drawing your attention.**

2. **Observe what effect this difficulty has on your physical body and emotions at the moment.**

3. **Listen to the difficulty as you would listen to a friend's problems, with a warm sense of empathy rather than criticism.**

4. **Say to yourself words like, 'It's alright. Whatever the difficulty is, it will pass, like everything else. Let me feel it for this moment.'**

5. **Accept the difficulty just as it is for the time being.**

6. **Breathe into it and stay with the sensations, even if they seem to grow larger at first. With practice, stay with the feeling of the difficulty for longer.**

7. **When you're ready, gently go back to the focus of the meditation.**

Everyone experiences difficulties of varying degrees from time to time. Mindfulness is here to help you to be with the difficulty if you can't change the circumstances that are causing it.

Understanding why you're bothering

In the middle of your mindfulness meditation practice, you may start thinking, 'Why am I bothering to do this?' and 'I'm wasting my time.' This is quite normal and part of the process of learning to meditate. Simply notice the thought, gently say to yourself 'thinking, thinking', and turn your attention back to the breath or other focus of meditation. When you practise for a while and begin to see the benefits of meditation, your trust in the process grows and your doubts diminish.

If you feel as if you've forgotten why you're practising meditation in the first place and are lacking motivation, refer to Chapter 3.

Realising that setbacks are inevitable

When I first learnt to meditate, I tried too hard. I thought I had to *get* something. I sat up extremely straight in a stiff way, rather than comfortably. Each time my mind wandered away from the breath, I hauled it back instead of kindly guiding it back to the breathing. I waited for an experience. I kept trying to clear my mind completely. Sometimes it felt wonderfully blissful, and I thought I'd got it! But then it went away. So, there I was again, trying to *get* it. I felt I was going through setback after setback.

In fact, I was going through a learning process, beginning to understand what meditation was all about. You can only have a setback if you're trying to get something or go somewhere. If you have no goal, you can't really have a setback. Ultimately, meditation is about letting go of goals and being in the here and now.

Imagine you're sitting at home and you decide you're going to go home. What do you need to do? You guessed it: nothing! You're already there. The journey of mindfulness is like that. You feel as if you're getting closer to true meditation, but really *each moment you practise* is true meditation, no matter what your experience.

Meditation maestro

Meditation is similar to training to be a musician. You may love playing music, but you need to put in the practice every day. Some days are great, and wonderful sounds emerge from your instrument – you feel at one with the harmony of the piece. Other days are tough. You don't want to practise, you can't see the point, you feel like giving up. But the musician still perseveres. Deep down you know the magic of music and trust that your practising will pay off. You play music because you love music.

Meditation is the same. You have good and bad days, but if you know deep down that it's important for you, you keep putting in the time. That depth of motivation and vision is the secret to making the most of meditation.

Setting realistic expectations

If you think that mindfulness meditation is going to make you feel calm and relaxed and free of all problems straight away, you're going to have a hard time. When you first learn to drive, you don't expect to be an expert after one lesson. Even after you pass the test, it takes years to become a good driver. Meditation, like any other learning experience, takes time too. Have realistic expectations about meditation.

Here are ten realistic expectations to reflect on:

- 'My mind will wander around. This is what happens in meditation, even if it's for a few breaths.'

- 'There's no such thing as a good or bad meditation. It's like when a small child does a scribble for drawing. It just is what it is.'

- 'Mindfulness isn't about getting certain experiences. It's about being with whatever arises, moment to moment, with acceptance.'

- 'I'll sometimes feel calm and sometimes feel agitated and tense in meditation. With time, the calmness will increase.'

- 'Meditation is a long-term practice. I'll gradually learn to let go of my expectations as I practise.'

- 'It may be difficult to motivate myself to practise every day, especially at the beginning. Some days I may forget to practise. That doesn't mean I should immediately give up.'

- 'Sometimes I may feel worse after the meditation than before. This is part of the learning process that I need to understand.'

- 'I can never know how I've benefited from meditation. I can only practise every day and see what happens.'

- 'Even after years of meditation, I may sometimes feel I haven't progressed. This isn't a fact but an idea. Meditation works below conscious awareness, and so I can't know what's happening there.'

- 'The more I practise, the easier it gets.'

Looking at change

Humans are creatures of habit. Once you get into a habit, you effortlessly do it day after day without a second thought. So, for change to last and become effortless, it needs to become a new habit – in this case, the habit of mindfulness. When you establish a pattern of mindfulness, your brain immediately begins to change, gradually transforming your experience of life for the better.

Creating a new habit pattern results in new neurons firing in your brain. And neurons that fire together, wire together. As you practise regularly, the neural pathways in your brain involved in being mindful begin to link up, thereby creating a healthy habit.

To create a habit of mindfulness meditation try the following:

1. **Decide on a plan of action: how long you'll meditate for every day and at what time.**

2. **Stick to the plan whether you feel like it or not.**

3. **If you forget to meditate on the odd day, don't give up.** Slipping up is natural. Pick up and start again. As I keep emphasising, be kind to yourself rather than berating yourself.

4. **Assess your progress after four or eight weeks, and make changes if necessary.** Make a new plan, perhaps meditating for a longer duration.

Creating a habit of mindfulness meditation sounds so simple. However, the difficult bit is Step 2. You listen to thoughts saying things like 'Don't bother today,' or you give in to feelings of tiredness or restlessness. This is your moment to challenge the usual way in which you behave. You can practise what you committed to, or you can follow the old habit pattern. Listen to what you decided to do in the first place, and stick to the practice as best you can. As soon as you've established the habit of mindfulness, you find yourself becoming mindful without even thinking about it – the neurons in your brain have wired together. Step by step you can change.

Part IV
Reaping the Rewards of Mindfulness

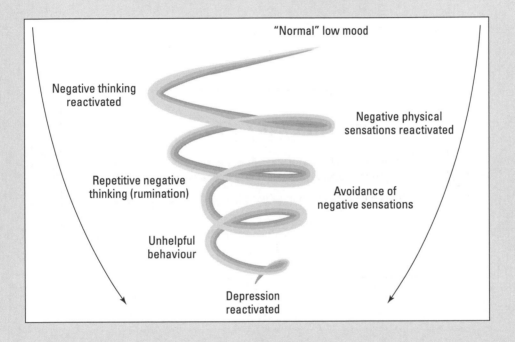

For a great bonus article about mindfulness, head online and take a look at www.dummies.com/extras/mindfulness.

In this part . . .

✔ Discover the wonderful ways in which mindfulness can help you, from boosting your happiness to dealing with anxiety.

✔ Try some of the techniques used in mindfulness therapy to combat depression.

✔ Find out how to teach mindfulness to children and pick up some useful tips on mindful parenting.

Chapter 11

Discovering Greater Happiness

I'd just started my career. I had a job with a proper salary going straight into my bank account – much more money than any pocket money or student loan I'd received. The feeling was exhilarating: I'd made it! All those years at school, all those exams at university, slogging away, and now I'd made it. Now what? Spend it of course, I thought. So I went out and spent it. A new car, clothes, the latest gadgets and gizmos – and yet the pleasure was short lived. Before long, that sense of emptiness I'd unconsciously been running from returned. Something was missing. Chasing after stuff wasn't the way to happiness, even though the whole of society seemed to advertise that it was. My search for real and lasting happiness began.

This chapter explores the relationship between the science of happiness (positive psychology) and the art of mindfulness. By applying the findings of what makes a happy life along with the contemplative exercises of mindfulness, you can explore ways to be more content and peaceful in your life.

Discovering the Way to Happiness

The Dalai Lama, often giggling or smiling with others, says: 'I believe that the very *purpose* of our life is to seek happiness.' That's a huge statement. Imagine living as if your very purpose is to seek happiness. A life where your decisions and choices are based on whether your happiness will be increased or decreased. What would your life be like? How would it be different? Is it even possible? If the sole purpose of life is to seek happiness, then you need to find the best way to greater wellbeing.

Whether happiness is the key purpose of life or not, happiness has scientifically proven benefits:

✔ **Happiness improves your relationships.** You have more friends and get on better with them.

✔ **Happiness boosts your intelligence.** No matter how smart you are, you use those brain cells well.

✔ **Happiness makes you more optimistic.** You see the bright side in most situations. And your optimism makes you feel happier too.

✔ **Happiness makes you live longer and more healthily.** You have lower blood pressure and fight off diseases more effectively.

✔ **Happiness supercharges your creativity.** You're capable of coming up with new and innovative ideas for home and work.

Exploring your ideas about happiness

Some people describe themselves as extremely happy, whereas others claim to be unhappy. Happiness seems to be at different levels from person to person and from moment to moment.

Ask yourself the following question:

Considering everything, how are things these days: are you very happy, pretty happy, or not too happy?

If you rate yourself as not too happy, don't despair! This chapter is designed to help you work towards greater wellbeing. You can use a whole range of well-researched approaches right away.

An interesting way of finding out your ideas about happiness is a technique called sentence completion. Complete the following sentences quickly with five or six different answers, without thinking too much:

The things that truly make me happy are . . .

To be 5 per cent more mindful in my life, I need to . . .

To be 5 per cent happier in my life I need to . . .

Keep your answers handy. Practise this exercise daily for a few weeks to see what kind of answers you get. You may need to act on them, or you may not. Just by becoming aware of your responses, you naturally begin to move towards becoming happier.

Challenging assumptions about happiness

The most common assumption about happiness is that *pleasure equals happiness*. By maximising the number of positive feelings and minimising the number of negative ones, a happy life is created. It turns out that this is a very small part of the picture. Research shows that pleasure alone doesn't lead to any greater sense of life satisfaction. So, although nothing's wrong with staying in luxurious hotels and enjoying your favourite food, these activities just result in a fleeting feel-good effect.

That money equals happiness is another popular belief. The relationship between happiness and money is really interesting, because society gears itself towards acquiring more money and therefore hoping for more happiness. One experiment compared the happiness of big lottery winners with the happiness of people who had been in a serious accident and become paralysed. That's a serious test: what a comparison! The results showed that after two years, the people who won the lottery went back to the happiness level they'd been at before. The same happened with the paralysed accident victims. Isn't that amazing? Whether you become paralysed or win the lottery, you end up with the same level of happiness in the long term. I think that's incredible. It shows that the power of your mindset and attitude is stronger than circumstances.

Imagine that you're able to sell your happiness. Once you've sold it, you'll never be happy again – your happiness will be gone. Will you sell your happiness, and for how much? Maybe £1,000? Most people say no. How about £50,000? That gets people thinking, but usually the answer is no. How about a million pounds in cash – crisp £50 notes – in exchange for your happiness? Think about that for a moment. A million pounds. Will you sell it? A million pounds can buy you a lot of stuff, but you'll get no happiness in return. How about a billion pounds?

I find the question of selling happiness an interesting one because it really gets you to reflect on how much you value happiness. But you sell your happiness very easily in the short term. You sell your happiness when you can't find a parking space, if your partner irritates you, or a demanding manager is rude to you. It's easy to forget how much your happiness is worth. Perhaps it's priceless?

In the wonderful book called *Happiness*, Buddhist monk Matthieu Ricard states that wellbeing is a deep sense of serenity that *underlies and permeates all emotion states*, including joy and sorrow. This sense of being, or well-*being*, is cultivated through 'mind training' (meditation). Mind training involves becoming aware of destructive emotions like jealousy and anger. Rather than acting on them, which just reinforces the self-perpetuating process, watch them arise in your awareness, without judgement. As you watch the negative feelings rise up in you and refrain from acting, or reacting, these feelings naturally subside in their own time. This doesn't mean you spend all day trying to force a grin on your face (although apparently that actually helps), but you see different emotional states as opportunities to find out about them and create an emotional balance between them. You're not pushing them away or grabbing hold of them – just calmly observing them, from moment to moment.

A happiness recipe

I found a sense of happiness through the following 'recipe':

- A **regular practice** of mindfulness

- An attitude of **gratitude** for what I have

- **Valuing social relationships** and practising forgiveness when things go wrong

- **Letting go** of anything outside my control and accepting life as it is in the present moment

- Having **meaningful goals** in my life that are in line with what I believe is important, and enjoying the journey towards achieving them rather than getting fixated on results

- Seeing things in a **positive light**

- Having a light-hearted approach – **laughing** uncontrollably from time to time!

- Working with a **sense of service** for the community

I'm not perfect, and some days tend to go better than others of course. However, the practice of mindfulness is always available to me and helps me to access my deep inner resources for healing, wellness and peace. Consider what your happiness recipe is, and write it down. Which ingredients do you need to be truly happier?

Applying Mindfulness with Positive Psychology

Positive psychology is the science of wellbeing – it's concerned with people's strengths, improving normal lives, and building healthy organisations. Mindfulness is one of the most powerful tools in the positive psychology toolkit, because evidence demonstrates a link between mindfulness practice and levels of happiness.

Psychology traditionally studied people's problems. Psychologists were interested in conditions like depression, anxiety, schizophrenia, and psychosis. This is certainly not a bad thing and has resulted in a number of mental illnesses now being treatable. Through talking treatments and drugs, psychology has helped people to reduce their sadness. The problem is that in their rush to help suffering people, psychologists forgot about how to make relatively normal human beings happier. So psychologists can move people from unhappy to neutral, but they haven't considered how to go from neutral to happy. If you drive a car, you know that you can't get very far in neutral! Positive psychologists focus on moving people towards greater happiness.

Understanding the three ways to happiness

'Happiness is not something ready made. It comes from your own actions.'

Dalai Lama

Positive psychology describes three different ways to happiness. You can use all three interchangeably.

Pleasure

Maximising the amount of pleasure you experience leads to feelings of happiness. Eating your favourite chocolate, going out to watch a film, or going shopping are all examples of seeking pleasure. Being grateful for the experiences you're having or have had can help to enhance the happy experience and make it more long lasting. Pleasant experiences make you feel happy temporarily, but if you keep repeating them they become unpleasant. For example, eating one bar of chocolate is delicious, but not 100 bars of chocolate!

Engagement or flow

With flow, you give 100 per cent of your attention to and are at one with whatever you're doing, whether pleasurable or not. Flow usually requires some effort on your part. The activity involved is just challenging enough to hold your relaxed attention. Refer to Chapter 5 for a complete description of flow.

You can develop a state of flow in anything you do, if you give it your full attention. This is where mindfulness comes in: developing a relaxed, calm, focused awareness from moment to moment. Even washing the dishes or walking the dog is an opportunity to live in this state of flow, a condition of happiness. Give full attention to whatever you're doing, whenever you remember.

Meaning

Living a meaningful life involves knowing your strengths and using them in the service of something larger than yourself. We live in an individualistic society, and the word 'service' isn't often thought to be attractive. However, helping others is the core ingredient for a happy life.

Don't worry: you don't necessarily have to change your job or lifestyle to lead a meaningful life. You just need to make a genuine *attitude* shift. If you're a lawyer who wants to make as much money as possible, that severely limits your overall sense of happiness. The same work can offer more meaning, with the right motivation. Justice, equality, the inner desire to help others – all give you a much greater sense of meaning and purpose in such a career.

Other ways of creating greater meaning include volunteer work or joining a religious or spiritual group. Simply performing acts of kindness wherever you can gives life greater meaning. You don't have to make a massive world-changing difference: cracking jokes with friends, making tea for everyone at the office or organising a group holiday all count.

Using your personal strengths mindfully

Positive psychologists carefully analysed a range of strengths and virtues, and found 24 of them to be universally significant across cultures. By discovering and using your strengths in your work and home life you achieve a greater sense of wellbeing because you're doing something you're good at and that you love doing.

Table 11-1 shows the 24 key signature strengths under six key categories. Scan through the list and reflect on what you think are your five main strengths or virtues.

Table 11-1	The 24 Signature Strengths				
Wisdom	*Courage*	*Love*	*Justice*	*Temperance*	*Transcendence*
Creativity	Bravery	Intimacy	Responsibility	Forgiveness	Appreciation
Judgement	Perseverance	Kindness	Fairness	Self-control	Gratitude
Curiosity	Integrity	Sociability	Leadership	Humility	Optimism
Love of learning	Enthusiasm			Caution	Humour
Perspective					Spirituality

The great thing about discovering your signature strengths is finding a strength you never knew you had. I found out that one of my strengths was kindness. I never thought of that as a strength, but it is. And it makes me happy to offer kindness to others. You too can dust off your undiscovered strengths and apply them to your life.

Looking on the funny side of life

One of my top five signature strengths turns out to be humour. Now, let me make it clear, that doesn't mean I'm going to be the next big hit on the comedy circuit. It means I particularly love laughing and making others laugh. I never thought of it as a strength until I discovered that I rated highly for it in the signature strengths test I did online. Now I know that, I value time to be with friends and colleagues who like to see the funny side of life. I also use it to see life in a light-hearted way when things aren't going my way, and let myself clown around regularly. I've recently even trained to be a laughter teacher and run creativity workshops combining mindfulness with laughter yoga. I'm not joking!

Mindfulness is an important practice, but if you take it too seriously you miss out on an important attitude. By discovering your own signature strengths, you can spend more time developing them in a mindful way. When I'm coaching clients in mindful living, I sometimes recommend identifying strengths as an beneficial approach.

Link your strengths with your mindfulness practice by becoming more aware of when you do and don't use your strengths. Also, notice what effect mindfulness meditation has on your signature strengths – for example, you may find that you become better at leadership as your confidence grows, or that your general level of curiosity increases.

For example, say one of your undiscovered strengths is a love of learning, but your job is boring and seems to involve repeating the same thing every day. How can you use your love of learning? Well, you do an evening course, start a master's degree or make time to read more. Or you can integrate your strength into your work in a mindful way. Become aware of each of the tasks you do and think about what makes that task boring. Look at co-workers and discover what attitudes others have that make them feel differently about the job. Discover something new about the work every day, or research ways of moving on to a more suitable career. By doing so, you use your strength and feel a bit better every day.

To increase your day-to-day feelings of happiness, try this:

✔ Discover your signature strengths. You can discover your own strengths for free at www.authentichappiness.org.

✔ Use your signature strengths in your daily life wherever you can and with a mindful awareness.

✔ Enjoy the process and let go of the outcome.

Writing a gratitude journal

The human brain is designed to remember things that go wrong rather than right. This is a survival mechanism and ensures that you don't make the same mistake again and again, which may be life-threatening if you live out in the jungle and need to remember to avoid the tigers. If you don't live in the jungle, focusing on the negative is a problem. The antidote for the human brain's tendency to look for what's going wrong is to consciously focus on what's going well – in a nutshell, gratitude. And research has found gratitude to be very effective.

A gratitude journal is a powerful and simple way of boosting your happiness. The journal is simply a daily record of things in your life that you're grateful for. Research has found that if, at the end of each day, people reflect on what made them grateful, their levels of gratitude increase and people feel significantly happier. It works!

Here's how to write an effective gratitude journal:

1. **Get a book or diary in which you can make a daily record.** As long as it has sufficient space for you to write three sentences every day, that's fine.

2. **Every evening, before you go to bed, write down three things that you're grateful for.** Try to vary what you're grateful for. Writing that you're grateful for your cat, apartment, and car every single day isn't as effective as varying it, unless you really mean it and feel it. You don't have to choose huge things: anything small, even if you feel only slightly grateful about it, will do. Examples include having a partner (or not having a partner!), enjoying a conversation at work, a relaxing drive home, a roof over your head. You're training your gratitude muscle. The more you practise, the better you get at focusing on what's going well in your life.

3. **Notice what effect your gratitude diary has on the quality and quantity of your sleep and how you generally feel throughout the day.** By checking in on how you're feeling and what effect the exercise is having, you're able to fine-tune it to work for you. Noticing the benefits of gratitude also helps to motivate your practice.

4. **Continue to practise regularly if you find it beneficial.** After a while, gratitude will become a pleasant habit.

Through practising mindfulness meditation, you may naturally find that you're grateful for the simpler things in life and feel happier as a result. Writing a gratitude journal complements your daily mindfulness practice very well (refer to Chapter 9 for a daily routine). Both gratitude and mindfulness are proven to boost your happiness, so you're sure to feel more emotionally resilient over time. You can even write the journal together with a loved one, to deepen your relationship.

If you don't like writing a journal, simply think about what's going well in your life as you drift off to sleep, or even on your morning commute.

The *gratitude visit* is a very popular experiment among positive psychologists, because it's so powerful. Think of someone who made a big difference to your life who you haven't properly thanked. Write a letter to express your gratitude to that person. If you can, arrange to visit the person and read the testimonial to him. Even three months later, people who express their gratitude in this way feel happier and less depressed. Add mindfulness to this exercise by simply being aware of your thoughts and feelings that arise as you do the exercise. See what happens.

Savouring the moment

Savouring the moment means becoming aware of the pleasure in the present time by deliberately focusing attention on it. Here are some ways of developing this skill:

- ✔ **Mindfulness.** Being aware of what you're doing in the moment is the only way of ultimately savouring the moment. If your mind and heart are in two different places, you miss the joy of the moment – the breeze that passes through the trees or the flower on the side of the pavement. Most of the exercises in this book help you to grow your inner muscle of mindfulness.

- ✔ **Sharing with others.** Expressing your pleasure to those around you turns out to be a powerful way of savouring the moment. If you notice a sunset or beautiful sky, share your pleasure with others. Letting someone know about the pleasure it gave you helps to raise the positive feeling for both of you. However, don't forget to look carefully at the beautiful thing first – sometimes it's easy to get carried away talking and miss the beauty of the moment itself.

- ✔ **Seeking new experiences.** Vary your pleasurable experiences rather than repeating the same ones over and over again – it's a happier experience. And if you like ice cream, eat it once in a while and with full mindful awareness rather than feeling guilty about it.

Helping others mindfully

Of the three ways of achieving satisfaction in life (pleasure, engagement, and meaning), engagement and meaning are by far the most effective, and of the two, *meaning has been found to have the most effect.*

Painting joy

Last year I decided to paint the walls my living room. Now, you may see this as a boring task with no particular opportunity apart from getting the room painted, or you may see it as a fantastic chance to be absolutely 100 per cent mindful of the task.

I felt the bristles on the brush as I dipped the brush into the thick paint, connected with the sensations in my arm as I moved the brush over to the edge of the wall, and enjoyed watching the colour magically release itself from the brush and onto the surface. As I got into a calm, rhythmic movement, I gradually lost my usual sense of self and was at one with the painting. By the time I finished, I felt energised and uplifted. I'd been fortunate enough to enter the state of flow, or mindful awareness.

Think about a task that you find boring or repetitive, try to give the task your full mindful awareness and see what happens.

To achieve deeper meaning, you work towards something that's greater than yourself. This involves doing something for others – or, in other words, helping others. A meaningful life is about meeting a need in the world through your unique strengths and virtues. By serving a greater need, you create a win–win situation: the people you help feel better, and you feel better for helping them.

Compassion motivats us to relieve others of suffering. Research shows that compassion has deep evolutionary benefits. Your heart rate slows down, and you release the social bonding hormone called oxytocin and experience feelings of pleasure. Research on even short courses in cultivating compassion has found that people report long-term feelings of happiness.

Going back to the Dalai Lama, he states:

> *'If you want others to be happy, practice compassion. If you want to be happy, practice compassion.'*
>
> *Dalai Lama*

I often attend talks by the Dalai Lama or volunteer for his public events. The Dalai Lama almost radiates warmth and compassion in the way he speaks to and interacts with others. Recently, I watched him speaking with a bishop on stage in Italy. As the Dalai Lama spoke to the bishop, he held his hand as if the two were good friends. The Dalai Lama stated that he'd love to attend one of the bishop's religious ceremonies. And he shared the importance for us all to respect each other's religion to create greater harmony in the world. These are all acts of compassion.

Here are the Dalai Lama's suggestions to develop greater compassion and therefore happiness in your life:

✔ **Understand what true compassion is.** Compassion isn't desire or attachment. When you're genuinely compassionate for your partner, you wish for him to be happy. The ultimate form of compassion for your partner means that even if he behaves negatively or leaves you, you're happy for him if he's happy. That's not easy! Just start by imagining yourself in his shoes when he goes through a tough time, and wish for his difficulties to end soon.

✔ **Realise that, like you, everyone wants to be happy and not suffer.** Once you begin to see how we're all the same underneath our thin layer of skin, you feel greater compassion for others. Compassion grows when you see how everyone's essentially the same, with the same desires and the same essential needs.

✔ **Let go of anger and hatred.** You can do this by investigating your feelings of anger and hatred for others. Do they serve you? Do they make you feel happier? Even when you think that your anger gives you the energy to act on injustices, look more closely: anger shuts down your rational brain and can make your actions destructive and unkind. Investigate and observe mindfully for yourself. Notice the difference between acting as if you're angry and actually being angry. The former is less destructive.

✔ **See compassion as strong, not weak.** Compassion and patience are mistakenly thought of as weak. Actually they offer great strength. People who react quickly with anger are not in control of themselves. Whereas someone who listens, is patient and compassionate is tremendously resilience and strong. The science agrees on this too.

✔ **Be grateful for your enemies.** If you want to learn tolerance and patience – qualities of compassion – you can't learn from your friends. You need a challenge. So when someone annoying comes into your life, be thankful for the opportunity to cultivate compassion! Understand that this person has a deep desire for happiness, just like you do. He may be looking for happiness in the wrong way. Wish that he finds a better path to happiness and therefore doesn't suffer so much. If he suffers more, he may just cause more pain for others.

✔ **Treat whoever you meet as an old friend, or as a brother or sister.** That makes you feel happier straight away!

✔ **See beyond people's outer appearances.** They may look different, dress differently, or act differently. But remember that underneath we're all the same. We're all part of the same human community.

By cultivating compassion, you make a positive contribution to the world. When you feel a little happier, you make the world a happier and more peaceful place to live. The planet is our home, and the best way to protect it is through compassion – positive relations with others. Ultimately, it's vital for the survival of our species.

Testing selfish and selfless happiness

In positive psychology classes, teachers sometimes give students the task of doing something for their own happiness followed by doing something to make someone else happy.

Students who do something for their own pleasure – like watching a film, eating out in a restaurant, or surfing on the Internet – find the happiness to be short-lived and lacking in depth.

The students then do something that will make someone else happy, such as giving their partner a massage or complimenting a friend. Students always find that making others happy is far more enriching and fulfilling than just making themselves happy, with the sense of happiness lasting for much longer.

Why not try making someone happy today?

Doing things just for your own happiness doesn't really work. Imagine cooking a meal for the whole family and then just eating it yourself and watching the rest of the family go hungry. Where's the fun in that? The food may taste good, but without sharing you miss something really important. Happiness is the same. If you practise mindfulness just for your own happiness and for no one else, the meditation has a limited effect. Expand your vision and allow your mindfulness to expand to benefit all, and you'll find it far more fulfilling. Each time before you practise, recall the positive effect mindfulness has on both yourself and those around you, ultimately making the world a better place to live in. (Refer to Chapter 6 for an exercise in metta meditation, which encourages kind feelings for yourself and others.)

Generating Positive Emotions with Mindfulness

Mindfulness is about offering a warm, kind, friendly, accepting awareness to your moment-by-moment experience, whatever that may be. For this reason, any practice of mindfulness, in the long term, develops your ability to generate positive feeling towards your inner (thoughts, emotions) and outer (world) experience. To develop this further, try the exercises in this section.

Mindfulness practice is like training in the gym. You may feel uncomfortable at first, but through regular practice you get better at being mindful in each moment. Because it's such a gradual process, you may not notice any change at first, but just trust in the process and give it a decent try. Keep going to the brain gym!

Breathing and smiling

'A smile makes you master of yourself. When you smile, you realise the wonder of the smile.'

Thich Nhat Hanh

Research has found a connection between the muscles you use to smile and your mood. You smile when you feel good – but interestingly, simply smiling makes you feel good. It works both ways.

You can test this out for yourself. Try smiling right now and simultaneously think a negative thought. Can you? I find that smiling certainly has an effect over negative mood.

Smiling's contagious: have you noticed how infectious a smile is? If you see someone smiling, you can't help but do the same. It also reduces stress: by deliberately becoming aware of your breathing and smiling, you act against the body's automatic defence mechanism and allow a more restful and calm state to occur.

Thich Nhat Hanh, a world-famous meditation teacher, has dedicated his life to the practice of mindfulness. One of his recommended practices is breathing and smiling. He offers the following meditation. Try reciting these lines as you breathe in and out:

Breathing in, I calm body and mind.

Breathing out, I smile.

Dwelling in the present moment

I know this is the only moment.

Have a go at this mindful smiling exercise, which is available as an audio track (Track 19):

1. **Sit in a really nice warm and cosy place, where you feel safe and comfortable.**

2. **Take a few moments to stretch your arms. As you do so, gently smile.**

3. **Come back to a relaxed seated posture, or any other posture that feels right for you.**

4. **Gently close your eyes. Hold that gentle smile on your face, even if you don't actually feel happy or smiley at the moment.**

5. **Enjoy the feeling of each in- and out-breath. Imagine your breath has the quality of happiness within it. With each in-breath, you're breathing in smile energy.**

6. **As you breathe in, say to yourself: 'Breathing in, I calm my body and mind.'**

7. **As you breathe out, say to yourself: 'Breathing out, I smile.'**

8. **While you continue this exercise, simply say to yourself 'breathing' on each in-breath and 'smiling' on each out-breath.**

9. **Persevere for a few minutes to see what happens. The process may feel fake, contrived, or uncomfortable. Or it may feel great!**

10. **Stop this exercise after around five to ten minutes. Notice how you feel having completed this process.**

Smile, especially when you don't feel like it or it feels unnatural. Even if you don't feel great, smiling has a small effect. You're planting the seeds of happiness. With time, the seeds are sure to grow.

Mindful laughter

Everyone enjoys a good laugh. A good belly laugh has physical, mental, and social benefits.

Mindfulness increases happiness: The proof

Jon Kabat-Zinn of the University of Massachusetts Medical School, and Richard Davidson, Professor of Psychology and Psychiatry of University of Wisconsin-Madison, and their colleagues have proved that mindfulness increases happiness.

The researchers randomly split a group of employees at a biotech company into two groups. The first group did an eight-week course in mindfulness-based stress reduction (MBSR), and the others did nothing. The electrical activity of their brains was studied before and after the training.

After eight weeks, the people who did the mindfulness training had greater activation in a part of the brain called the left prefrontal cortex.

This part of the brain is associated with positive emotions, wellbeing and acceptance of experience. Left prefrontal cortex activated people normally describe themselves as interested, excited, strong, active, alert and enthusiastic. In comparison, right prefrontal cortex activated people describe themselves as afraid, nervous, scared, upset and distressed.

The experiment showed that just eight weeks of mindfulness meditation training in a busy workplace environment can have positive effect on happiness. Other studies with more experienced meditators suggest that these changes in the brain become a permanent feature – explaining the mild grin on the faces of experienced meditation practitioners.

Physically, laughter relaxes your whole body, decreases your stress hormones, releases endorphins (your body's natural feel-good hormone), and improves heart and blood vessel function. Mentally, you'll feel less anxious and be more resilient to life's stressors. And socially, laughter brings people closer to you, and through it you can defuse conflict more easily and enhance teamwork.

I've combined mindfulness practice with laughter yoga (developed by Dr Madan Kataria) to enhance the process. In this way, you don't have to find a reason to laugh: you can laugh any time!

Here are a few of the key principles:

- ✔ **You don't need a reason to laugh.** You don't need to have jokes, comedy routines, or anything like that. You can if you'd like, but it's not necessary – simply having a playful attitude and creating sounds of laughter is sufficient.

- ✔ **Fake it until you make it.** The idea is to do fake laughs. If they turn into real laughs, great. If not, that's fine too! With practice, you'll get better at it. It'll feel very strange at first, but just persevere and you'll find yourself laughing for real at the silliness of the whole thing!

- ✔ **Be conscious and enjoy the experience, however it goes.** Most people aren't used to laughing much. And many people don't laugh at all. So it'll take time at the beginning. With experience, you'll be laughing more easily. It's just a matter of getting used to it. Because the neurons in your brain that fire together, wire together, with practice you'll be able to enjoy and laugh more easily at life's ups and downs.

Have a go at this mindful laughter exercise. You can do this exercise with a friend or even with a group of friends or family members:

1. **Begin by doing a mindfulness exercise together with a smile on your face.** Any mindfulness meditation from this book is fine. The breathing and smiling exercise above is a good one.

2. **Now look someone in the eye and, as you clap, say, 'Ho, ho, ha, ha, ha.'** Make the sounds of laughter. Be as playful with this as you can. Be non-judgemental and let go of your inhibitions if you can. Be like a child for just the next few minutes.

3. **Try the handshake laugh. As you and your friend shake hands, look each other in the eye and do some fake laughs.** You may find yourself finding it funny. But if not, no worries. You're just warming up.

4. **Take a few moments to just calmly breathe between these laughter exercises.**

5. **Now sit in a circle or facing each other and laugh.** Any kind of fake silly laugh will suffice. Have eyes open or closed. Listening to the laughter of others can kick off your own laughter. Laughter is contagious. Let the joy bubble up inside you. And remember: there's no need to think you're doing it incorrectly if your laugh isn't a real one at the moment. You're just starting the journey of mindful laughter. Get serious about laughter by seriously laughing!

6. **Finish with another mindfulness exercise in this book.** It can be simply mindfulness of breath or some relaxing mindful walking. Or lie down and try doing the body scan meditation.

If you really don't enjoy this approach to laughter, try to watch more comedies or spend time with people who make you laugh. See the funny side of things, and avoid taking things too seriously, by asking, 'Is there a more light-hearted way of seeing this situation?'

Releasing Your Creativity

What is creativity? Where does creativity come from? How can you become happier and more creative? Good questions! The act of creativity is a deep mystery. If creativity is a mechanical process in which you do such and such, it ceases to have its intrinsic uniqueness.

For example, I'm being creative by writing this book. I simply type the words that come into my mind. I don't know where the thoughts are coming from: they seem to arise into awareness and vanish again in the same mysterious way. Creativity is a beautifully magic process that seems to be a natural part of the Universe. By using ways to calm your mind, you find the creative process naturally unfolds itself, which increases your happiness.

Exploring creativity

Play is an important aspect of creativity. If you're willing to play and have fun, creativity is sure to follow on. When you play, you engage the more creative right side of the brain. You let go of the usual rules. If you stick to the normal rules, you can't come up with something new. The new is born from transforming the way you see things.

Let's say, for example, that you're trying to think of something different to do with the family this weekend. Here's one way to get the creative juices flowing:

Moments of genius

Arguably one of the greatest scientific creative thoughts in the last hundred years didn't occur in a lecture theatre or seminar with top scientists. It arose in the relaxed, curious, open and questioning mind of a teenager. Einstein's greatest moment of genius occurred to him when he was 16 years old, strolling along and dreaming about what it would feel like to ride on a beam of light – which led to his famous theory of relativity. I call that state of mind 'mindfulness of thought': Einstein allowed the mind to wander but was aware of thoughts and ideas arising.

Inventors need to be aware to spot everyday problems that need a new invention. James Dyson was vacuuming in his home when he realised the top-of-the-range vacuum cleaner was losing suction and getting clogged up.

He became aware of this (mindfulness) and then went on to design over 5,000 different prototypes before coming up with his famous bagless vacuum cleaner.

Another inventor, George de Mestral, embodied the mindful attitude of curiosity. He was walking his dog on a beautiful summer's day in Switzerland and returned home to find burrs – plant seed sacs – stuck to his dog and his own trousers. With his burning curiosity, he examined the burrs under a microscope to discover that they were covered in tiny hooks which clung onto the loops in his trousers. In that moment, he had the idea to invent Velcro, made of hooks on one side and loops on the other. Genius!

1. **Write down what you want to achieve.** For example, I'm looking for an exciting weekend getaway with the whole family, to cheer us all up and so that we can have fun together.

2. **Let go of the problem.** Allow the mind to slow down and connect with the breath for five minutes or more.

3. **Write down several things you've done at weekends for fun.** For example, staying over at your sister's place, going to the nearest beach, staying over at your friend's house, going to local museums, playing different sports.

4. **Change your perspective. Imagine you're very rich or you don't have a family, or you live in a forest. What would you do then?** For example, if you were very wealthy, you might fly to a bigger city for the weekend; if you didn't have children, you might book a romantic weekend getaway; if you lived in the forest, you might start building a tree house.

5. **Now see what ideas can be used from that.** For example, you can travel by train or budget airline to a relatively cheap hotel in a city you haven't been to before, you can ask your neighbours whether you can stay at their country home for the weekend, or you can find a hotel that caters for children while you spend some quality time with your partner.

To be highly creative, you need to calm the mind completely. Many research papers show that a calm and relaxed mind is far more creative than an anxious and stressed one. When you're calm, your thoughts aren't firing off too often, so you have space for creative ideas to rise to the surface. Creativity is a bit like looking for treasure at the bottom of a lake. If the water is choppy and murky, you can never see the treasure below. But if the lake is clear and calm, you can easily see it. Mindfulness gives space for the mind to become calm, and at the same time raises your level of awareness. You're not forcing calmness, you're just creating the right conditions for it to happen.

I often get new ideas when practising informal mindfulness. I can be going for a stroll through my local park, looking at the trees, or enjoying the blueness of the sky when a new idea pops into my head. I usually carry around a small notebook in which to jot ideas down. I don't do this when I'm doing formal mindfulness meditation, however, because that would be a distraction. I don't *try* to get ideas or force them to come up.

Keep your mind engaged in the moment, and ideas naturally arise. Imagine you're trying to remember where you left your keys, and no matter how hard you try, you can't recall where they are. Then you forget about it, and whoosh – the location shoots into your head.

Look at Figure 11-1.

Figure 11-1:
Optical
illusion.

If you haven't seen this illusion before, you probably see a series of random dots. Now try feeling your breath, becoming aware of the feelings and sensations in your body for a few moments, and then look again in a more relaxed way. As best you can, let go of any frustrations or desires to 'get it'. Spend a few minutes doing this. Look at the image just as it is. Has it changed? Can you see it from a different perspective? Be patient and see what unfolds. I'm going to tell you now, are you ready . . . it's a Dalmatian. If you still can't see the dog, what can you do? You can ask someone else, come back to it later, or try looking from different angles – in other words, you look for creative alternative ideas. Can you see how getting frustrated may be a natural reaction but isn't helpful?

This shows how the same thing (that picture) can be seen in two different ways. One seems random, and the other a fairly clear image of a dog. We create our reality. If you let go and look deeply, other realities can unfold. The interesting thing is, once you've 'seen' it, you can't forget it! Sometimes you may do this with problems too: seeing the same problem instead of new and innovative approaches to a solution. Try letting go of the obvious answer: walk away, meditate, do something else, and come back to the challenge later on with a refreshed and therefore more creative and happier mind.

Creating conditions for originality

You can do this meditation to kick-start your creativity. The meditation helps you to consider your challenge, allows time for incubation, and makes the space for new ideas to arise. As an example, I'm going to use this exercise to think of new ways to better serve mindfulness teachers who I've already trained and who currently get a monthly coaching call from me.

Here's how:

1. **Consider the challenge and state it clearly in a sentence in your mind.** For example, 'I'm looking for a simple, powerful way to better serve my existing mindfulness teachers so they become happier and more effective mindfulness teachers.'

2. **Sit or lie down in a comfortable posture, with a smile.** Have a gentle smile on your face to remind yourself to have fun and be playful – the foundations of creativity.

3. **Be mindful of whatever you like.** For example, right now I'm in a park, and so am enjoying being mindful of the sounds of the birds. You can choose what you prefer – your breathing, your body sensations, your thoughts – whatever is predominant for you now. Practise for a least a few minutes.

4. **After your meditation time is up, see which ideas pop into your head.** As I did this exercise, an idea arose in my mind: to offer an advanced mindfulness teacher training programme online for those who've done my basic course. That would help them improve the quality of their teaching. I could also offer to train them to teach compassion-type meditations rather than just mindfulness-based approaches. Did any ideas come up for you?

5. **If no ideas come to mind, do the exercise again.** Remember to see whether you can enjoy the mindfulness exercise rather than making it a struggle.

6. **If you still have no ideas or feel agitated, try going for a mindful stroll or have a mindful cup of tea or coffee.** You may just need to give your brain a rest!

Through this exercise you begin to allow your inner creative space to fill with fresh, new ideas. You clear out the old limiting ideas to make space for the brand new ones. Feel free to interrupt the meditation at any time to write your ideas down, because this isn't a formal meditation practice but a creativity exercise – allow yourself to have fun with it and experiment.

Chapter 12

Reducing Stress, Anger and Fatigue

Difficulties are part and parcel of life – you can't stop them, unfortunately. What you *can* stop is the way you meet and relate to challenges. Perhaps you habitually go into denial, or maybe you throw yourself in head first and end up overly tired. If you can face the difficulty in the right way, you can take the heat out of the problem and even use the energy generated by the issue to manage your emotions and activities.

Mindfulness offers you the opportunity to become more intimate with your own habitual patterns of operation. If you haven't really noticed how you currently meet challenges, you're bound to have a hard time assessing whether your approach is useful. Whether the way you react is helpful or not depends on what effect your reaction has. If you have no clear idea of the effects, you're not benefiting from experience – you're just replaying a record again and again. As this chapter shows, by becoming even slightly more mindful, your awareness grows and something can shift – and the smallest shift can make the biggest difference. As astronaut Neil Armstrong said (sort of): one small step for you; one giant leap for your wellbeing!

Using Mindfulness to Reduce Stress

Research shows that mindfulness reduces stress, in the short and long term, even well after people have completed training in mindfulness. This is because many people choose to continue to practise some form of mindfulness as part of their daily routine years later, because they found it so helpful. In this section I explore the various ways stress creeps up on you, and how mindfulness can help you say goodbye to unmanageable levels of stress.

Understanding your stress

Stress is a natural and everyday occurrence. Whenever you have a challenge to meet, doing so triggers the physiological reaction of stress. Stress isn't an illness, but a state of body and mind. However, if your stress level is very high, or goes on for too long, then you can suffer from both physical and mental ill health.

Stress isn't always a bad thing: when you or someone near you faces a physical danger, stress is helpful. For example, if you see a child running out in the street, the stress response provides you with the energy and focus you need to run and stop her. However, if you're lying in bed, worrying about your tax bill, stress isn't helpful: the result is that you don't sleep. If this stress goes on for too long, your health is likely to suffer.

Stress researcher Richard Lazarus found that stress begins with you *interpreting* the situation as dangerous or difficult and rapidly deciding what resources you have to cope with the challenge. If you interpret an event as dangerous or difficult and you feel you don't have the resources to cope, you experience a stress reaction. This is why one person loves going on a rollercoaster, whereas for another the experience is a living nightmare.

When you interpret a situation as challenging, your body's primitive nervous system is hard-wired to automatically begin a chain of reactions in your body. This includes stress hormones being released into the bloodstream, your pupils enlarging, perception of pain diminishing, attention becoming focused, blood moving from the skin and digestive organs into the muscles, breath and heart rate rising, blood pressure increasing, and more sugars being released into your system, providing you with an immediate source of energy.

In this state of body and mind, called the *fight–flight–freeze response*, you see almost everything as a potential threat. You're in an attack mode and see things from a survival, short-term point of view, instead of seeing the long-term impact of your words and actions. You fight the situation, run away or simple freeze, unable to take action.

Imagine that your boss tells you how poor your last presentation was, and that you're not working hard enough. If you *interpret* this as a personal attack, your blood pressure rises, your pupils dilate, you sweat and feel anxious. Your body behaves as if you're about to be attacked by a life-threatening bear, and you're ready to fight, flee, or freeze. However, if you interpret the situation as 'the boss is in a bad mood' or 'she says the same to everyone – it's no big deal', you're less likely to trigger so great a stress reaction. The interpretation is far more important than the 'reality' of the situation, from a stress point of view.

Research shows that everyone has an optimum level of stress. Think of stress levels like the pressure of a pencil on a piece of paper. If you push too hard (high levels of stress), you tear the paper or snap the pencil. If you press too lightly (too little stress), nothing you draw can be seen, which is dissatisfying. The optimum balance is between the two. Then a beautiful drawing can emerge. Too little stress leads to a lack of motivation, and too much leads to over-stimulation and ill health. Mindfulness can help you cope with higher levels of pressure before your stress reaction becomes too highly activated.

Here I break down the forms of stress into the following categories and offer some mindful ways to ease them:

- **Physical stress:** This is when your body is under too much pressure. You may be sitting in one position for long periods, or lifting very heavy weights or exercising your body excessively. Reduce this by simply trying to take more time off and by practising the body scan (Chapter 6) to learn to be kinder to your body.

- **Mental stress:** This arises if you have too much work to do in too short a space of time. Time pressure can cause stress. Thinking too much and worrying are sources of mental stress. Reduce this stress by practising mini meditations regularly (Chapters 7 and 8) and perhaps mindful walking (Chapter 6).

- **Emotional stress:** This is often due to relationship issues. Perhaps you've had a communication breakdown with someone or feel very depressed, anxious, or lonely. Practising compassion meditations (Chapter 6) or forgiveness meditation (Chapter 4) can really help here.

- **Spiritual stress:** Your life lacks a sense of meaning or purpose. You may feel disconnected from other people or nature. The compassion meditations (Chapter 6) and meditating in nature can help. Reading mindfulness books, spending more time with friends or getting some life coaching may help too.

Noticing the early signs of stress

How do you know when you're *beginning* to get stressed about something? What are your early warning signs? Does your eye start twitching, or do you begin to get a headache? Perhaps you lose patience easily, or begin worrying. By becoming more aware of your early reactions to stress, you can begin to take appropriate action before the stress spirals out of control.

When the pressure gets too much for me, my shoulders tense up and I find it harder to smile, I'm less likely to chat to friends, and generally begin to take life far too seriously! I remember being like this the last time I had a really tough deadline to meet and had far too much work to get done in the allocated time.

Regular mindfulness meditation and doing your daily activities with a mindful awareness makes you more aware of your own thoughts, feelings, bodily sensations and behaviour. You're more likely to be aware when stress levels begin to rise, and you can then take appropriate action.

Take a few moments to reflect on the last time you were stressed. Did you notice what was happening to your body? Which parts became tense? Was it your tummy or jaw? How did your behaviour change? Did you call up your drinking buddies or some other particular friend? What sorts of emotions did you feel? Anxiety or sadness? What thoughts were going through your mind? Negative thoughts about yourself or others? Look out for these changes when facing your next challenge. Then you can use mindfulness to reduce your stress to more acceptable levels.

Assessing your stress

You may find that a stress diary is a useful way of assessing your level of stress from day to day. Stress diaries make you more mindful of the areas in your life that cause you stress in the short term, as well as your own reaction to the stress. This knowledge makes you more aware of the onset of stress and your response to it, allowing you to make more helpful choices to lower your stress levels if they're too high, or at least to view your stress in a more useful way.

Designate a notebook as your stress diary, and try the following. Write down:

- ✔ How stressed you feel on a scale of one to ten, with ten being extremely stressed

- ✔ What caused the stress

- ✔ The thoughts going through your mind, your emotions, and bodily sensations like headache or tense shoulders

- ✔ How you're responding to the stress – in other words, your actions

Moving from reacting to responding to stress

When experiencing stress, I call the things that you do automatically, without even thinking about it, stress *reactions*. If you're lucky, some of your reactions may be helpful and therefore dissipate the stress. More often than not though, reactions to stress are unhealthy and lead to further stress. A *response* is more mindful, includes some time for reflection, is aware rather than automatic, and tends to be more helpful.

Your reactions to stress are partly based on what you assimilated in child-hood, are partly genetic, and partly based on your own experiences with stress. If whoever brought you up reacted in a certain way to stress, you have a greater chance of behaving in a similar way. Your own experience of ways of dealing with stress also comes into the equation. Perhaps you've always drunk several cups of coffee when you're feeling stressed, and find the caffeine helps you to get your work done. Although you may feel that this is effective, caffeine is a stimulant, and the more you drink the *more* stressed you'll probably become. Changing these small habits can make a big difference.

Reacting automatically implies a lack of choice. Through practising mindful-ness, you begin to have a greater choice of ways to respond, and can thereby achieve a more satisfactory outcome.

Make a list of the unhelpful and helpful ways in which you deal with stress:

- ✔ Unhelpful reactions may include drinking too much alcohol or caffeine, negative thinking, zoning out, working even harder, or eating too much or too little food.

- ✔ Helpful responses may include going for a walk, exercising, meeting up with friends, meditating, or listening to music.

As you make your list, don't been too hard on yourself. Instead, laugh or at least smile at your shortcomings. Hey, no one's perfect!

Become more aware of the choices you make following a stressful event, and begin choosing small helpful strategies such as going for a walk. Make use of mindfulness skills to help you make wiser choices. Remember to give your-self a nice big pat on the back when you make a positive choice, even if you'd normally think of it as too small or insignificant an event to reward yourself for. Every little helps!

Here's the two-step mindfulness process for responding rather than reacting when you feel your stress levels rising:

1. **Notice your current reactions.** What are your body, mind, and emotions doing? Are they showing the signs of stress? Acknowledge the fact that you're suffering from stress. Observe how you're reacting to the stress. Your *body* may be tense in certain places. Perhaps you're suffering from indigestion or have had a cold for weeks. Your *behaviour* may be differ-ent to usual. You may be snapping with anger for the smallest thing. You may not be making time to meet up with friends. Your *emotions* may be fluctuating. You may feel tired or out of control. Your *thoughts* may be predominantly negative. You may have trouble concentrating. At this stage, you just need to become aware of what's happening, without

judging the situation as bad or wrong – just be aware, without the judgement if you can. By becoming aware of what's happening within you, *the experience is already transforming*. This is because you're *observing* the stress, rather than *being* the stress. As the *observer* of an experience, you're no longer tangled up in the emotions themselves. You can't be what you observe.

2. **Choose a mindful response.** Now, from an awareness of the level of stress you're experiencing and how you're currently coping with that stress, you can make a wise, mindful choice as to the best way to cope. You know yourself better than anyone else does – you need to decide how best to cope with the stress. As you become aware of your own inner reactions, you make space for creative action to arise, rather than the habitual, well-worn paths you've chosen many times before.

   Here are some suggestions for a mindful response to your stress:

   • **Take as many mindful breaths as you have time for.** Even one nice big deep breath has positive physiological benefits, and everyone can do that.

   • **Do a three-minute mini meditation (refer to Chapter 7) or practise a formal mindfulness meditation for a more extended period.**

   • **Go for a walk, perhaps in the park, or do some yoga, tai chi. or stretching exercises.**

   • **Avoid excessive alcohol, caffeine, drugs, and sugary or fatty foods.** And if you do indulge by mistake, see whether you can forgive rather than berate yourself. You're human after all.

   • **Talk to someone or socialise.** Even sending a little text message is better than nothing.

   • **Watch a hilarious comedy. Or just laugh for no reason.** See Chapter 11 on mindful laughter.

   • **Observe the stress rise up in your body and mind and then fall away.** Consider yourself as the witness of stress – whole, complete, and free just as you are. Pretend that the stress is separate from you, which it is in some ways.

   • **Do some vigorous but mindful exercise such as running, swimming, or cycling.**

   • **See stress positively.** Think about how stress energises you, releases oxytocin (a hormone that encourages connection with others) and gets you moving. A recent major study found that if you can shift your mindset about stress, the stress goes from being destructive to healthy. Seeing stress in a positive way was even shown to increase people's life expectancy by many years!

Washing away stress with RAIN

Mindfulness groups sometimes take an approach with the acronym RAIN for a mindful way of dealing with emotions. Just as rain falls equally on everyone and provides for your body, so can RAIN help to transform your inner world. Follow these four steps next time you find yourself getting too stressed, anxious, angry or any other overwhelming experience for you.

✒ **R**ecognise that a strong emotion is present.

Often, you can easily be swept up by the emotion itself, and immediately begin acting on it. Emotions can be such an integrated part of who you are that you don't give the feeling due credit. Begin with recognition of the emotion.

✒ **A**ccept that the emotion is there.

With strong emotions, sometimes the natural reaction is to pretend that the feeling isn't really present. In this step, you accept that at this precise moment, you're experiencing anger. You can even say to yourself, 'I'm experiencing a strong feeling at the moment.' You aren't being passive and giving in to the feeling. If you don't accept what's here now, you can't hope to manage the emotion in any way.

✒ **I**nvestigate thoughts, feelings, and bodily sensations.

In this third step, you're not trying to analyse, but instead to observe what's going on in your mind, heart, and body. What thoughts are running through your head? What feelings are you mindful of? What areas of your body feel tense, or burning, or warm, or relaxed? How does your body feel as a whole? Do you have a burning, throbbing, unpleasant sensation, or is the physical expression of the emotion quite pleasant? Where is the core of the emotion located exactly, and what effect does a sustained mindful awareness have on the physical aspect of your experience? Simply observe the sensations.

✒ **N**on-identification with the passing emotion.

Emotion has the word motion in it. Emotions are always moving, fluxing, and changing. No emotion stays completely fixed forever. This final step is to try to distance yourself and create a space between yourself and your emotion. By you offering a space, the emotion is more likely to do what emotions do quite naturally, which is to keep moving. Remember that you're not your anger. Emotions come and go, but you don't come and go: you're always here. Another way of seeing this is like clouds in the sky. The clouds come and go; some are black, some are white and fluffy. No matter what happens to the clouds, the sky itself remains unaffected. In the same way, emotions come and go, but your awareness, like the sky, is free.

Breathing out your stress

Your breath is a particularly helpful ally in coping with stress. Many relaxation programmes are well aware of the power of the breath in regulating stress, and recommend deep breathing to manage it.

Usually, in mindfulness, you simply need to be aware of your breath and don't have to change your breathing rate. However, here are some different techniques you can use to help relieve stress:

- **Diaphragmatic or belly breathing.** You can do this lying down, sitting up with your back straight, or in whatever position suits you. Take a natural breath and allow your belly to fill up with air. Allow the breath to release as you normally do. Repeat for as long as you feel necessary. Feel each breath coming in and going out of your body. (See Chapter 6 for more about diaphragmatic or belly breathing.)

- **Counting your breaths.** Adopt a comfortable posture and close your eyes if you want to. Feel your breath coming in and out. Each time you breathe out, count. Begin with one, and work your way up to ten. When you reach ten, start again from one. If at any point you lose count, begin again at one. You may find it difficult to get past the number two or three before your mind goes off into worries or dreams – no problem. All that matters is that as soon as you notice that your mind's drifted off, you start again at one, *without criticising yourself if you can.*

- **Breathing and smiling.** Sometimes your joy is the source of your smile. And sometimes your smile is the source of your joy. So if you feel stressed, lift up the corners of your mouth as you feel your breathing. For more on breathing and smiling, see Chapter 11.

- **Deep mindful breathing.** Take a deep breath and allow your belly to fill up with air. Hold your breath for a few seconds and then slowly release the breath. Repeat for as long as you feel comfortable. As you breathe out, allow yourself to let go of all tension and stress as best you can. If you can't, you don't need to worry – just try again later.

- **Mindful breathing with other activities.** Mindful breathing while engaging in day-to-day activities provides a calming and nourishing antidote to stress. If you're doing a simple or repetitive activity, become aware of your breathing as you do it. For example, as you walk, feel your breath and notice how your breathing rate changes. If you're waiting for your computer to start up, or you're in a queue, or hanging up the clothes on the washing line, simply allow some of your awareness to go to the feeling of your breath.

As you practise, you may become great friends with your own breath. You look forward to being with the breath and noticing its calming, rhythmic flow.

Using your mind to manage stress

Stressors don't cause stress on their own. First, you need to interpret the stress as a problem that may have a negative impact on you. Then the stress reaction occurs. This simple but fundamental process can be seen in Figure 12-1 below.

Remembering that you're the observer of your stress rather than the stress itself helps you to become free, and stress becomes less of a problem.

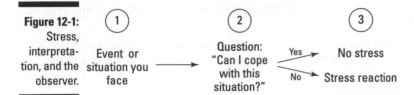

Figure 12-1:
Stress, interpretation, and the observer.

Use the following tips to lower your level of stress by becoming aware of how you interpret challenges:

- **Write down the thoughts that are causing you stress.** For example, if you've just suffered a relationship breakdown, just keep writing whatever comes into your head. Nobody else but you needs to see what you write, so be totally honest. The process of writing helps to slow your mind down, and enables you to tackle the stressful thoughts one at a time. Having written them, remember that thoughts are just thoughts – not necessarily facts. Your stress is caused not so much by the thoughts, but *because you believe them to be true.* Seeing thoughts as just sounds and images that pop in and out of consciousness reduces their impact significantly.

- **See the big picture.** What effect does seeing things from a different angle have on the situation? How would you feel if you were in someone else's shoes? This may be the person who seems to be causing the stress, or someone else – you choose! Or, imagine you're zooming up into the sky, away from your life. See your own town, your region, your country. Keep imagining that you're zooming out of the planet to the solar system and beyond! Is your stress still such a big issue?

- **Consider what's the worst that could happen.** Sometimes you may imagine the situation to be worse than it actually is. By considering the worst, you may realise things aren't that bad.

- **Break down the problem.** If you have a big problem and can't face up to the issues, try splitting the problem into small steps. Then take things one step at a time. For example, if you've lost your job and are short of cash, the first step to getting a new job may be to rewrite your CV (résumé). You can even break that down to phoning a friend to help you write one, or getting a book from your local library on writing CVs.

- **See problems in a different way.** If you see difficulties in life as challenges, your mind may automatically begin to start searching for helpful solutions. If all you see are problems, you're more likely to feel drained and stressed by their weight on your shoulders. See challenges as opportunities to discover new things about yourself and your resilience, rather than problems to be avoided or coped with. Think of this challenge as something that's come into your life to teach you a wiser, kinder way of living.

✔ **Discuss the cause of the stress with someone.** The process of talking about your issue is likely to help you to see aspects you never even thought of. And even if you don't, the very act of talking about the issues you're facing helps to dissipate their potency.

✔ **Let go of perfectionism.** Perfectionism is a common reason for high levels of stress. Understand that being perfect is impossible to achieve. Adjust your standards by lowering them a little. You can try aiming for 80 per cent perfection and see whether that helps. Notice how the imperfection of a tree with its wonky branches and lack of symmetry is also its beauty. In the same way, see the beauty of your imperfections. This is the ancient Japanese philosophy of *wabi-sabi*.

✔ **Appreciate what's going well.** Think of all the things that are going well for you at the moment and write them down. They don't need to be big things – anything you're even slightly grateful for will suffice. Doing so encourages you to feel less stress. You're still breathing? You have a roof over your head? You have a friend? Anything is fine.

Life is the way you see

How often you experience high levels of stress is at least partly, if not completely, dependent on the way you see things. This old Muslim mystical (Sufi) story illustrates the point beautifully.

A young traveller from another country entered a new territory. She saw an old man sitting under a tree and asked the man, 'What are the people like in this country?' The old man looked up and asked, 'How do you find the people in your own country?' The young woman enthusiastically replied, 'Oh, they are kind, hospitable and generous.' 'Well,' replied the old man with a gentle smile, 'you'll find the people of this country to be kind and friendly too.'

A little later on in the afternoon, another traveller was passing through into the country. He too spotted the old man under the tree, and asked, 'Hey, what are the people like in your country?' The old man asked, 'What are they like in your own country?' 'Terrible,' he sighed. 'They're always fighting, often inhospitable and sly.' The old man answered, 'I'm afraid you'll find the people of this country to be the same as in yours.'

The secret to transforming the level of stress you experience is to change the way you see life.

Cooling Down Your Anger

Anger can be healthy if the emotion is controlled and used sparingly. For example, if you're being treated unfairly, you may need to *act* angrily to ensure that you're treated justly and with respect. However, being out of control when you're angry can cause tremendous harm both to yourself and to your relationships with others. Cooling down anger isn't an easy process and requires a clear decision, effort, and support from others. Mindfulness can help, as this section shows.

Understanding anger

Anger is a normal human emotion. If you're mistreated, feeling angry is perfectly natural. The problem is knowing what to do with the emotion that arises if you hurt yourself or others with the anger.

Anger arises when you feel something *should* happen but it *doesn't*, for example if you receive poor customer support for something you've bought, or you see how much crime has gone up in your city and feel angry because the government *should* be taking more action.

I don't really have outbursts of anger. The last time I had to *act* in an angry way was during a visit to India a few years ago. A shoe polisher insisted that she wanted to polish my shoes, so we agreed a price and she polished them. Then she tried to charge me ten times more. I refused. She then wouldn't give my shoes back. So I decided to act as if I was angry to get my shoes back! It worked. I had to raise my voice, and I attracted a little crowd. I then gave the shoe polisher the agreed price, which she promptly threw back at me. I was a bit disappointed with her but felt sorry for her too. She was poor, and perhaps I should have given her more money. But this is a simple example of how acting angry can help you get your shoes back!

Acting angry and *being* angry are different. When you act angry, you don't experience a lack of control or a loss of reason. You can switch straight back to smiling when you need to.

Different situations make different people angry. Like all emotions, anger depends on the *interpretation* of the situation, rather than the situation itself. If someone at a checkout gives you the wrong amount of change and you see this as a mistake, you probably forgive her straight away and think nothing of the oversight. However, if you think that she did this to you on purpose, you're more likely to become annoyed, frustrated or angry. So, it's *your interpretation* that causes the anger, not the situation itself.

Anger in the aisles

A manager at a supermarket overheard an employee who was helping a customer pack her bags with groceries. The customer said, 'Do you know when you'll get some?' The bagger replied, 'No, I don't know. We may not have any all week, or maybe even longer.' The customer said, 'Oh. Okay, thanks. Bye,' and walked off.

The manager glared at the bagger and chased after the customer saying, 'We'll have some in tomorrow. Don't worry, I'll guarantee we'll get it for you.' He then turned back to the bagger and was furious. 'Don't ever, ever say that we don't have something. And if we don't have it, say we'll have it in by tomorrow. That's the policy. You're useless! What did she want anyway?' 'She wanted rain,' replied the bagger.

When you're stressed out, you're more likely to see things the wrong way.

Anger arises from a thought or series of thoughts. Anger doesn't just come up on its own. You may not be aware of the thought causing the anger you feel, but a thought must have arisen for the emotion to surface. For example, if you think 'That cashier is out to rip me off', you feel anger surging through your body almost instantly afterwards.

You experience certain physical sensations when angry, such as tensing your shoulders, tightening your stomach, a headache, clenching your hands or jaw, poor concentration, feeling sweaty, increasing your breathing rate, restlessness, and a fast heart rate.

Coping when the fire rises up

You arrive home and your partner hasn't cooked any food. You were working late, and you begin to feel anger rising up in you. What do you do? You know that logically you're far better off talking calmly about the issue and resolving the conflict rather than spoiling the evening with an argument. Here's how:

1. **Become aware of the physical sensation of anger in your body.** Notice the sensations in your stomach, chest, and face. Become aware of your rapid heart and breathing rate. Observe whether your fists or jaw are clenched. Witness the tension in the rest of your body.

2. **Breathe.** Breathe into the physical sensations of your body. Close your eyes if you want to. You may find counting out ten breaths helpful. Imagine the breath entering your nose into your belly, and as you breathe out, imagine the breath going out of your fingers and toes, if you find this useful.

3. **Continue to stay with the sensations as best you can.** Bring a sense of kindness and gentleness to your feelings of anger. Look at the discomfort in the way you would look at scenery – taking your time and being with the landscape of your inner self. Try to see the anger as an opportunity to understand about the feeling, how the burning rises up in your being, and how the breath may or may not have a cooling effect on the flame within you.

4. **Notice your thoughts.** Thoughts like 'It's not fair' or 'I'm not having this' feed the fire of anger. Notice what effect you have by letting go of these thoughts, for your own health and wellbeing more than anything else. If you can't let go of the thoughts, which is common, just continue to watch the way thoughts and feelings feed into each other, creating and recreating the experience of anger as well as other feelings like guilt, frustration, and sadness. If you have lots of energy pumping through your body, try walking around the room and feeling the contact between your feet and the ground. Alternatively, instead of walking, you can try slow, mindful stretching, feeling the body as you extend your various muscle groups.

5. **Step back.** Take a step back from your internal experiences. Notice that you're the observer of your thoughts and emotions and not the thoughts and emotions themselves. Just as images are projected onto a screen, but the screen itself is unaffected, so thoughts, emotions, and sensations arise in awareness, but you, as awareness, are untouched.

6. **Communicate.** As soon as the main force of your anger has dissipated, you may need to communicate your feelings with the other person. Begin with 'I' statements instead of 'you' accusations. If you blame the other person for your feelings, you're more likely to make her act defensively. If you say 'I felt angry when you didn't cook dinner' rather than 'You made me angry when you didn't cook dinner,' you're taking responsibility for your feelings. As you continue to communicate, stay aware and awake to your own feelings, and let go of any aggression if you can – less aggression and more honesty are more likely to lead to a harmonious and productive conversation and result.

Coping with anger is a challenging task, and nobody can follow these steps perfectly. The idea is to keep these steps in mind and follow them with small levels of frustration rather than outright anger. When you do, you become more adept at cooling the flames of anger.

Some other ways of managing your feelings of anger are to:

✔ **Be mindful of the thought patterns that feed your anger.** These include:

  • **Over-generalising** by using sentences like 'You *always* ignore me' or 'You *never* respect me.' Be specific instead.

- **Mind-reading** by thinking you *know* what the other person is thinking, and often predicting the thoughts as negative, such as 'I know you think I nag you too much.' Try to avoid making assumptions like this.

- **Blaming** others for your own anger with thoughts like 'You always make me angry' or 'It's all their fault.' Instead, take responsibility for your anger.

✔ **Take mindful physical exercise.** By exercising regularly, you build up a greater resilience to stress, and this may dissipate some of your anger. By exercising mindfully (see Chapter 7), paying attention to all the physical sensations as you perform an exercise, you simultaneously build up your mindfulness muscles too, leading to greater levels of awareness and less reactive, automatic-pilot behaviour.

✔ **Connect with your senses.** Listen to the sounds around you or listen mindfully to some music. Smell some of your favourite calming scents. Eat a snack as slowly as you can, chewing and tasting with as much awareness you can muster. Have a shower or bath and connect with the sensations on your skin. Look out of your window and enjoy the sky, clouds, trees, or rain.

✔ **Question your reaction.** Ask yourself questions like: 'Is this worth it?' 'Is this important in the big picture?' 'How else can I respond in this situation?' 'What is a more helpful thing to do now?'

Figure 12-2 shows how you can use mindfulness to dissipate the anger cycle.

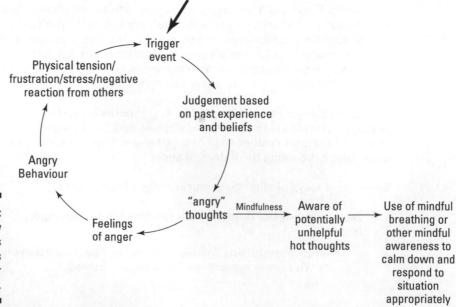

Figure 12-2:
Seeing how mindfulness dissipates the anger cycle.

Dealing with the roots of anger

If you have a short fuse, you may wonder why you get angry so easily. For many people, the reason is a difficult upbringing. If those who cared for you were often angry, being angry is the only way in which you understood how to react to situations. If your parents or carer treated you badly, you're bound to have feelings of anger trapped inside. Highly stressful and traumatic events can also lead to anger.

If you easily react with anger, you may be using the anger to cover up other, deeper feelings. The anger acts as a protection, to prevent you from becoming aware of more subtle feelings of fear, shame, guilt or embarrassment.

By becoming mindful of the feelings behind your anger, you can begin to unlock the emotional chains that may be controlling you. One way of doing this is by feeling the emotion as you notice it arising, and being aware when it manifests itself in your body. By feeling this with openness and kindness rather than criticising yourself, you begin the healing process within yourself.

Coping with your anger as the emotion arises is a bit like fire-fighting. Dealing with the cause of the anger when you're not in the midst of the emotion is like fitting a smoke alarm and acting before things become out of hand.

Powerful ways of dealing with the roots of anger include meditation and forgiveness meditation. Loving kindness meditation, or metta meditation, can also be very effective (covered in Chapter 6).

For an entire book's worth of tips and strategies on coping with anger, see *Anger Management For Dummies* by Gillian Bloxham and W Doyle Gentry (Wiley).

Reducing Fatigue

If you're full of energy, getting your daily tasks done is a doddle – you may come home from work brimming with energy, able to cook, clean, go out with your friends, socialise, and generally have a good time. If you're lacking in the energy department, everything becomes a drag – right from getting out of bed in the morning, to getting back into bed at the end of the day. You can find some helpful tips to reduce your fatigue in this section.

Assessing your energy levels

Begin by assessing your energy levels in a typical week or month. You can do this by simply making a note in your diary or journal. You'll find several benefits of doing this:

- You discover how your energy levels change from one day to the next.
- You see at what times of the day you have the most energy available to tackle your more challenging tasks.

■ ✔ You may begin to see patterns: certain foods or certain physical activities may be boosting or draining your energy levels.

Practise some mindfulness meditation on a daily basis, just to see what effect the exercise has on your energy levels. Mindfulness isn't a short-term fix but a long-term way of meeting life in a healthy way; any improvements in energy may take some time but be long lasting, so persevere with your practice.

Discovering energy drainers

Some activities are similar to energy leeches – they suck energy out of your system. By discovering and mindfully reflecting on what takes energy out of you, you can begin to reschedule your lifestyle, or reduce your intake of energy drainers. Energy drainers include:

✔ **Too much stress.** If you allow yourself to become overly stressed out and don't take steps to manage the stress, you stand to burn lots of your energy. This is because the stress reaction, or fight or flight response, pushes all your energy reserves out of your digestive and immune system and into your muscles. If you keep engaging the stress reaction again and again, your energy reserves gradually become more and more depleted. Use the mindfulness tips earlier in this chapter to help combat stress.

✔ **Too much thinking.** If you take your thoughts too seriously, you give your mind undue attention. This tends to feed the mind and encourages you to think more and more. The brain uses a massive 20 per cent of all your energy – if you give thoughts too much attention, they spiral out of control, zapping your energy. Take a step back from thoughts, and don't let thoughts become your master.

✔ **Too much sugar.** Although sugar may seem to uplift your energy in the short term, your energy levels soon plummet. Reduce your intake of refined sugar and watch out for low-fat foods that contain high levels of sugar to make them taste good. Read *Mindful Eating For Dummies* by Laura Dawn (Wiley) to learn how to be more mindful with food.

✔ **Skipping breakfast.** Lots of research shows the benefits of eating a healthy breakfast. In fact, people who don't eat breakfast not only lack energy but are also more likely to put on weight due to overeating later on in the day.

Finding what uplifts you

You can take control of your energy levels by taking active, healthy steps to raise your liveliness. Keep in mind that you want the kind of energy that's revitalises you rather than the kind that makes you overly excited! Too much of a 'high' eventually results in you crashing out as you burn your energy rapidly. That's okay from time to time when you want to have fun, but not all the time.

Do the following with a mindful, gentle awareness:

- ✔ **Engage in mindful physical exercise.** Rather than draining your energy, regular exercise actually gives you a boost. This may be due to the release into your brain of a chemical called serotonin that helps you feel better and less frustrated or stressed. Health organisations recommend 30 minutes of vigorous physical exercise on a daily basis, which can include a brisk walk to the shops and back. Anything that gets your heart beating, your breathing rate up, and makes you a bit sweaty and out of breath is classified as a vigorous exercise. Read Chapter 7 for more about mindful physical exercise.

- ✔ **Enjoy mindful, regular meals.** Eating smaller portions on a regular basis rather than having a few big meals is healthier and helps to maintain your energy levels. Wholegrain rye bread, porridge, pasta, beans, lentils and noodles all contain energy that is released slowly into your body, helping to sustain you throughout the day. Eat mindfully too, by looking at your food, tasting as you eat, eating one mouthful at a time and not doing anything else when eating.

- ✔ **Drink plenty of water.** Aim to drink six to eight glasses of water a day, and more if you're exercising. Become more aware of your feeling of thirst, or better still, drink before the feeling arises in case you're already dehydrated. As you drink, remember how lucky you are to have water available to you, and feel the water in your mouth and how it has a cooling effect as it goes down into your stomach.

- ✔ **Find your joy.** Make time for activities that you enjoy. You may simply be working too hard. If you can't change that, see what small things you can do to make your work more fun. Spend time with friends and family that are 'mindful' – whatever that means for you. Try smiling more and do mindful laughter exercises (see Chapter 11). Tell someone a joke. Move towards laughter. Act in a silly or childlike way from time to time. Try and see the funny side of life if you can.

- ✔ **Meditate.** Both informal mindfulness and a formal meditation on a daily basis help to increase your energy levels. This is because mindful awareness helps ultimately to lower the stress you experience. As you continue to practise on a daily basis, your tendency to become stressed in the first place diminishes and therefore your energy levels increase to a healthy level. As your ability to be calm and focused increases, your energy becomes calm and focused too.

Using meditations to rise and sparkle

Here's an energising meditation, which is available as an audio track (Track 20), that you can practise whenever you want to focus on increasing your energy levels:

1. **Sit or lie down in a suitable posture for yourself in this moment.** You may choose to sit up straight in a chair, or lie down on your bed.

2. **Adjust your intention of this meditation to simply be with whatever arises without trying to push things away or grab hold of experiences.** Let your attitude be one of curiosity and kindness.

3. **Feel the gentle rhythmic sensations of your own breathing.** Feel the sensations of the breath from moment to moment, non-judgementally. Just allow the breathing to happen by itself. As you breathe in, imagine you're breathing in nourishing, fresh, energising oxygen into your body. Get a sense of this nutritious oxygen permeating your whole body, feeding each cell generously. As you breathe out, imagine any toxins being released out of your system. Breathe out anything that's troubling you, and let go of unhelpful thoughts, emotions, ideas, or sensations.

4. **With each breath you take, feel more energised and uplifted.** Essentially you're a container of energy, interchanging with the energy all around. Get a sense of this as you continue to breathe. Feel the exchange of energy with your surroundings – both a give and take process; a cycle.

5. **Now come back to a sense of awareness of the breath: breathing itself.** Enjoy the in-breaths and out-breaths with a spirit of acceptance, caring, and empathy.

6. **As you come towards the end of this meditation, notice your transition into a normal, wakeful state.** Continue to be mindful of this exchange of energy taking place with your surroundings as you go about your daily activities.

A couple of other helpful meditations to provide an energy boost are:

✔ **Body scan.** You can do this practice no matter how tired you feel. You simply need to listen to the *Mindfulness For Dummies* Track 9 while lying down on the floor, a mat, or a bed. Even if you're unable to concentrate for much of the time, something will shift. You may drop a stressful idea, you may drift into a restful sleep, or you may feel immediately energised by the end of the practice. (See Chapter 6 for a full description of the body scan.)

✔ **Three-minute breathing space.** This meditation (Track 17) is ideal if you don't have much time available. If you can find the time and discipline to practise this exercise several times a day, you'll begin to become aware of the kinds of thoughts and emotions running through your system, sapping your vital energy. (Refer to Chapter 7 for a description of the breathing space.)

Chapter 13

Using Mindfulness to Combat Anxiety, Depression and Addiction

In This Chapter

▶ Finding out about depression and anxiety

▶ Discovering ways in which mindfulness reduces depression and anxiety

▶ Exploring specific techniques

"You are not your illness."

Depression, anxiety and addiction present serious challenges in our society. According to the World Health Organization, depression is the planet's leading cause of disability, affecting 121 million people worldwide. About one in six people suffer from clinical depression at some point in their lives. About one in fifty people experience *generalised anxiety* at some point in their lives – feeling anxious all day.

Medical evidence suggests that mindfulness is very powerful in helping people with recurrent depression, and studies with anxiety and addiction look extremely promising too. If you suffer from any of these conditions, following the mindfulness advice in this chapter can really help you.

If you think that you suffer from a medical condition, please ensure that you visit your doctor before following any advice here. If you currently suffer from depression as diagnosed by a health professional, wait until the worst of the illness is over and you're in a stronger position to digest and practise the mindfulness exercises in this chapter. Often mindfulness can work well together with other therapy or medication – again check with your doctor before you begin, so he can best advise and support you.

Dealing Mindfully with Depression

Of all mental health conditions, recurring depression has most clearly been shown to respond to mindfulness. If the body of evidence continues to grow, mindfulness may go on to become the standard treatment for managing depression all over the world. This section explains what depression is and why mindfulness seems to be so effective for those who have suffered from several bouts of depression.

Understanding depression

Depression is different to sadness.

Sadness is a natural and healthy emotion that everyone experiences from time to time. If something doesn't go the way you expect, you may feel sad. The low mood may linger for a time and affect your thoughts, words and actions, but not to a huge extent.

Depression is very different. When you're depressed, you just can't seem to feel better, no matter what you try.

Unfortunately, some people still believe that depression isn't a real illness. Depression *is* a real illness with very *real symptoms*.

According to the NHS, if you have an ongoing low mood for most of the day every day for two weeks, you're experiencing depression and you need to visit your doctor. The symptoms of depression can include:

- A low, depressed mood
- Feelings of guilt or low self-worth
- Disturbed sleep
- A loss of interest or pleasure
- Poor concentration
- Changes to your appetite
- Low energy

Understanding why depression recurs

Depression has a good chance of being a recurring condition, and to understand why, you need to understand the two key factors that cause mild feelings of sadness to turn into depression:

- **Constant negative thinking (rumination).** This is the constant, repetitive use of self-critical, negative thinking to try to change an emotional state. You have an idea of how things are (you're feeling sad) and how you want things to be (feeling happy, relaxed or peaceful). You keep thinking about your goal and how far you are from your desired state. The more you think about this gap, the more negative your situation seems and the further you move away from your desired emotion. Unfortunately, thinking in this way – trying to fix the problem of an emotion – only worsens the problem and leads to a sense of failure as depression sets in. Rumination doesn't work, the reason being that emotions are part of being human. To try to fix or change emotions by simply thinking about what you want doesn't work. Rumination is a hallmark of the *doing mode* of mind, explained in Chapter 5.

- **Intensely avoiding negative thoughts, emotions and sensations (experiential avoidance).** This is the desire to avoid unpleasant sensations. But the process of experiential avoidance feeds the emotional flame rather than reducing or diminishing the emotion. Running away from your emotions makes them stronger.

When you first suffer from depression, you experience negative thoughts, a negative mood and sluggishness. When this occurs, you create a connection between these thoughts, feelings and bodily sensations. Even when you feel better, the underlying connections are still there, lying dormant. Then, when by chance you feel a little sad, as everyone does, you begin to think, 'Here we go again. Why is this happening to me? I've failed,' and so on. The negative thoughts recur. This triggers the negative moods and low levels of energy in the body, which creates more negative thinking. The more you try to avoid your negative thoughts, emotions and sensations, the more powerful they become. This is called the downward mood spiral, as shown in Figure 13-1.

Using mindfulness to change your relationship to low mood

One of the key ways in which depressive relapse occurs and is sustained is through actively trying to avoid a negative mood. Mindfulness invites you to take a different attitude towards your emotion. Depression is unpleasant, but you see what happens if you approach the sensation with kindness, curiosity, compassion and acceptance. This method is likely to be radically different to your usual way of meeting a challenging emotion. Here are some ways of changing your relationship with your mood and thereby transforming the mood itself.

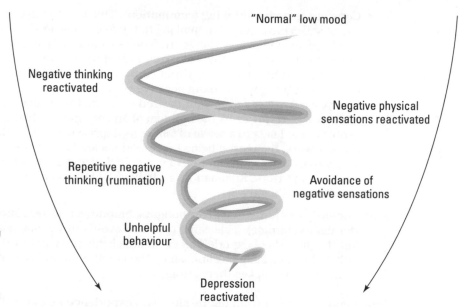

"Normal" low mood

Negative thinking
reactivated

Negative physical
sensations reactivated

Repetitive negative
thinking (rumination)

Avoidance of
negative sensations

Unhelpful
behaviour

Depression
reactivated

Figure 13-1:
Downward
mood spiral.

When you experience a low mood, try one of these exercises as an experiment and see what happens:

- **Identify where in your body you feel the emotion.** Is your stomach or chest tight, for example? What happens if you approach that bodily sensation, whatever the sensation is, with kindness and curiosity? Can you go right into the centre of the bodily sensation and imagine the breath going into and out of the sensation? What effect does that have? If you feel too uncomfortable doing that, how close can you get to the unpleasant feeling in your body? Try playing with the edge of where you're able to maintain your attention in your body, neither pushing too hard nor retreating away. Try saying to yourself: 'It's okay, whatever I feel, it's okay, let me feel it.'

- **See yourself as separate from the mood, thought or feeling.** You're the observer of the sensation, not the sensation itself. Try stepping back and looking at the sensation. When you watch a film, you have a space between yourself and the screen. When you watch the clouds going by, a space separates you from the clouds. A space also exists between you and your emotions. Notice what effect this has, if any.

✔ **Notice the kinds of thoughts you're thinking.** Are they self-critical, negative thoughts, predicting the worst, jumping to conclusions? Are the thoughts repeating themselves again and again? Bring a sense of curiosity to the patterns of thought in your mind.

✔ **Notice your tendency to want to get rid of the emotion.** See if you can move from this avoidance strategy towards a more accepting strategy, and observe what effect this has. See whether you can increase your acceptance of your feelings by 1 per cent – just a tiny amount. Accept that this is your experience now, but won't be forever, so that you can temporarily let go of the struggle, even slightly, and see what happens.

✔ **Try doing a three-minute breathing space as described in Chapter 7.** What effect does this have? Following the breathing space, make a wise choice as to what is the most helpful thing for you to do at the present moment to look after yourself.

✔ **Recognise that recurring ruminative thinking and having a low mood are a part of your experience and *not part of your core being.*** An emotion arises in your consciousness and at some point diminishes again. Adopting a de-centred, detached perspective means you recognise that your low mood *isn't* a central aspect of your self – of who you are.

Understanding avoidance and approach modes

The more you try to avoid an emotion, the greater the emotion grasps hold of you and strengthens. However, by approaching the emotion, you begin to open up the possibility of releasing yourself from its hold. By approaching the sensations with a sense of kindliness, compassion and gentleness, you create the possibility of allowing and accepting your present-moment experience as it is. You let go of the possibility of a downward mood spiral created by an avoidance mode of mind.

Professor Richard Davidson, top neuroscience professor at the University of Wisconsin-Madison and friend of the Dalai Lama, has shown that the avoidance mode of mind is associated with activation of the right prefrontal cortex part of the brain (commonly seen in those in depression), and the approach mode of mind is associated with greater activation in the left prefrontal cortex part of the brain (commonly seen in more positive people). He's also shown that mindfulness helps to move people's brain activation from right to left, in other words from avoidance mode to approach mode. This creates a healthier, more open, detached stance towards emotions, thereby allowing them to operate in a more natural way. In a nutshell, mindfulness can train your brain to become healthier!

Discovering Mindfulness-Based Cognitive Therapy (MBCT)

Mindfulness-based cognitive therapy (MBCT) is an eight-week group programme based on the mindfulness-based stress reduction (MBSR) course described in Chapter 9. The MBSR course has been found to be very helpful for people with a range of physical and psychological problems. MBCT was specifically adapted for those who've suffered repeated episodes of depression. Research so far has proven that MBCT is 50 per cent more effective than the usual treatment for those suffering from three or more episodes of depression.

MBCT is a branch of a more general form of therapy called cognitive behavioural therapy (CBT), which holds that thoughts, feelings and actions are intimately connected. The way you think affects the way you feel and the activities you engage in. Conversely, the way you feel or the activities you undertake affect the way you think, as shown in Figure 13-2.

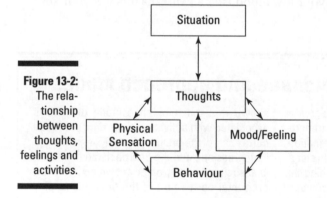

Figure 13-2: The relationship between thoughts, feelings and activities.

Traditional CBT encourages you to challenge unrealistic negative thoughts about yourself, others or the world. (Discover more in *Cognitive Behavioural Therapy For Dummies* by Rhena Branch and Rob Willson (Wiley).) Mindfulness-based cognitive therapy takes a slightly different approach. Rather than deliberately considering alternative thoughts, you move towards your unpleasant thoughts, emotions and physical sensations in a more de-centred, kind, curious and compassionate way – in other words, mindfully. The emphasis isn't on changing the experience but on being with the experience in a different way. You develop the ability to do this through mindfulness meditation.

Seeing the scientific basis of mindfulness

A recent survey in the USA found that more than 40 per cent of mental health professionals do some form of mindfulness therapy to encourage healing in both the body and mind. In group clinical settings, mindfulness is applied mainly through two programmes:

✔ Mindfulness-based stress reduction (MBSR): An eight-week training in mindfulness meditation for reducing stress in those with a wide range of medical conditions.

✔ Mindfulness-based cognitive therapy (MBCT): Based on the eight-week MBSR course, with added elements of cognitive behavioural therapy, developed to address the problem of relapse in clinical depression, and now being tested and used for a wide variety of ailments.

Dr Jon Kabat-Zinn and colleagues developed MBSR in a hospital setting at the University of Massachusetts Medical School in 1979.

The scientific evidence proving the medical benefits of mindfulness is impressive.

Here's a small sample of the research on mindfulness so far:

✔ More than 200 patients with chronic pain were referred for mindfulness treatment, and large overall improvements in physical and psychological wellbeing following MBSR were observed for the majority.

✔ A study on the use of MBSR for patients with anxiety disorders showed significant reductions in anxiety and depression scores for more than 90 per cent of the patients.

✔ In an experiment, some patients with psoriasis were given a guided mindfulness meditation to listen to while in a light box. Those patients healed four times faster than the patients without the mindfulness audio in the light box. This shows that mindfulness itself seems to accelerate the healing effect.

✔ Several trials have shown that MBCT is effective in preventing relapse in depression, showing that in patients with three or more previous episodes of depression, MBCT reduced the recurrence rate by 55 per cent.

Chapter 9 explores MBSR.

If you want to do the MBCT course on your own using this book, you can follow the eight-week MBSR course described in Chapter 9, and in addition do the activities in this chapter. This isn't the same as doing a course with a group and a professional teacher, but gives you an idea of what to expect and certainly may help you.

Pleasant and Unpleasant Experiences

In everyday life, you experience a whole range of different experiences. They can all be grouped into pleasant, unpleasant and neutral experiences. Pleasant experiences are the ones you enjoy, like listening to the birds singing or watching your favourite television programme. Unpleasant experiences may include having to sit in a traffic jam or dealing with a difficult customer at work. Neutral experiences are the ones you just don't even notice, like the different object in the room you're in at the moment, or the taste of the tea or coffee you're drinking. Mindfulness encourages you to become curious about all aspects of these experiences.

You can probe your experiences through the following exercise, which is normally done over two weeks:

Take a sheet of paper, or use your journal, and create four columns. Label them 'experience', 'thoughts', 'feelings', 'bodily sensations'. Under each column heading, write down one experience each day that you found to be pleasant. Write down the thoughts that were going through your head, the feelings you experienced at the time, and how your body felt under the appropriate columns. Continue this each day for a whole week.

The following week, repeat the exercises, but this time for an unpleasant experience each day. Remember, you don't need to have very pleasant or unpleasant experiences – even a small, seemingly insignificant experience will suffice.

The purpose of this exercise is to:

✔ Help you to see that experiences aren't one big blob. You can break down experiences into thoughts, feelings and bodily sensations. This makes difficult experiences more manageable rather than overwhelming.

✔ Notice your automatic, habitual patterns, which operate without you even knowing about them normally. You learn how you habitually grasp onto pleasant experiences with a desire for them to continue, and how you push away unpleasant experiences, called experiential avoidance, which can end up perpetuating them.

✔ Learn to become more curious about experiences instead of just judging experiences as good or bad, or ones you like or dislike.

✔ Encourage you to understand and acknowledge your unpleasant experiences rather than just avoid them.

Interpreting thoughts and feelings

You can do this visualisation exercise sitting or lying in a comfortable position:

1. Imagine you're walking on one side of a familiar road. On the other side of the road you see a friend. You call out his name and wave, but he doesn't respond. Your friend just keeps on walking into the distance.

2. Write down your answers to the following questions:

- What did you feel in this exercise?

- What thoughts did you have?

- What physical sensations did you experience in your body?

If you think, 'Oh, he's ignored me. I don't have any friends,' you're more likely to feel down, and perhaps your body may slump. If you think, 'He couldn't hear me. Oh well, I'll catch up with him later,' you're unlikely to feel affected by the situation. The main purpose of the exercise is to show that your *interpretation* of a situation generates a particular feeling, rather than the situation itself.

Almost all people have a different response to this exercise, because they have a different *interpretation* of the imagined event. If you're already in a low mood, you're more likely to interpret the situation negatively. Remember: *thoughts are interpretations of reality, influenced by your current mood.* Don't consider your thoughts to be facts, especially if you're in a low mood. *Thoughts are just thoughts, not facts.*

Combating automatic thoughts

Mindfulness encourages you to recognise and deal with negative automatic thoughts that can prolong depression or cause it to worsen.

Consider the following statements (adapted from Kendall and Hollon's 'Automatic Thoughts Questionnaire', Cognitive Therapy and Research, 1980):

✔ I feel as if I'm up against the world.

✔ I'm no good.

✔ I'll never succeed.

✔ No one understands me.

✔ I've let people down.

✔ I don't think that I can go on.

✔ I wish I were a better person.

✔ I'm so weak.

✔ My life's not going the way I want it to.

✔ I'm so disappointed in myself.

- ✔ Nothing feels good anymore.
- ✔ I can't stand this anymore.
- ✔ I can't get started.
- ✔ Something's really wrong with me.
- ✔ I wish I were somewhere else.
- ✔ I can't get things together.
- ✔ I hate myself.
- ✔ I'm worthless.
- ✔ I wish I could just disappear.
- ✔ I'm a loser.
- ✔ My life is a mess.
- ✔ I'm a failure.
- ✔ I'll never make it.
- ✔ I feel so helpless.
- ✔ My future is bleak.
- ✔ It's just not worth it.
- ✔ I can't finish anything.

How much would you believe these thoughts right now if any one of them popped into your head? How much would you believe them if any one of them popped into your head when you were in your lowest mood? *These thoughts are attributes of the illness called depression, and aren't to do with your true self.*

By considering depression in a detached way, you become more detached from the illness. You see depression as a human condition rather than something that affects you personally and almost no one else. You see depression as a condition that's treatable through taking appropriate steps.

Alternative viewpoints

Alternative viewpoints are the different ways in which you can interpret a particular situation or experience.

This exercise from MBCT shows how feelings affect thoughts, and thoughts affect feelings. The exercise is similar to the 'Interpreting thoughts and feelings' exercise earlier in the chapter, but focuses more on how you interpret situations depending on how you're already feeling.

Consider the following scenario: You've just been *criticised* by your boss for your work, and you feel low. You walk past one of your colleagues and are about to say something to him, and he says he's really busy and can't stop. Write down your thoughts and feelings.

Now consider a different scenario: Your boss has just *praised* you for doing an excellent job. You walk past one of your colleagues and are about to say something to him, and he says he's really busy and can't stop. Write down your thoughts and feelings.

You probably found very different thoughts and feelings in the two different circumstances. By understanding that your thoughts and feelings are influenced by your interpretation of a situation, you're less likely to react negatively. Mindfulness allows you to become more aware of your thoughts and feelings from moment to moment, and offers you the choice to respond to a situation in a different way, knowing that your thoughts are just thoughts, or interpretations, rather than facts.

De-centring from difficult thoughts

Practise the three-minute breathing space meditation (explained in Chapter 7) and then ask yourself some or all the following questions. Doing so helps you to de-centre or step back from your more difficult thoughts and helps you to become more aware of your own patterns of mind. The questions are:

- Am I confusing a thought with a fact?
- Am I thinking in black and white terms?
- Am I jumping to conclusions?
- Am I focusing on the negative and ignoring the positive?
- Am I being perfectionist?
- Am I guessing what other people are thinking?
- Am I predicting the worst?
- Am I judging myself or others overly harshly?
- What are the advantages and disadvantages of thinking in this way?
- Am I taking things too personally?

Listing your activities

Make a list of all the typical activities you do in a day, such as preparing food, getting dressed, travelling to work, interacting with others, hobbies, sports, evening classes and so on. Then label each activity as nourishing or depleting.

Nourishing activities make you feel uplifted and enthusiastic, giving you energy and joy. Depleting activities drain your energy, making you feel low in vitality and dull in attention. Consider what you can do to increase the number of nourishing activities and decrease the number of depleting activities in your daily routine.

Now list activities that give you a sense of mastery or pleasure. Activities that offer a sense of mastery are those that are quite challenging for you, such as tidying up a cupboard, making a phone call you've been avoiding, or forcing yourself to get out of the house to meet a friend or relative. Activities that offer pleasure may include having a hot bath, watching a film or going for a gentle stroll.

When you feel stressed or low in mood, choose a 'mastery' or 'pleasure' activity. Prior to making your choice, carry out the three-minute breathing space meditation to help bring mindfulness to the experience.

Making wise choices

When experiencing a low mood, a depressing thought, a painful sensation or a stressful situation, practise the three-minute breathing space and choose what to do next, which may be:

- ✔ **Mindful action.** Go back to doing what you were doing before, but in this wider, more spacious, being mode of mind (Chapter 5 explains a being mode of mind). Do each action mindfully, perhaps breaking the activity into small, bite-size chunks. The shift may be very small and subtle in your mind, but following the breathing space, you'll probably feel different.

- ✔ **Being mindful of your body.** Emotions manifest in your physical body, perhaps in the form of tightness in your jaw or shoulders. Mindfulness of body invites you to go to the tension and feel the sensations with an open, friendly, warm awareness, as best you can. You can breathe into the sensation, or say 'opening, acknowledging, embracing' as you feel the uncomfortable area. You're not trying to get rid of the sensations, but discovering how to be okay with them when the sensations are difficult or unpleasant.

- ✔ **Being mindful of your thoughts.** If thoughts are still predominant following the breathing space, focus your mindful awareness onto what you're thinking. Try to step back, seeing thoughts as mental events rather than facts. Try writing down the thoughts, which helps to slow them down and offers you the chance to have a clear look at them. Reflect on the questions listed in the section 'De-centring from difficult thoughts'. Bring a sense of curiosity and gentleness to the process if you can. In this way, you're trying to create a different relationship to your thoughts, other than accepting them as 100 per cent reality no matter what pops up in your head.

✔ **A pleasant activity.** Do something pleasant like reading a novel or listening to your favourite music. While engaging in this activity, primarily engage your attention on the activity itself. Check in to notice how you're feeling emotionally and how your body feels, and be mindful of your thoughts from time to time. Try not to do the activity to force any change in mood, but instead do your best to acknowledge whatever you're experiencing.

✔ **A mastery activity.** Choose to do something that gives you a sense of mastery, no matter how small, such as washing the car, going for a swim or baking a cake. Again, give the activity itself your full attention. Notice whether you're trying to push your feelings out, going back to habitual doing mode (Chapter 5), and instead allow yourself to accept your feelings and sensations as best you can, which is being mode (Chapter 5). Bring a genuine sense of curiosity to your experience as you go about your activity.

Using a depression warning system

Writing out a depression warning system is a good way of nipping depression in the bud rather than letting it spiral downwards. Write down:

1. **The warning signs** you need to look out for when depression may be arising in you, such as negative thinking, oversleeping or avoiding meeting friends. You may want to ask someone close to you to help you do this.

2. **An action plan** of the kind of things you can do that are helpful, such as meditation, yoga, walking or watching a comedy, and make a note of the kind of things that would be unhelpful, too, that you need to try to avoid if you can (perhaps changing eating habits, negative self-talk or working late).

Calming Anxiety: Let It Be

Anxiety is a natural human emotion characterised by feelings of tension, worried thoughts, and physical changes like increased blood pressure. You feel anxious when you think that you're being threatened. Fear is part of your survival mechanism – without feeling any fear at all, you're likely to take big risks with no concern about dangerous consequences. Without fear, walking right on the edge of a cliff would feel no different to walking in the park – not a safe position to be in!

Anxiety and panic can be due to a combination of factors, including your genes, the life experiences you've had, the current situation you're in, and whether you're under the influence of drugs, including caffeine.

This section looks at how mindfulness can help with managing your anxiety and fear, whether the feelings appear from time to time or whether you have a clinical condition such as generalised anxiety disorder (GAD), where you feel anxious all the time.

Feel the fear . . . and make friends with it

Eliminating fearful thoughts isn't easy. The thoughts are sticky, and the more you try and push them out, the stronger the worries and anxieties seem to cling on. In this way, you can easily get into a negative cycle in which the harder you try to block out the negatives, the stronger they come back.

Mindfulness encourages you to face up to all your experiences, including the unpleasant ones. In this way, rather than avoiding anxious thoughts and feelings, which just makes them stronger and causes them to control your life, you begin to slowly but surely open up to them, in a kind and gentle way, preventing them building up out of proportion.

Perhaps this analogy may help. Imagine a room filling up with water. You're outside the room trying to keep the door closed. As more and more water builds up inside the room, you need to push harder and harder to keep the door shut. Eventually you're knocked over, the door flings open and the water comes pouring out. Alternatively, you can try opening the door very slowly at first, instead of pushing the door shut. As you keep opening the door, you give the water a chance to leave the room in a trickle rather than a deluge. Then you can stop struggling to keep the door shut. The water represents your inner anxious thoughts and feelings, and the opening of the door is turning towards the difficult thoughts and feelings with a sense of kindliness, gentleness and care, as best you can.

Using mindfulness to cope with anxiety

If you worry a lot, the reason for this is probably to block yourself from more emotionally distressing topics. For example, you may be worrying whether your son will pass his exams, but actually your worry-type thoughts are blocking out the actual feeling of fear. Although the worry is unpleasant and creates anxiety, the thoughts keep you from feeling deeper emotions. However, until you open up to those deeper emotions, the worry continues.

Worry is an example of experiential avoidance, described earlier in the chapter. Mindfulness trains you to become more open and accepting of your more challenging emotions, with acknowledgement, curiosity and kindness. Mindfulness also allows you to see how you're not your emotions, and that your feelings are transient, and so it helps you to reduce anxiety. Mindfulness encourages you to let go of worries by focusing your attention on the present moment.

Here's a mindful exercise for anxiety:

1. **Get comfortable and sit with a sense of dignity and poise on a chair or sofa.** Ask yourself: 'What am I experiencing now, in the present moment?' Reflect on the thoughts flowing through your mind, emotions arising in your being, and physical sensations in your body. As best you can, open up to the experiences in the here and now for a few minutes.

2. **Place your hand on your belly and feel your belly rising and falling with your breath.** Sustain your attention in this area. If anxious thoughts grasp your attention, acknowledge them but come back to the present moment and, without self-criticism if possible, focus back on the in- and out- breath. Continue for a few minutes.

3. **When you're ready, expand your awareness to get a sense of your whole body breathing, with wide and spacious attention as opposed to the focused attention on the breath alone.** If you like, imagine the contours of your body breathing in and out, which the body does, through the skin. Continue for as long as you want to.

4. **Note your transition from this mindfulness exercise back to your everyday life.** Continue to suffuse your everyday activities with this gentle, welcoming awareness, just to see what effect mindful attention has, if any. If you find the practice supportive, come back to this meditation to find some solace whenever you experience intrusive thoughts or worries.

Mindfulness isn't about trying to get rid of your anxiety, or any other difficult experience. Mindfulness offers the possibility of developing a healthy stance towards your unpleasant experience. The unpleasant experience is here, whether you want it or not. You can try distracting yourself in the short term, but this is tiring and tends not to work in the long term. The invitation of mindfulness is a radical one: to take a courageous, challenging step towards the difficulty, whatever the difficulty is, and see what unfolds. This act of acknowledgement changes your relationship with the anxiety and therefore gives freedom for that emotion to move on, when you're ready.

Welcoming the noisy neighbours

Your anxious thoughts are like the music from a noisy neighbour. Mindfulness isn't so much about trying to force the neighbour to stop, which may or may not work, but about listening to the noise in a different way. When you're listening to your favourite piece of music, you let the sounds come into you, you open yourself fully to the rhythm. In the same way, you need to open up and listen to your thoughts and feel the underlying emotions without trying to fix or change them — just acknowledging them as they are.

Training your mind like this isn't an easy process and takes practice. The 'music' (your anxious thoughts) may or may not change — all you can control is your attitude towards them. Let the attitude be one of curiosity and kindness as far as you can.

Being with anxious feelings

If you want to change anxiety, you need to begin with the right relationship with the anxiety, so you can be with the emotion. Within this safe relationship, you can allow the anxiety to be there, neither suppressing nor reacting to it. Imagine sitting as calmly as you can while a child is having a tantrum. No tantrum lasts forever, and no tantrum stays at exactly the same level. By maintaining a mindful, calm, gentle awareness, eventually and very gradually the anxiety may begin to settle. And even if it doesn't go away, by sitting calmly next to it, your experience isn't quite such a struggle.

You don't need to face anxiety head-on straight away. You can take these steps over a period of days, weeks or months:

1. **Observe how you normally react when anxiety arises; or if you're always anxious, notice your current attitude towards the emotion.**

2. **Consider the possibility of taking a more mindful attitude towards the anxiety.**

3. **Feel the anxiety for about a minute with as much kindness and warmth as you can, breathing into it.**

4. **Notice the colour, shape and texture of the feeling. What part of your body does it manifest in?** Does the intensity of the sensation increase or decrease with your mindful awareness? Explore the area somewhere between retreating away from and diving into the anxiety, and allow yourself to be fascinated by what happens on this edge with your kindly, compassionate awareness.

5. **Watch the feeling as you may look at a beautiful tree or flower, with a sense of warmth and curiosity. Breathe into the various sensations and see the sensations as your teacher.** Welcome the emotion as you may welcome a guest, with open arms.

This isn't a competition to go from Steps 1 to 5 but is a process, a journey you take at your own pace. Step 1 is just as important, significant and deep as Step 5. Remember that these steps are a guide: move into the anxiety, or whatever the emotion is, as you see fit. *Trust in your own innate wisdom to guide your inner journey.*

Overcoming Addiction

An addiction is a seemingly uncontrollable need to abuse a substance like drink or drugs or to carry out an activity like gambling. Addictions interfere with your life at home, work or school, where they cause problems.

If you're suffering from addiction, remember that you're not alone. In the USA, for example, 23 million are addicted to alcohol or other drugs. And over two-thirds of people who suffer from addiction abuse alcohol.

The good news is, help is available. If you've tried and failed at overcoming your addiction, don't give up. There's hope, with all the support out there. Mindfulness is one of many ways to overcome addiction.

Not sure whether you're suffering from addiction? It can be hard to admit if you're addicted to something. But recognising and accepting your addiction is the first step in change. Ask yourself the following questions:

- ✔ Do you use more of the substance or participate in the activity more now than in the past?

- ✔ Do you experience urges or withdrawal symptoms when you don't have the substance or activity?

- ✔ Do you ever lie to others about your use of the substance or your behaviour?

If the answer is yes, consider consulting a health professional for a more accurate evaluation and appropriate advice. A health professional can refer you to all sorts of support – many organisations can help in treating addiction. Cognitive behavioural therapy (CBT) and motivational enhancement therapy (MET) have been found to be very effective treatments.

Mindfulness itself is an ancient practice, going back at least 2,500 years. But, clinically speaking, mindfulness is a new approach for overcoming addiction, and the evidence for the approach is at the very early stages of being gathered, although it's positive so far.

Understanding a mindful approach to addiction

Once you're addicted, your actions are the opposite of mindful: they're automatic. This example describes a process that happens almost unconsciously each time you smoke a cigarette:

1. You're sitting at work on your desk and you feel a bit lethargic and tired.

2. You feel the urge to smoke a cigarette. It's actually a physical sensation in your body, but usually you don't know where the sensation is in your body.

3. You immediately think: 'I need to smoke.' (You don't often consciously register this thought – it just happens in your brain.)

4. You very quickly find yourself standing up and walking out of the building with the packet of cigarettes and a lighter in your hands (usually without awareness – a conscious choice is rarely made).

5. The act of taking a cigarette out, lighting it and drawing in the smoke happens quickly and automatically (you may be lost in other thoughts).

6. The urge is satisfied for now and the lethargy gone. You're rewarded with a feeling of pleasure (dopamine is released in your brain). The cycle repeats again in a few hours.

Mindfulness offers you a way to identify the thoughts and emotions that are driving your addiction, and gives you a *choice* rather than just the automatic compulsion and action of depending on the addictive behaviour.

You discover that just because you have an urge to do something doesn't mean you have to do it. You can just experience the urge until it passes.

Discovering urge surfing: The mindful key to unlocking addiction

One brilliant way of managing the urges that arise in addiction is called *urge surfing*. It's a different way of meeting the reactive behaviour of addiction. Acting on strong cravings, when in an automatic pilot mode, doesn't help you in the long term. By urge surfing, you don't have to act on the urge or craving that you experience.

Addiction and the brain

Most scientists now consider addiction a long-term disease. This is because addiction changes the structure and function of the brain. Just as a piece of clay changes when you squeeze it, so the brain's internal structure changes with addiction.

Changes happen in the brain due to the experience of pleasure and consequent action. When you experience anything pleasurable, the brain releases dopamine. A delicious meal, receiving money or taking a drug all result in a dopamine release. The greater the intensity, speed and reliability of dopamine release, the greater the chance of addiction.

Drugs cause a massive surge of dopamine in your brain. This begins to make changes in the way the memory, motivation and survival system areas of your brain work. This is how just wanting the substance turns into a compulsion. Addiction is much more than just a desire.

The huge surge of dopamine creates the experience of pleasure and overwhelms your brain. Your brain isn't designed to deal with so much dopamine. The ability to experience pleasure diminishes as your pleasure system gets overloaded and, to some extent, damaged. You need more of the substance or activity to get the same experience of pleasure.

At this point, compulsion takes over. Your memory reminds you of the past pleasure you experienced, and you are compelled to recreate that experience by taking more of the substance or further engaging in the behaviour.

This is why addiction is so powerful and how everyday willpower doesn't seem to help.

Listen to the urge surfing meditation (Track 21). The steps when you have an urge are:

1. **Find a comfortable posture.** You can sit, lie down, or even walk slowly – whatever you prefer. See whether you can relax your body a little and let go of any areas of tension. Begin by taking a deep breath and slowly breathing out.

2. **Notice that you have an urge to smoke, drink, gamble or whatever else it is for you.**

3. **Be mindful of your body.** Turn your attention to your physical bodily sensations. Where do you feel this urge in your body? Is it in one particular place or is it all over your body? What's does the urge actually feel like?

4. **Be mindful of your thoughts.** Notice and acknowledge the thoughts that are arising for you right now. Is it a familiar pattern of thoughts? Are they negative or judgemental thoughts? See whether you can step back from those thoughts, as if you're an observer of the experience, rather than getting too caught up in the thoughts, if you can. Watch the thoughts like bubbles floating away.

5. **Be mindful of your feelings.** Notice the feeling of the urge. The feeling may be very uncomfortable. That doesn't make it bad or good – it's just the nature of the feeling. Notice your judgement of 'I like this experience' or 'I don't like this experience'. Remember that the feeling isn't dangerous or threatening in itself.

6. **Allow the experience to be as it is.** See whether you can be with the experience without a need to get rid of it or to react to it by engaging in the behaviour that's not helpful for you. Just practise being with the experience, the urge, the craving, the compulsion, in the present moment.

7. **Notice how the urge is changing.** Perhaps the urge is increasing or decreasing for you. Maybe it's staying just the same.

8. **If the urge is increasing, imagine a wave in the ocean approaching a beach.** The waves rises higher and higher. But once it reaches its peak, it begins to come down again. Imagine your urge is like the wave. It'll continue to grow in intensity but will then naturally go down again. It won't keep growing forever. See whether you can just be present with the urge as it rises and falls. Ride the wave. You may even like to imagine yourself surfing the wave, the urge. Make use of your breathing. Keep 'surfing that urge'. Perhaps see your breath like a surf board that supports you as you surf the wave of your urge.

9. **Notice how you've managed to surf this urge for all this time.** This tool is always available for you, no matter how strong your urge or however intense your emotion or whatever thoughts arise for you.

Try reflecting on what you really want when you're in the midst of your craving. Usually it's not the substance or behaviour you're craving. Maybe you're feeling lonely or stressed? Or maybe you want freedom from circumstances or emotions at this time?

Think of your urge like a tantrum that a child has. If you give the child a sweet, they'll quieten down. But they've learnt to be rewarded for screaming. So before long they'll have another tantrum. So what's the solution? Just to be nice to them, but don't to give them any sweets. Eventually the tantrum will stop. The next time they start screaming, if , again, you just hold them or hug them but don't give them any sweets, the tantrum will end sooner. Eventually they'll stop having tantrums altogether. Being kind to the child without giving them sweets is like being mindful of your urge without satisfying your urge.

Each time you ride out your urge, your craving gets weaker. Each time you satisfy that urge with a smoke or a drink, for example, you strengthen your craving. Every small effort you make counts.

Smoker's hell?

In one fascinating experiment, researcher Sarah Bown from the University of Washington asked a group of smokers to come into a lab. Half were taught the urge-surfing approach and the other half weren't.

Then the whole group sat around a large table and the smokers were asked to take over 20 minutes to light a single cigarette. Each process was slowed down, guided and made mindful: taking the new packet out of the pocket, taking the cellophane off, smelling the new packet, looking at the packet, choosing a cigarette, taking it out of the packet, smelling the cigarette, putting it in the mouth, taking out the lighter, looking at the lighter, lighting the lighter, lighting the cigarette and experiencing smoking the cigarette. That's torture for a smoker!

After the experiment, even though the group weren't asked to reduce the number of cigarettes they smoked, the part of the group that had been taught urge surfing had cut back by 37 per cent. The other group smoked as much as before.

If you want to boost your willpower, try one of the following ideas suggested by Kelly McGonigal, author of a fabulous book called The Willpower Instinct, Avery Publishing Group, 2013:

- ✔ Get enough sleep. Aim for around eight hours if possible.
- ✔ Mediate daily.
- ✔ Exercise. Even a few minutes of walking is a great idea. You don't have to be too intensive. Make it mindful walking to make it even more powerful.
- ✔ Slow down your breathing to four to six full breaths a minute – that can boost your willpower when you need it.

Managing relapse: Discovering the surprising secret for success

As someone once told me: 'I've been a smoker for 20 years. I've given up hundreds of times.'

Most people who want to give up an addiction are able to stop for a short period, but in a moment of difficulty or mindlessness they begin using the object of their addiction again. This is to be expected. Everyone's human and will mistakenly go back to the drug, drink or whatever.

How do you treat yourself when you have a relapse? Most people think that if they're hard on themselves when they accidently relapse, they'll get better. In fact, amazingly, the opposite has been found to be true in research.

Studies have found one of secrets of those that manage to give up long term: self-compassion. For example, people addicted to alcohol were less likely to have a major relapse if they were more forgiving of themselves when they had a drink.

The more kind and forgiving you can be with yourself when you relapse, the more likely it is that the relapse be a one-off. But if you beat yourself up, thinking, 'Oh, I'm such an idiot. I can't even give up drinking. I'll never do it,' the worse you feel. And the worse you feel, the more you feel the need to find some false comfort in your addiction.

This is a powerful approach if you're dealing with an addiction. When you do manage to give up, let's say a drug, for a few days, congratulate yourself each day. And when you end up relapsing on a bad day, tell yourself that you've made a one-off mistake and can go back to being drug-free again. Remind yourself that you've had four days of no drugs and one day having taken the drug. That's four out of five – pretty good!

See whether you can manage a few more days without the substance – see whether you can sit with that urge a bit longer. See whether you can take the time to meditate, perhaps simply feeling your breathing, for a couple more minutes today. Be extra nice to yourself.

Chapter 14

Getting Physical: Healing the Body

• •

• •

Mindfulness for people with serious medical problems was initially adopted in the USA, and now the approach is rapidly being adopted all over the world. Doctors who'd exhausted all traditional medical routes referred patients to a stress-reduction clinic that used mindfulness to help people cope with pain, anxiety and stress.

As the patients engaged in mindfulness, they began to discover a different way of relating to their challenging experiences. They began to feel better, despite their medical problems. The symptoms didn't necessarily disappear, and the aim of mindfulness wasn't to make them go away. The patients found a different way of coping with the illness: from a state of wholeness and wisdom, rather than fear and disharmony.

This chapter explores why mindfulness may be beneficial for those suffering from a chronic health condition, and offers a variety of different ways of beginning that journey. You certainly don't have to be ill to benefit from mindfulness, but thousands suffering from serious medical conditions have found relief through mindfulness.

Contemplating Wholeness: Healing from Within

The word 'heal' is related to the Old English word for whole ('hal'). The word 'health' originally meant wholeness.

Get a sense of what being whole means for you, and as you read this chapter, continue to reflect. Mindfulness is about going to that capacity you have to be aware, whole and free, no matter how broken you feel your body to be. This is a totally different way of seeing what healing truly means, but seems to lead to a peace of mind conducive to feeling better.

Physical disease, or dis-ease, isn't just a problem with the body, but a problem for the mind too. As I explore in this section, your mind and body are inseparable – a whole. When you suffer from a disease, you need to look after both your body and mind to best manage your difficulties. You also need to consider how a sense of being whole can come about whatever happens to your body. Everyone's physical body perishes in the end – how can you live so that this process is dignified rather than full of stress, anxiety and the feeling of being broken?

When you practise mindfulness, you practise an act of love. You're befriending yourself, slowly but surely. You're engaging in an activity for yourself, to look after and nurture your own health and wellbeing.

In mindfulness meditation you may at some point connect with your own deep, innate sense of wholeness. You begin to touch a depth of relaxation, of peace, of calm, that you may not have been aware of beforehand. This encounter with your own wholeness is profoundly healing in the sense of feeling at peace with yourself and with an inner conviction that things are going to be okay, however they work out. Your ill heath, your body, your thoughts, the emotions that arise and pass away, aren't everything. They're a part of the whole. The thought, 'It's all my fault; I'm completely useless,' is just a thought, not a fact. When you begin to touch this inner wholeness, your illness becomes less threatening. You become more optimistic in both the present moment and the future. From your more detached, free and light-hearted stance, your perception of your predicament shifts, and you allow more space for your body to heal as best it can, while taking all the medical treatment as appropriate.

Mindfulness helps you to see things from a bigger perspective. If, due to your disease, you feel low and down, out of control, and that you just can't dig yourself out of the hole that you're in, you probably feel depressed, isolated, lonely and afraid. However, consider the same situation from a bigger perspective: remember that you're suffering in the same way as many others. You can become aware of both the suffering you feel and those aspects of you that are healthy and well. Although you may have a bad back, what about the parts of your body that are functionally well? Mindfulness shifts the fixed patterns of the mind and enables you to see from eyes of wholeness. Then perhaps you can forgive yourself for feeling down – you're human after all.

Seeing the Connection between Mind and Body

Imagine you're scared of spiders. As you walk downstairs before dawn, you can see a shape on the floor in the gloom. 'It's a spider!', you think. Your heart starts pounding and you begin to sweat. You're not sure whether you should even move, in case you disturb the spider. Your thoughts go wild. Then you look again and notice that the shape doesn't look quite right. You switch on the light to discover it's only a mark on the carpet! You feel relieved.

When you saw the mark as a spider, a whole series of changes took place in your body. You experienced the changes because of what you thought and interpreted the mark to be – in other words, because of your mind. When you realised it was just a stain on the carpet, a set of calming reactions took place. The object remained exactly the same. The way you changed your bodily reaction was by bringing curiosity to your experience and then switching on the light. Through awareness and curiosity, you begin to interpret things differently, to see them as they actually are rather than what you *think* they are.

By becoming more skilful in the way you use your mind, you can create the conditions to help rather than hinder the healing process. High levels of stress reduce the strength of your immune system, so any creative ways of reducing stress are bound to have some positive effect.

Here's a very short exercise you can try that clearly demonstrates the link between your mind and body:

1. **Make yourself comfortable sitting or lying down and close your eyes if you want to.**

2. **Imagine you are hungry and are about to eat your favourite food.** You can smell the food and see it on your plate. Take a few minutes to imagine what the food looks and smells like. You take a piece of the food and begin eating. Imagine the taste of the delicious food in your mouth.

3. **Notice any changes happening in your body.** Are you salivating? Do you feel the desire to have this food now? Do you feel certain emotions manifesting themselves in your body? Are some parts of your body becoming tense or relaxed?

This short exercise (or form of torture, with all this talk about food!) again shows how your mind can directly have an effect on your body. All you did in this exercise was use your mind to create images in your head. And yet all sorts of physical changes took place in your body. You may now even go off to cook this food you've been imagining. In the same way, using your mind in the right way can go on to create positive, healing effects in your body.

Appreciating the power of placebos

A *placebo* pill is a non-active substance, usually made of sugar, which has no actual medicine in it. Whenever scientists want to test a new drug, they compare the drug with a placebo. Amazingly, many studies show that patients feel better after taking a placebo rather than the real medicine. How? The answer lies in your belief system. If you believe that a pill is going to help you, the positive belief seems to accelerate the healing process.

Here are some interesting facts about placebos:

✔ Placebos seem to release natural painkillers from your body into the bloodstream, if you *believe* that the pill is a painkiller. This can have the equivalent effect of that of a moderate dose of morphine!

✔ Expensive placebos work better than cheap ones. I love this fact! In one experiment, researchers gave patients a placebo, telling half the patients that the pill cost $2.50, and telling the other half it cost 10 cents. The group that thought they had the more expensive pills experienced less pain when given a mild electric shock in their hands. Ouch!

✔ Placebo surgery is where the patients think they've had surgery, but no actual surgery has taken place. For ethical reasons placebo surgery is rarely carried out. In a study done in 2013, published in the New England Journal of Medicine, 146 patients with a particular form of knee damage were randomly assigned to have either actual surgery or placebo surgery. After 12 months, at no point did the actual surgery group report less pain or better function than the placebo surgery group.

The placebo effect is powerful and proves how the mind can actually affect the healing process.

Acknowledging Your Limits

You have a certain amount of time and energy on this planet. If you didn't have any limits on time, you'd live forever. If you didn't have any limits on your energy, you'd never need to sleep. So, how can you best use the time and energy you do have? If you try to do more and more, you eventually break down. You're better off becoming aware of your limits and acknowledging them, but continuing to push those boundaries every now and then, in a healthy and mindful way.

At one point in my career, I believed that I could do anything and everything. I took on more and more jobs and responsibilities. I was doing more but achieving less. By the end of the day I was exhausted, my energy levels were very low and I was just about finding time to meditate, just to keep going. One day I woke up and thought 'enough is enough' – why sacrifice my health and wellbeing for the sake of yet another promotion and a bit of extra cash?

I began to reduce the responsibilities that I could reduce, and looked for more efficient and creative ways of doing the things I had to do. In this way, I enjoy challenging myself, and testing my limits, but I don't overdo it.

Don't confuse accepting or acknowledging your limits with feeling defeated. If you suffer from a long-term health condition for example, you don't have to give up and curl up in the corner for the rest of your life. Accepting your limits means accepting that your body isn't well and you need to start taking small steps to begin improving your condition, as your doctor advises. You may need support from a group, or from your own friends or family. You also need to remember that you won't magically transform, and that therefore you need to work at accepting your limits slowly but surely.

Accepting limits reminds me of what bees do. When a bee is stuck in a room, it continues to fly into the closed window, thinking that it can go through. If the bee could see that the window is a limit, and it's not possible to get out that way, it wouldn't keep knocking into the window until it died. If you find yourself hitting limits again and again, and getting frustrated, be imaginative and try a different approach – don't keep flying into the window just because the view looks great on the other side. Try a radically different approach.

Rising above Your Illness

To rise above your illness means to separate yourself from your illness rather than to identify yourself with the disease. In this way, you may become less overwhelmed by your condition.

Dana Jennings, who suffered from cancer, wrote in a *New York Times* blog:

> *Being able to laugh in the face of cancer lets you continue to own yourself, as hard as that might be, rather than ceding ownership to the disease. A good laugh reminds you that you are not your cancer.*

You are not your illness. Laughter may be one way of reminding yourself of that fact, and mindfulness is another. Some days are better than others. Some days may be dark, and you may need just to hang on until things lighten up a bit. Remembering that 'I am not my illness' may help.

Recently, when I was practising a mindful meditation, my body felt lighter and lighter, in a pleasant way. I felt completely calm and at ease. Everything was okay with the world. At that point in time, I didn't identify with my body and yet I felt completely at ease and fine with the experience. In fact, I felt as if I was truly myself. Experiences such as this remind me that my body isn't as solid and real as I normally think. I like to think: 'I am not my body but

I am aware of my body. I am the awareness – aware of thoughts, feelings, my body and the world around me.' In this sense of wholeness, you experience a freedom from the chains of thinking 'I'm ill' or 'I'm incomplete,' to achieve the freedom of being, of resting, in the sense of 'I'm alone.' In this context, I mean alone as in 'al-one' or 'all one', the original meaning of the word alone. This is the opposite of feeling lonely and isolated. It's a feeling of being connected to yourself and the world around you.

Don't use mindfulness to try to chase certain pleasant experiences. Whatever you experience in mindfulness practice is okay – the meditation isn't good or bad. The sense of wholeness is your true nature, right here and right now, not just in some exotic mindful experience. Experiences come and go, but awareness is always here, whether you want to be aware or not. Identify with that presence and you're immediately reminded of your own sense of wholeness.

Using Mindfulness to Manage Pain

Acute pain is a sharp pain lasting for a short time, sometimes defined as less than 12 weeks. Medicine is quite good at treating acute pain. *Chronic pain* is pain that lasts for over 12 weeks, and doctors have a much harder time treating such a condition. Many consider chronic pain as one of the most underestimated health-care problems in the world today, having a massive effect on both the patient and being a major burden on the health-care system.

The World Health Organization found that between a half and two-thirds of people with chronic pain struggle to exercise, enjoy normal sleep, perform household chores, attend social activities, drive a car, walk or have sexual relations.

It has repeatedly been found that those who complete an eight-week mindfulness programme find their level of pain reduced. This is surprising, because mindfulness asks you to go into the place that hurts and allow the sensation to be there, rather than to fight with the pain itself. The following sections explain how this may work.

Knowing the difference between pain and suffering

Pain is inevitable. Suffering is optional. Pain is a sensation that you're bound to experience from time to time. In fact, pain is often a very useful sensation – without pain, you'd go around damaging yourself without realising it. If you've ever been anaesthetised in your mouth by your dentist, you know how easy it is to bite the inside of your cheek, even making it bleed, without realising.

Suffering is different. Suffering is something you create yourself, often unknowingly. Say you suffer from arthritis. Each morning, when you wake up, for a split second you just experience the raw sensation – the pain of having arthritis. Then, within a second or so, your mind begins to interpret the experience: 'That stupid disease. Why me? I bet I got it because of the unhealthy food I used to eat. It's not fair. I'm so annoyed! It's all my fault. What will happen in the future?' Unhelpful judgements, interpretations and predictions all lead to suffering.

A useful formula to remind you of the difference between pain and suffering is:

Pain x Resistance = Suffering

In other words, the more you resist or fight or deny or avoid your pain, the greater the suffering you experience. I'm not saying it's going to be easy to reduce your urge to resist pain – resistance is the automatic response to pain. But through the tools and approaches in this book, you can learn to reduce that reaction and therefore begin to find relief from your suffering.

Dealing with a headache

As I write, my head is aching. So, what do I do? Mindfulness is about awareness, so I become aware of the sensation in my head. I notice that my shoulders are tensing up due to the pain, so I breathe into them, and the tension seems to melt a little. I also take frequent breaks and drink lots of water. I remember that I'm not my headache. The headache arises and at some point is going to pass away. The actual experience of pain only exists in this moment. I don't need to 'tolerate' the pain, because even if I stop tolerating it, the pain is still there. Tolerating is a state of extra unnecessary tension. I can also become aware of the shape, size, colour and texture of the pain sensation in my head.

I breathe into the pain, and some resistance eases around the pain. I know that the pain only exists from one moment to the next. I notice and let go of the desire for the headache to go away.

This may give you some idea of the spirit with which to practise mindfulness when coping with a painful sensation. The idea is to turn your attention towards the difficulty and become really curious about it – but not to try and get rid of it. I suppose it's a bit like trying to soothe a crying baby: getting angry usually doesn't help. By giving the baby your attention, although it's uncomfortable when she's crying, you're able to meet her needs.

Being inspired by others

Here are some of the kinds of things my clients with chronic pain conditions say about the effect of mindfulness, which may help you to cope with your pain, and offer you some ways to apply mindfulness.

'I suffer from a chronic pain condition – if I move around for an hour or so on one day, my body is in agony the next day. Mindfulness is pretty much the only thing that has helped relieve the pain I've suffered in the last six years. I can't really move my body, and most therapies require some sort of movement. With the body scan, or mindfulness of breathing, I can lie down on the floor and do the meditation without actually moving. That's a wonderful thing. By the end, I feel really tired, but also as if I've released lots of tension I've been holding for weeks or even months.'

'I have severe lower back pain. The pain goes shooting down my leg every time I move. I thought the pain was there 24 hours a day, seven days a week. Having done the mindfulness training, the biggest thing I've realised is that there are moments in the day when I have no pain. That's really important for me.'

Pain can be emotional: feelings of sadness, loneliness, grief, anxiety or anger. Suffering is the way you meet those emotions. If you're curious about them and almost welcome them rather than trying to push them away, fight or block them, you're unlikely to create much suffering. However, if you avoid the emotions through addictions like drugs or excessive alcohol use, to avoid these feelings, you're likely to increase your own suffering.

All the avoidant strategies can't make the pain go away, they just numb it for the time being. This can be helpful in the short term to help you to cope, but by avoiding the painful sensations or emotions, you sustain and feed them. Suffering is something you can begin to manage and control by looking more carefully at the thoughts and feelings you're experiencing – the very act of turning towards painful experiences begins to change the level of suffering you have.

Here's a quote from Nisargadatta, a famous Indian spiritual teacher. He experienced the pain of throat cancer in the latter years of his life:

Pain is physical, suffering is mental. Beyond the mind there is no suffering. Pain is essential for the survival of the body, but none compels you to suffer. Suffering is due entirely to clinging or resisting; it is a sign of our unwillingness to move on, to flow with life. As a sane life is free of pain, so is a saintly life free from suffering. A saint does not want things to be different from what they are; he knows that, considering all factors, they are unavoidable. He is friendly with the inevitable and, therefore, does not suffer. Pain he may know, but it does not shatter him. If he can, he does the needful to restore the lost balance, or he lets things take their course.

Coping with pain

Here are a few things to remember about pain when applying mindfulness to the condition:

- ✔ **Pain can only exist in the present moment.** You only need to cope with this moment now. By worrying about the rest of the day, week, month or year, you begin to create suffering for yourself.

- ✔ **Tension increases pain.** By becoming aware of the sensation of pain and imagining the breath going into and out of the area of pain, the tension naturally begins to release, thereby reducing the pain. However, if the tension stays, that's okay too – your intention is all you can control here. Become aware of the actual sensation of the pain itself. Notice where the pain is located in the body. Does it have an associated shape, size, texture or colour?

- ✔ **Trying hard to reduce pain doesn't really work.** (This is just like how trying to relax can create more tension.) By discovering how slowly but surely to acknowledge and accept your pain, your experience may change for the better.

Here's a mindfulness meditation you can try to help you through your pain:

1. **Adopt any position that you feel comfortable in for a few minutes.**

2. **Feel the sensation of your own breathing.** Be aware of your breath with a lightness, a kindness and a sense of gratitude as far as you can.

3. **Notice how the pain grabs your attention time and again.** Try not to criticise yourself for this. Understand that this is a difficult practice and guide your awareness gently back to the feeling of the in-breath and out-breath around the nose, chest, belly or wherever else you find it most easy to focus on. Continue for a few minutes.

4. **Now bring your attention to the sensation of the pain itself.** This may feel frightening, or you may be very reluctant to try moving your attention to the pain. However, if you've never done this before, why not give it a go? Imagine your breath going into and out of the centre of the pain, or however close you can comfortably move to the pain.

5. **You may find saying the following words to yourself helpful, as you breathe in and out.** You may want to make a nice, slow recording of it – perhaps with music in the background if you like – and play the recording back to yourself:

Breathing in, I am aware I am breathing in,

> *Breathing out, I am aware I am breathing out.*

Breathing in, I am aware of pain,

> *Breathing out, I am aware of pain.*

Breathing in, I am aware of pain,

> *Breathing out, I know I am not my pain.*

Breathing in, I am aware of tension,

> *Breathing out, I know I am not my tension.*

Breathing in, I am aware of anger,

> *Breathing out, I know I am not my anger.*

Breathing in, I am aware of sadness,

> *Breathing out, I know I am not my sadness.*

Breathing in, I am aware of anxiety,

> *Breathing out, I know I am not my anxiety.*

Breathing in, I take things moment by moment,

> *Breathing out, this is the only moment.*

Breathing in, I know I am awareness,

> *Breathing out, I know I am free.*

You can change the wording to whatever you feel comfortable with. Feel free to experiment. Practise at least once a day and note the effect.

The butterfly of the mind

The Diving Bell and the Butterfly is the title of a book by Jean-Dominique Bauby that was later made into a film. Bauby, editor of the French *Elle* magazine, wrote the whole book after becoming paralysed, communicating by blinking his left eye when his companions spoke the correct letter of the alphabet. He explores the value of the simple things in life, and the experience of feeling trapped in his body, like being in a diving bell, while his mind flits around like a butterfly. The book is a reminder of what you have rather than what you don't have – of how precious life is, despite the pain and suffering. As one critic said: 'Read this book and fall back in love with life.'

Using Mindfulness during Ill Health

In the mindfulness-based stress reduction clinic, a popular saying is: 'If you can breathe, there's more right with you than wrong with you.' You don't even have to be able to sit up or to move to benefit from mindfulness. Mindfulness is mind training, and so no matter what the condition of your body, you can still train your mind.

Mindfulness is used to support those with cancer, heart disease, diabetes and a whole range of other chronic conditions. How does it support you when you have such a physical disease? Here are some ways:

- ✔ Mindfulness offers you a way to support yourself and build some inner resilience so you aren't overwhelmed by the looming decisions you may need to make and difficulties you may meet. Making choices about your treatment is an extra stressor when you're unwell. With mindfulness, you can access a greater clarity of thought.

- ✔ Mindfulness offers a way of connecting with something other than just your physical body, making you feel more grounded. The illness may have a physical impact and cause changes to your appearance. Your whole sense of personal identity and self-worth can be questioned when you look different as you gaze at yourself in the mirror.

- ✔ Ultimately, mindfulness is about realising that you're more than just your body, mind and heart. You're more than your fleeting thoughts and fluxing emotions. You're more than your illness. Through the practice of mindfulness and a natural self-enquiry that arises, you begin to discover a different dimension of yourself, a dimension in which illness no longer overwhelms you.

- ✔ Mindful awareness can help you to spot unhelpful and untrue thoughts, thereby defusing their potency. If you're ill, stress increases not only for you but also for your family and friends, when you all need greater support and calm. Some people even believe that they've brought the disease upon themselves due to stress. This belief leads to further distress.

- ✔ The space offered in mindfulness may help you to uncover a direct experience of an understanding through which life and death begin to make sense on some level. Serious illness puts you face to face with the prospect of death. Facing death may force you to reflect on your priorities, on what is most important in your life.

Illness isn't all negative. Surprisingly, research has shown there are positive effects of terminal illness. Some patients report increased spirituality, a deeper appreciation and a generally more positive perception of partners and significant others. Some people report greater compassion and willingness to express emotions. Higher levels of spirituality indicate that the patient senses that the illness is part of a bigger picture, and is more likely to be at peace amidst such challenging life circumstances. The phenomenon of this re-prioritisation and personal development seems to occur when people overcome their trauma, and is called post-traumatic growth.

You can develop mindfulness in two main ways, even when you're feeling ill: either by practising mindfulness exercises and meditations, or by living in a mindful way whenever it comes to mind in the moment. So when you're lying in bed waiting for the doctor, you can try and enjoy some deep, mindful breaths. When you're waiting for your test results, you can slowly walk up and down and feel the sensations in your feet – that's mindful walking. When you spot yourself saying negative, harsh words to yourself, you can try soothing yourself with some words of self-kindness, or remember that you're not alone with this condition – many others are in a similar or worse situation all over the world. You don't need to beat yourself up just because you can't find the time or motivation to meditate. Any short mindful exercise counts.

Aiding the healing process

When you sit down to meditate, any aches, pains and physical discomfort that you may have managed to ignore during the course of the day become more apparent. The practice of mindfulness is about allowing and managing these uncomfortable feelings rather than totally distracting yourself from them; you use them in a positive way.

Mindfulness can make you feel empowered. Even if you can't move a muscle in your body, you're able to do something within your mind that may do you some good. In this way, you're able to be proactive at a time in your life when you feel most powerless. Mindfulness can feel like a lifebuoy when you're struggling to stay afloat. What a relief!

I can't guarantee that mindfulness will help you heal – but there's a chance it can, so it's worth a shot, especially if the practice makes you feel a bit better.

All the mindfulness exercises in this book can help you at a time of illness – choose whatever appeals to you. A selection of some practices you can do to help reduce stress and aid the healing process are:

- ✔ **Mindfulness of breath.** Practise focusing your attention on your breathing. If you find focusing on the breath too difficult due to any pain you feel, try counting your breaths or saying 'in' and 'out' to yourself as you breathe in and out. Even managing just one mindful breath is a great start. Allow yourself to become aware of the natural, life-giving energy of your breathing as it finds its instinctive rhythm. As you breathe, you may become aware of a physical tightness in the body that restricts the breathing process. Allow and accept this, and breathe into the tension. If the tension melts, fine; if the tension doesn't, that's also fine.

- **Mindfulness of body.** Being mindful of your body is a particularly important stage if you're unwell. Bring as much kindness as you can to your experience. If you aren't too overwhelmed by the sensation of pain, allow and accept it as far as you can. Feel the sensation of pain in a neutral way, staying with the feeling and doing nothing else. In addition to kindness, bring some curiosity to your experience, as best you can. The more nurturing and gentle you can be in your relationship with your body, the better. Try some yoga, stretching or tai chi if they help to soothe the pain.

- **Mindfulness of thoughts and emotions.** In mindfulness, you can welcome your thoughts and emotions rather than resisting them. You may want to use your breath to anchor yourself in the present moment every now and then when you find yourself swept away by thoughts, as happens very often. Notice the nature of your thoughts. Are they catastrophic? Are they always about the illness? Do they focus on the future all the time? What about your emotions? Allow yourself to move into your emotions rather than resist them. Notice in what part of the body they manifest themselves and use your breath to soothe them. Trust in your own capacity to heal, to make whole.

- **Mindfulness of being.** Become aware of your own sense of identity – be aware of the sense of 'I am'. Experiment with letting go of your identification with your body, your mind, your emotions, your health and illness, your desires and fears. Keep coming back to the sense of being, the sense of 'I am'. Rest in this state of 'beingness'. If you find yourself getting lost in thoughts, imagine that your thoughts are simply dancing on top of your awareness. Remember that your thoughts and feelings are like waves in an ocean of being that is you. Expect thoughts to arrive rather than resisting or fighting them. Just as clouds aren't distractions for the sky, so thoughts aren't distractions for your mindfulness practice. Just be.

Chapter 15

Coaching Children in Mindfulness

*O*nce you've begun to develop your own mindfulness practice, you can consider how to coach your children in mindfulness too. Mindfulness can help children to become calmer and more focused. Mindfulness is a very natural process that children can practise from a young age. In this chapter you can find lots of fun exercises to train your child or teenager in mindfulness, as well as some mindful parenting tips to help keep your family smiling in the challenging but rewarding art of bringing up children.

Children and Mindfulness: A Natural Combination

Young children are naturally experts at mindfulness. Babies are like mini Zen masters! Since they haven't learnt language, they see things as they are. A set of keys, a light bulb, or the eyes of another human being are awe-inspiring for them. All actions they take are spontaneous. One moment they can be crying, and the next moment they completely let go of the past and laugh. They eat when they're hungry, sleep when they're tired, and walk when they want to walk. Their minds are full of curiosity – they can't help but explore. They're naturally full of love and affection, which you can see beaming out of their eyes. Babies are often happy just to 'be'. They can look around and shake their legs and arms, and that's enough. They love to play and don't take things too seriously. Babies don't see themselves as separate individuals; they simply do what they do and go with the flow. Many of these qualities are the essence of mindfulness.

Having a mindful pregnancy and childbirth

Pregnancy and childbirth are usually both exciting and scary times. But one thing's for sure: being pregnant is an emotional rollercoaster.

Pregnancy can be a joyous experience but is often painful too. Medication isn't normally recommended during pregnancy, which makes the pain more challenging to cope with. Because mindfulness has been found to help with chronic pain, mindfulness is being researched for pregnancy as an approach to pain management. One of the most common areas of concern for women is the feeling of losing control and not being able to cope. Mindfulness helps women to decouple the physical sensation of pain from their negative thoughts and emotions. With this approach, women experience less anxiety, and that may have a positive knock-on effect of reducing the feeling of physical pain.

The value of mindfulness extends to the birth, too. Research has found that some women are able to manage labour without the pain relief that's offered. Further questions have revealed that such women have more positive empowering experiences from labour rather than resisting labour. They tend to use expressions like 'going with the flow', 'being present' and 'pain is your friend not your enemy'. These are mindful approaches that these women seem to naturally possess. But the research shows that all women can learn these skills.

Mindfulness offers a middle path during childbirth: it gives women permission to be mindful and aware of the experience of labour, but not to feel self-judgemental if they need pain relief. Another helpful aspect of mindfulness around pregnancy is in managing depression. Over one in ten suffer depression around the time of pregnancy and childbirth and afterwards. With mindfulness being used to prevent the reoccurrence of depression during pregnancy, this can be a great time to learn about mindfulness to manage the challenging feelings.

Here are three little tips if you're pregnant right now:

✔ **Slow down.** Pregnancy is a great time to take things easy. Try not to overschedule. Enjoy naps in the afternoon, and take naps more often. Once your child is born, you'll be busy. Do just one thing at a time. Enjoy relaxing while you can.

✔ **Get enough sleep.** If you're struggling to sleep, which is common in pregnancy, try doing some soothing body scan meditations. Mindful body-awareness exercises can be relaxing while lying down. Bring a self-compassionate attitude to the mindfulness practices – in other words, bring a feeling of affection towards yourself and your baby as you meditate.

✔ **Adapt your routine.** If you're used to doing a long mindfulness practice in the mornings, but are now struggling to achieve this, adapt. You'll need to adapt again when your baby's born, so doing this is good practice. Thirty minutes of mindful yoga may need to turn into a five-minute stretch and then some ten-minute body scan meditations through the day when you can fit them in.

As babies grow up and begin to develop individuality, they begin to lose the sense of focused calm and can end up going from one thing to another, looking for a source of entertainment but lacking the attention to stay with it. When your child is age 5 upwards, you can begin to teach him some very simple mindfulness exercises to help give him some relief from his overactive mind, helping him to find out how to calm himself down. Often, children enjoy becoming calm and may even ask for the mindfulness exercise if feeling agitated.

As children approach their teenage years, they battle with a huge influx of hormones and struggle with the demands that the world makes upon them. They become more serious as individuality takes a firm hold, and begin to suppress emotions. In this challenging transition into adulthood, the innocence of being a baby seems distant and almost a dream. Some simple mindfulness exercises, like mindful breathing for a few minutes, can offer your child a method to focus the mind inwards and not spiral out of control each time something doesn't go his way.

Teaching Mindfulness to Children

Before you attempt to teach your children the art of mindfulness, consider how they learn. By adopting the right attitude to this important and challenging endeavour, you're more likely to avoid unnecessary frustration. Follow these tips when teaching mindfulness:

- **Be light-hearted.** Children don't like taking things too seriously, so bringing an element of play and fun is important. At the same time, be clear in your mind what the purpose of each mindfulness exercise is, and explain it to your children. (See the next section for ideas for exercises.)

- **Keep the sessions short.** Children's attention spans just aren't as long as those of adults. You need to adjust the length of the session as appropriate for the child.

- **Reduce talk and increase action.** Avoid talking about how much meditation helps you and how wonderful it is. You're better off practising more meditation and letting your child learn from what you do rather than what you say.

- **Remember that some days will be better than others.** Children don't do meditation, the meditation comes to them. Some days you may feel as if nothing works – then suddenly, your child may sit quietly without distraction, for no apparent reason.

✔ **Avoid using force.** If your child doesn't want to meditate, you can't force him. This just creates a negative idea about meditation. Meditation isn't like learning the piano, or maths. Mindfulness requires a desire to practise with a sense of curiosity, and using force can't generate the right attitude. Instead, be creative and try something completely different. (See the later exercises in this chapter for ideas.)

Setting an example

Children learn far more from what you *do* than from what you *say*. Children love copying others, especially people they respect. If a child sees you meditating, he's likely to be curious about what you're doing and why you're doing it. In this way you draw your child towards meditation, rather than forcing meditation upon him.

If you practise very little mindfulness, but think that your child would benefit from the practice, you may have a hard time convincing him of the benefits. He may have seen you react to your stress in unhelpful ways, getting unnecessarily angry and becoming frustrated over small things. Your child may pick up on these reactions and unconsciously begin copying them instead.

If you practise mindfulness on a regular basis and genuinely put in the time, effort and energy to develop it in your life, your child is going to pick up on this too. He'll notice how you try to calm down when you become upset; how you take mini meditations when things become overwhelming for you; how you're firm when you need to be firm, and light-hearted at other times. If your child sees you making genuine efforts to cultivate mindfulness, he's likely to pick up on this. Even if he doesn't show calm and controlled behaviour at the moment, the memory of his positive perceptions of mindfulness will stay with him, and is likely to flower as he gets older.

Taking baby steps

Don't expect your child to start with a 30-minute, mindful-breathing exercise the first time you teach him. You may not even be able to do the eating meditation with a raisin or any other food. (See Chapter 6 for the eating meditation.) If your child feels bored, he's likely to give up immediately and do something more interesting instead. You'd probably have a hard time trying to convince him to explore the boredom or to get interested in the cause of boredom!

If you have high expectations about your child practising mindfulness, you may be disappointed. Keep your expectations reasonably low and be happy with any small progress. Ultimately, meditation is about being in the present moment, so any time at all is very valuable and better than nothing.

Playing Mindfulness Games and Exercises

Children love games. Games help to focus your child's mind and at the same time have an element of fun. Then, in this more focused state of mind, you can do a short guided imagery for a minute or so – and with young children, that's enough. I know a couple of schools that do this, and the children really look forward to doing the meditations – they enjoy both the fun and the release of any anxieties and stresses in their systems.

Use your intuition to decide which games to use, but be brave too and try some that you initially doubt. You never know what will happen until you try! Some can be adapted for older children – just use more appropriate props, more adult language and extend the length of the mindful exercises slightly.

You can do these games with one child or more.

Memory game

This game helps to train attention and memory and focuses the mind before a meditation:

1. Put about 20 random items, such as pens, scissors, socks and toys, onto a tray.

2. Tell the child he has one minute to study the items and to try to remember as many as he can. He gets one point for each item he remembers.

3. Cover up the tray with a towel and ask your child to recall the items.

4. Praise your child for however many he gets correct, and challenge him to see whether he can remember one more next time you play.

Teddy bear

This exercise helps to encourage belly breathing, and also to focus the attention on the breathing:

1. Ask your child to lie down on the floor, a mat or a bed.

2. Place a teddy bear or any other favourite toy on your child's belly and ask him to become aware of the toy as it rises and falls.

3. Encourage your child to be curious about how often the teddy bear goes up and down. Can he make it go up and down a little more slowly? How does that make him feel inside?

Paper windmill spinning

This game is a way of focusing your child's attention on his breathing. The visual cue of a colourful paper windmill is far more interesting to your child than just feeling his breath alone.

The steps are:

1. Give your child a colourful paper windmill (pinwheel). Let him play with it for a while, and then tell him you're going to practise being curious together.

2. Ask him to blow as softly as he can and to observe what happens. Ask him to see how slowly he can make the paper windmill turn. How does this make him feel?

3. Ask him to blow as hard as possible, and see how fast the paper windmill turns. What happens to all the colours? How does this make him feel?

4. Ask him to experiment with a long or short breath, and notice how long the paper windmill turns for.

5. Ask him to breathe normally, and to watch what happens to the paper windmill. Again, ask him how he feels.

6. Finally, ask him to put the paper windmill down and feel his breath without it. Ask him whether he can feel calm and relaxed even without the paper windmill, just by feeling his own breath.

Curious mind

This works if you have several children sitting in a circle. The game feels a bit like playing pass the parcel, a popular party game. Although children are naturally curious, this exercise helps them to become aware of the sense of curiosity itself:

1. Find a beautiful, shiny object, wrap it up in layers of newspaper and place it in a box.

2. Now ask the children to try to guess what may be inside. They can shake the box, but nothing else. Let everyone have a guess.

3. Now ask them what it feels like to not know or to be curious. Ask them to look at the faces of the other children – their eyes may be wide open, and there may be smiles around. Encourage curiosity about curiosity!

4. Begin to slowly unwrap the object. Explain how mindfulness is about being curious about everyday experience and in this way reveals the unknown. Tell them that eventually they'll discover a jewel or other beautiful object inside themselves, and they'll enjoy looking inside every day.

Loving kindness meditation

This is a powerful exercise to practise with your children. If your children really like the exercise, they may be happy to do the meditation every day before going to sleep. They may find that they sleep more deeply and feel calmer and refreshed the next day. Pause after giving each instruction, to give your child plenty of time to experience the meditation.

For the loving kindness meditation:

1. Ask your child to find a comfortable, relaxed sitting or lying-down posture with his eyes closed, if that feels okay for him.

2. Ask him to remember something that makes him feel happy. He may recall a game he played with a friend, a favourite hobby or much-loved cuddly toy. Adjust according to the age of your child.

3. Ask him to place both his hands over his chest and imagine the feeling of warmth, peace and happiness grow from there to all over his body and even the room around him.

4. Tell him to imagine this happiness and loving kindness spreading to everyone in his family, then to all of his friends, all of the children in his class, his school and his town, even those he doesn't get on with very well. Then to all people on the planet, living in all the different countries. Then to all animals and plants on earth, including those that live high up in the air and down in the deepest oceans.

Some children may find difficulty in wishing happiness to people they don't like or to animals such as spiders. Explain that loving kindness includes every living thing, and just as they want to be happy, so do others want to be happy too.

Bubble meditation

I've tried this meditation with children from age 10 upwards, and they all seem to like it. You can also try the meditation for younger children too – just simplify the language a little.

The steps are:

1. Ask your child to sit or lie down in a comfortable position. Allow him to use pillows and blankets to make himself cosy. You don't need to ask him to sit up straight for this meditation. He can close his eyes if he's okay with that.

2. Say to him: 'Imagine you have a small, shiny bubble in your hand, that can't be burst. Imagine dropping that bubble on the floor in front of you, and watching it gently expand until it's so big you can step inside it. In fact, the bubble is the size of a large, spacious room. Then, step inside the bubble. Now, imagine you can instantly decorate the inside of this bubble in any way you like. You can cover it with blankets of your favourite colour or paint the walls and ceiling just as you like. You can have games machines, expensive televisions, and your favourite music playing in the background – whatever you want. Your favourite food is available whenever you need it. Consider all the sights, sounds, smells, tastes being just how you like them to be inside your bubble. You feel really relaxed, comfortable and safe inside this bubble of yours.' Allow him time to really enjoy his own personal bubble that he's created for himself. Children often like imagining what to put inside their bubble, and so you can extend this for more than five minutes.

3. Now allow some time to practise mindfulness. Say to him: 'Notice how your body feels right now. Which parts feel relaxed? Become aware of your own gentle in and out breath. Enjoy the feeling of your breathing. Feel how soothing the experience is. Breathe in any feeling of happiness and breathe out any stress.'

4. Say to your child: 'Now you've created and enjoyed your own personal bubble, you're ready to keep this personal bubble of yours for later on. You step out of your bubble and see the bubble shrinking so you can hold the bubble in your hand once again. Now imagine the bubble becomes so small it can move inside your hand and up your arm. Allow the bubble to go into the centre of your chest, where your heart is. You can keep your bubble here for safety, and any time you feel you need to go back into your bubble, you can.'

5. Bring the meditation to a close by asking your child to gently open his eyes, and then discuss how the practice went.

Mindful drawing

This exercise trains your child to be mindful of shape, colour, and light and shade. This is particularly helpful for children who resist traditional mindfulness meditation with their eyes closed, because drawing doesn't feel like meditation at all, and yet they're training their attention for detail with a sense of curiosity.

This exercise goes like this:

1. Ask your child to draw an object in the room. He can look at the object as he draws.

2. When he's finished, you can both compare the picture with the actual object. Which bits are close to the reality and which bits aren't quite right? Emphasise that this isn't a competition, more of an experiment to see what happens.

3. If the child wants to, you can repeat the exercise and see how much better the second drawing is through paying attention.

Mindful body scan

Children are far more likely to give their attention to the world around them rather than to their own bodies. This exercise helps to bring their attention back to their physical body, training their attention to focus on one part at a time; they also discover how to move their attention from one part of the body to another. Children can then use this capacity to hold and move their attention in their daily lives.

The steps for the mindful body scan are:

1. Ask your child to lie down in a quiet and relaxing place. He can close his eyes if he wants to.

2. Ask him to name each part of his body, beginning with his toes and moving up to his head. After naming each part, ask him to tell you how that part of the body feels. After naming the part of the body, the child can move it; this changes the feeling and brings a bit of fun to the exercise too.

3. When you get to the top of his head, gently ring a bell and ask him to put his hand up when he can no longer hear the bell. The bell is a way of expanding the attention from a sharp, focused one to a wider, more expansive and open awareness. By asking him to identify when the sound turns into silence, he is drawn naturally into the peaceful silence, and can feel more calm and refreshed.

Supporting Teens with Mindfulness

It's not easy being a teenager. If you cast your mind back to those days, you may recall mood swings, frustration with parents, annoying teachers, scary exams and the constant battle to fit in with your peers.

Teenagers often judge themselves harshly, with questions like: 'Why do I look fat? Why do I have a massive spot on my nose just when I managed to get a hot date? Why aren't I pretty? Why doesn't she fancy me?' With all these thoughts hijacking the brain, it's no wonder life is tough for teens.

The adolescent brain experiences more intense emotions than a child or adult's brain does. This has evolved in nature, because e*motions* are designed to create *motion*. In *Brainstorm: The Power and Purpose of the Teenage Brain* by Daniel Siegel (Published by Tarcher, 2014), the teenage brain has evolved to motivate the teenager to prepare to move away from home. So teenagers' mood swings are not their fault – it's the way their brains work.

Take a few moment to reflect on what your challenges were as a teenager. How may mindfulness have helped you? How would you have liked to be introduced to mindfulness?

About one in eight teens suffer from depression. And according to the US National Institutes of Health, a massive one in four teens suffer from an anxiety disorder, with one in twenty having a severe disorder. I think that, as a society, we need to do something about these alarming statistics.

Introducing mindfulness to teens

Mindfulness can be a great help to teenagers. With the cocktail of emotions that teens face, mindfulness can be used to help teens anchor themselves in the present by connecting with their senses, and thereby feel a little more in control.

When introducing adolescents to mindfulness, don't use it as a way make them behave better. If that's your attitude, it's likely to backfire. Instead, offer mindfulness for the sake of it.

The aim of mindfulness is not to feel better, but to get better at feeling.

Teenagers need you to treat them like adults. They're human beings, don't forget! The more respect you can show them, the better they'll be able to listen to you.

Offer short mindfulness exercises to teens. Around 10 minutes is a good length of time. A longer session of 15–20 minutes is acceptable for more relaxing exercises like the body scan, which can be done lying down.

With time, many of the mindfulness meditations offered in this book can work for teens.

These tips may help you:

✔ **Use appropriate language.** I think 'mindfulness' is quite a good word. The word 'meditation' has all sorts of connotations that may put teenagers off. Some people call it 'relaxation', but as I mention in Chapter 1, mindfulness is not really just relaxation. Teens may be interested if you explain the difference between mindfulness and relaxation.

✔ **Use examples and role models that they can relate to.** Think about the group of teenagers (or the individual teenager) you're speaking to, and what kind of things they're interested in. Tell them about famous personalities who are into mindfulness or meditation. Examples of meditators include Oprah Winfrey, Arianna Huffington, Bill Ford (executive chairman of Ford), Hugh Jackman (aka 'Wolverine'), Russell Brand and many more.

✔ **Respect them, like they're adults.** In my experience, the more you can show respect to teenagers as if they're adults, the better they'll respond. With the inner practice of mindfulness, you certainly can't force it upon anyone. By being mindful yourself, you set the stage and provide an example for them to follow you.

Here's a simple little exercise for teens to try:

1. **Mindful Three: Three things with three senses**

   Notice what you can see around you. Which three different objects can you see? Notice their colour and shape.

2. **Now listen.** Which three different sounds can you hear? Notice the pitch and volume.

3. **Now feel the physical sensations in your body.** Which three different sensations can you feel? What do the sensations actually feel like?

That's a quick, easy way to get into mindfulness using three senses.

Helping teens with exam stress

Being a teenager without the stress of writing exams is difficult enough. But the added pressure of relentless testing can tip teenagers into anxiety or depression. If you want to help your teenager manage the stress of exams, mindfulness can help.

You can introduce teens to mindfulness in several ways:

✔ Show them this or another appropriate book on mindfulness. Perhaps suggest a couple of specific chapters for them to look at.

✔ Give them a guided mindfulness audio from this book to try – aim for one that's between three and ten minutes long to begin with. Or invite them to practise mindfulness with you in a comfortable environment.

✔ Help them to find a time of day that's right for them – mornings, afternoons or early evenings are all good.

✔ Share the short mini mindfulness meditation, and let them use that several times a day, especially at times when they're feeling higher-than-normal levels of stress.

You can give these 'mindful' tips to your teenager in the run-up to exam day:

✔ Sleeping is like plugging your phone in at night. That's the best way your phone will work best if it's fully charged. The same goes for you. Make it a priority to go to bed on time. It's tempting to revise more and more, but the less sleep you have, the harder you make it for your brain to recall facts.

✔ Start the morning with a short mindfulness practice. You can do a short body scan or listen to the short mindfulness guided audio tracks that come with this book.

✔ Avoid last-minute revision. In my experience of doing last-minute revision, all I remembered was the stuff I revised at the last minute, and everything else somehow got lost! If you do revise at the last minute, observe to see whether it works for you or not.

✔ Do a mini mindful exercise just before you start your exam. Take three conscious deep breaths before you open the exam paper. Or if you feel pressured to open the exam paper when everyone else does, do so, but then do your three deep, mindful breaths. Then take your time over the first question. Exams are like building a house. You need to take your time to build nice solid foundations early on. The first question is your foundation upon which to build.

✔ If you're struggling to answer the questions, don't panic. Now's the time to stop writing for a few moments and gather yourself. Feel your body on the chair and your feet on the floor to bring you into the present moment. Try putting your pen down and opening and closing your hands a few times, noticing how that feels. Then make a fresh start with the next question, reading the question carefully. Don't give up!

✔ Treat your exam like you're a patient. When you go to see the doctor, do you want the doctor to rush or to listen carefully to your questions and answer them accurately? Of course you want the doctor to listen and take their time. Rushing exams will lower your grade, not increase it. Take your time and read each question at half the speed at which you normally read. See whether that helps you to answer the question more accurately.

Discovering 7/11 breathing

This is a nice, easy exercise for teenagers to use to deal with the anxiety of exams. Actually, younger children and adults can equally benefit from it. This breathing technique switches on your relaxation response, and if you notice the sensation of your breathing, the exercise can be a mindfulness experience too.

You can do this exercise anywhere: on a bus, on a train, sitting at home, lying down or even while gently walking. Here's how:

1. **As you breathe in, count to seven in your head.** Count at a rate that feels comfortable for your breath.

2. **As you breathe out, count to 11.**

3. **Repeat Steps 2 and 3.**

4. **Whenever you mind wanders off, just forgive yourself, smile and start again.** That's cool!

5. **Stop after five to ten minutes, or sooner if you feel too relaxed or light headed!**

As you do the 7/11 breathing exercise, consider these tips:

- ✔ You need to breathe in a bit faster than you breathe out. The in-breath is slightly harder, and the out-breath a little softer.

- ✔ This takes a bit of practice, like anything else. You'll get better at it after you've done it a few times. Eventually it may get so enjoyable it's slightly addictive, which is good!

- ✔ Combine this exercise with visualising yourself in a peaceful place if you like. That's what I call mindful visualisation, if you allow yourself to stay conscious within the experience.

Taking mindfulness into schools

Worldwide, there is a rapidly growing movement to bring mindfulness into schools.

If you're a parent or guardian and would like to see mindfulness offered in your child's school, try organising a conversation with the head teacher, or ask whether any other teachers are interested in mindfulness. Meeting with and suggesting your idea to teachers who are passionate about mindfulness may help to give the idea momentum. Sharing information and good quality books and articles about mindfulness in schools is like watering the seed of an idea. With a bit of luck, eventually the idea will sprout.

Either a teacher will convince the management it's a good idea, or the management itself will begin to take steps to organise an action plan within the school.

If you're a teacher and would like to learn to teach mindfulness and offer it to other teachers or students, see whether you can find a teacher training programme either online or in your local area. (You obviously need to have experience in practising mindfulness and experiencing the challenges and benefits of the practice before you can learn to share the approach with others.)

Mindful Parenting

I think that parenting is probably the most difficult, stressful, important and fulfilling responsibility in the world. A good parent needs not only to nurture the child with food, shelter and clothing, but to develop the child's mind too. Your behaviour as a parent often reflects what your own parents were like, even if you want to change and improve upon certain areas. However, parents often end up repeating the cycle in subtle ways, passing on unhelpful behaviours. Fortunately, mindful parenting can help to break the cycle.

Being present for your children

How can mindfulness help with parenting? Mindful parents are aware of and awake to their actions and the actions of their children. This is very important in bringing up a child. Children crave attention. For children, attention is like love. If they don't receive sufficient attention, they misbehave until they get that attention – even being told off is preferable to being ignored. Attention is a fundamental need for a child. How can you give that attention if you're not attentive yourself? Mindfulness offers ways to hone your attention skills to help bring up a child in a more harmonious and peaceful way.

Here are the benefits of parenting in the present moment:

- ✔ **You can meet your child's needs.** By living in the present moment, you're more able to meet your child's needs as necessary. You notice if your child needs to eat or sleep or just play. You notice if actually all that he needs is a hug. Each moment is different and fresh, and what worked yesterday may not work today. Your child is one day older and different – living moment by moment helps you to see this.

- ✔ **You can meet your own needs.** By being aware and awake to the present sensations in your own body, and noticing the way you react to situations, you're also better able to look after yourself. Parenting is very tiring, and when you're over-tired you can end up making decisions that just create more difficulties rather than solutions. Awareness of your own reactions helps you to sense when this is happening and to take whatever appropriate action is necessary.

- ✔ **You cultivate gratefulness.** Living in the present moment helps you to be grateful for what you have rather than ungrateful for what you don't. You may notice how much work you have to do, or how frustrated you are by your children's behaviour, but thinking about what isn't going according to plan is draining. Living in the present enables you to see what's going well and what you do have. You may have healthy children and a nice home; you may be having a spell of good weather; or you may have a supportive partner or friend.

✔ **You see things afresh.** One of the other key aspects of mindfully living in the present is adopting an attitude of 'beginner's mind'. (For more on seeing things afresh, jump to Chapter 4.) This involves seeing things freshly, as if for the first time. If you have a baby, you're able to see how he's always living in beginner's mind. Babies look around the room or area with wonder. By living with this same attitude, you're more able to meet the ever-changing challenge of parenting in the present moment.

✔ **You free yourself from worries.** Living and parenting moment by moment means you can let go of regrets about the past and worries about the future. Neither of them exist in the present moment. Do you have any problems at all, right now, if you don't think about them? All worries, concerns, fears and anxieties arise from leaving the here and now, the present moment. All you need to do is take things one day at a time – or, better still, one second at a time. You may be worrying about how your children will be tomorrow, or next week, month or year. All you can possibly do is your best, right here and now, and let go of what has happened or may happen.

Trying out tips for mindful parenting

Here are a few tips for practising mindful parenting:

✔ **Be present for your child.** The greatest present you can give your child is your presence. Live in the moment and as if everything in front of you is your teacher. Your child will observe and copy this on some level.

✔ **Find the balance between love and discipline.** If you're too lenient your children become spoilt, but if you're too harsh your children become overly cold and closed. Set clear boundaries, but ensure that you praise good behaviour and attitudes, and don't just criticise their errors.

✔ **Trust your intuition.** Your sense of the best thing to do is more intelligent than logical thinking – your intuition has access to all your unconscious learning that has operated in humanity for thousands of years. Use a combination of your head and heart in your decisions.

✔ **Look for a balance in situations.** You can't get your own way all the time, and neither can your child. But perhaps a place in between satisfies you both to a certain extent and feels right.

✔ **Imagine things from your child's perspective.** What's it like to be dominated by adults most of the time? How does your child feel if adults' seemingly silly desires are all they can think about? If you were your child, how would you want your parents to act towards you?

✔ **Take some time to meditate every day, even if for a short period of time.** Don't force your child to do the same, but answer his questions about meditation honestly and simply, and play mindful games with him when you can.

⮕ **Practise mindful listening.** Listen to your child as if you're listening to a piece of music or the sounds of nature. Listen with a gentle attentiveness and respond as necessary. Listening to your child can be like a mindfulness meditation.

⮕ **Observe your own behaviour as much as you observe your child's behaviour.** See how you like to do what you like doing, just as your child likes to do what *he* likes doing.

⮕ **Look after yourself.** Ensure that you eat properly, sleep enough (I know this can be difficult), and take exercise. You may need to be really creative to fit some of these things into your daily schedule.

⮕ **Be light-hearted.** You don't need to take things too seriously. If you made a mistake in your parenting, don't beat yourself up about the fault – instead see whether you can laugh or at least smile about it. You're human after all, and so is your child.

Mulla Nasruddin stories

Children love stories of Nasruddin, known throughout the Middle East. The stories seem to suggest that Nasruddin was foolish, but they all contain gems of hidden wisdom within. Here are a few examples:

⮕ Nasruddin was on his hands and knees one dark evening, under the light of a street lamp. A neighbour came out to ask what the problem was. Nasruddin said he had dropped his keys and so was looking for them. The neighbour helped him search but couldn't find the keys. In the end the neighbour asked: 'Where exactly did you drop them?' Nasruddin said, 'Over there,' pointing to his front door. The neighbour retorted: 'Then why are you looking under the lamp?'! Nasruddin replied: 'Because there's light here.'

⮕ One day Nasruddin went into his favourite coffee shop and said: 'The moon is more useful than the sun.' An old man asked: 'Why?' Nasruddin replied: 'We need the light more during the night than during the day.'

⮕ A friend asked Nasruddin: 'How old are you?' 'Fifty,' he replied. 'But you said the same thing two years ago!' 'Yes,' replied Nasruddin, 'I always stand by what I've said.'

⮕ 'When I was in the desert,' said Nasruddin to his friend, 'I caused an entire tribe of horrible and bloodthirsty people to run.' 'How did you do it?' 'Easy. I just ran, and they ran after me.'

⮕ Nasruddin, who wasn't used to public speaking, arose in confusion and said nervously: 'M-m-my f-f-friends, when I c-c-c-came here tonight only God and I knew what I was about to say to you. Now, only God knows!'

⮕ Nasruddin was sitting chatting with a neighbour, when his son came up the road holding a chicken. 'Where did you get that chicken?' Nasruddin asked. 'I stole it,' said his son. Nasruddin turned to his neighbour and said proudly: 'There's my boy. He may steal, but he won't lie.'

You can find more stories, in full, at www. nasruddin.org.

Part V

The Part of Tens

Enjoy an additional Part of Tens chapter online at www.dummies.com/extras/mindfulness.

In this part . . .

- Find ten tips for practising daily mindfulness.

- Explore ten different ways to practice mindfulness that can really help you.

- Discover ten common ideas about mindfulness that just aren't true.

- Investigate ten different resources including books, CDs and websites.

Chapter 16

Ten Top Tips for Mindful Living

In This Chapter

▶ Knowing the essence of mindfulness

▶ Discovering practical mindfulness exercises

▶ Exploring tips for applying mindfulness in daily life

Mindfulness is simple in essence – it's about cultivating present-moment awareness more than anything else – but the difficulty is in practising mindfulness consistently. This chapter gives you a series of short, easy ways of integrating the principles of mindfulness into your everyday life. Don't underestimate their value – they may take relatively little time and seem overly simplistic, but many of these tips have been proven to be effective. Try them out for yourself and hold back your judgement until you've given the tools a try for at least a few weeks.

Spending Some Quiet Time Every Day

Having some quiet time every day is the most important tip I can give you. I can't emphasise enough the importance of connecting with some form of mindfulness practice on a daily basis, preferably for ten minutes or more. By deliberately practising mindfulness every day, you strengthen your mind's ability to be more aware and awake.

If you want to be more mindful, you need daily training, just as when if you want to become fitter, you need to exercise your body on a daily basis. If you only exercised once a week, you wouldn't benefit as much. Your mind goes back to its original state even more quickly than the body does.

To practise mindfulness on a daily basis can involve sitting still and feeling the sensation of your breathing, or doing some yoga, or simply sitting in your garden and looking at the trees and birds with a warm drink before starting work.

Here are some ways to ensure that you remember to be mindful every day:

- ✔ **Practise at the same time and in the same place every day.** This way the mindfulness discipline becomes a routine like brushing your teeth, and you don't have to think about it.

- ✔ **Don't push yourself too much.** If ten minutes seems too long, just do whatever you can manage. You can gradually build up the time for which you practise.

- ✔ **Put reminders on your mirror, refrigerator, computer or phone.** When you see the reminder, do a little meditation.

Connect with People

In the first instant that you meet someone, within a split second, you judge her. You may think that she's too fat or too thin, you don't like her hairstyle, she reminds you of someone you don't like. Your mind instantly tries to categorise, which is why first impressions are so important in interviews. The moment you make an initial judgement of a person, you begin to look for evidence to support your theory. If she doesn't look you in the eye properly, or fails to say thanks, you take these moments as evidence about her, and your opinion becomes more fixed. Then you create an image in your mind. You think that you know this other person, when all you know are your own judgements of her.

When you meet someone, connect with your senses rather than your ideas. Look the person in the eye in a natural way. Listen to what she has to say, rather than thinking about what you're about to say. Be curious and ask questions rather than imposing your own perceptions so much. See things from the other person's point of view – what would you be like in that person's situation? How would you feel, and what would you want?

Mindfulness is about paying attention with a sense of warmth and kindness, as well as a sense of curiosity and openness. Bring these attitudes to the relationship and see what happens.

Enjoy the Beauty of Nature

The clearest way into the Universe is through a forest wilderness.

John Muir

Nature has a way of drawing a mindful awareness from you, rather than you forcing yourself to be mindful. Walking among old trees with their branches overhanging the path you're treading, smelling the scent of freshly cut grass, or listening to the birds sing and the twigs crunching under your feet, you can't help but be aware in the moment. Gardening is also a wonderful way of connecting with nature and experiencing 'flow' (explained in Chapter 5); absorb yourself in tasks such as weeding and planting and enjoy the fruits of your labours as you see tiny shoots grow into beautiful plants and flowers.

If you have a garden or live near a park or a bit of greenery, realise how fortunate you are. Take time to reconnect with mother nature – make time for doing so. Nature is a miraculous living being, and you're part of that life. As a child you may have loved to play in natural surroundings, jumping in puddles and sliding in mud. With your acute senses, perhaps you were quite happy to explore and observe all day long if permitted. Try reconnecting with a child-like innocence and visit a natural environment, whatever that means to you.

In a famous study in a care home, half the elderly folk were given a plant to look after themselves, and the other half were given a plant but told that the nurses would look after it. Those who had responsibility to water and nurture the plants lived significantly longer than the others. The study concluded that responsibility gave the elderly a sense of control, leading to longer life. The study also suggests that not only looking at nature in a passive way, but also growing plants and ensuring that they thrive as best you can, is a healthy and life-enhancing activity to engage in on a regular basis.

Change Your Daily Routine

Humans are creatures of habit. If you think about the things you've done today, they're probably the same things you've done many times before. One way of being more mindful is to change your routine. Yes, you have to get up, get dressed, go to work and so on, but you don't have to do all that in exactly the same way. And what about the way you spend your free time (if you're lucky enough to have free time!)? Do you always do the same hobbies, watch the same kind of movies, read the same type of books, meet the same sort of people, think the same sort of thoughts? The answer is probably yes.

Try changing your routine to boost your mindful awareness. When you're in your routine lifestyle, your mind goes into a sleep state. You're less likely to notice the good things happening around you. You're unable to think creatively.

By making just small changes in your routine, your brain wakes up. You gently nudge yourself out of your comfort zone. And in that more awakened state, you're immediately more mindful.

For example, today I had a cup of tea before my meditation practice, which I don't normally have. It's a small change, but it helped me stay present in my practice and has had a positive knock-on effect on my day!

Choose one of these options to help shift out of your automatic-pilot living.

- Meet up with a friend you haven't seen for ages.
- Drive to work without switching on the radio.
- Pick up a random book next time you're in a bookshop or library and read a chapter.
- Switch around your daily morning routine – maybe have breakfast before having a shower, or vice versa
- Do a random act of kindness today. Make tea for a co-worker. Pick up some litter from the ground. Or even just take extra care of some plants or your pet today.

See the Wonder of the Present Moment

Yesterday is history, tomorrow a mystery, today is a gift, that's why it's called the present.

This moment is the *only moment* you have, and you have it right now. Memories of the past come up in the present moment. Ideas of the future are shaped by past experience and projected into an imagined tomorrow. In reality, this present moment is all that's available.

If you're currently going through a difficult time, you probably don't think that the present moment is wonderful at all. That's okay. You can remember that you don't have to worry too much about the future and only need to cope with whatever you're facing here and now. In this sense, being in the present moment is helpful – you don't need to worry about the future.

To really appreciate the present moment, feel your senses. Connect with your sense of sight. Notice the range of different colours in front of you. Reflect on the fact that this experience of colour is partly due to a large amount of biochemical reactions rapidly turning into electrical impulses going into your brain, leading to this incredible experience called colour. What would it be like to see colour for the first time? How would you describe the experience to someone who'd never seen colour before? Try looking without naming objects or people – just connect with the bare awareness of light itself. Be grateful you have eyes that are able to see in the first place. Look with the effortless gaze of a child.

Another way to really connect with the present is to focus on your breathing. Think these words while breathing in and out, if you find them helpful:

- Breathing in: 'I am in the present moment.'
- Breathing out: 'This is a wonderful moment.'

Listen to Unpleasant Emotions

How do you see the wonder of the present moment if you feel down, upset or annoyed? In these situations, don't try to impose a different emotion on what you're experiencing. Be in the present moment and open up the emotion as best you can. Remember that all emotions have a beginning and an end – try to see the feeling as a temporary visitor. Additionally, see yourself as separate from the emotion. The emotion rises and falls, but you maintain a sense of stability and greater emotional balance.

Imagine that someone turns up at your front door and rings the doorbell. You decide to ignore the sound. The bell rings again and again. You get frustrated and try all sorts of ways of distracting yourself from the sound of the doorbell, but you can't. By simply opening the door and meeting the person ringing the bell, you can stop all your avoidance strategies. You're facing your fears. You're looking towards the unpleasant emotions rather than running away (which is an understandable response).

Moving towards the emotion, without forcing it to go away, often has the effect of dissipating the emotion. The emotion comes in, has a cup of tea or whatever, and off it goes. The emotion just wanted some mindful awareness. The idea is to offer just that – becoming aware of the emotions you spend so much time running away from with a kind, curious, open, non-judgemental awareness, as best you can. Explore and discover what effect this has on negative emotions in the long run, not to get rid of them, but to learn from them.

Chapters 12 and 13 are all about how mindfulness can help you deal with unpleasant emotions.

Remember That Thoughts Aren't Facts

If you had the thought, 'I'm a flying, pink chimpanzee,' you obviously wouldn't believe it. That's a crazy idea. Then why do you believe thoughts like 'I'm useless' or 'I'll never get better' or 'I can't go on'? They're thoughts too, that have just popped into your head. Don't believe everything you think. Your mind often makes assumptions and inferences that simply aren't true. 'I'm feeling low at the moment' may be true, but 'I'll always be depressed' is not. 'I find it annoying when she doesn't do her chores' may be true, but 'She never helps me' is unlikely to be true.

As you discover how to observe the nature of your mind in meditation, you realise from experience that thoughts are always arising in your mind, no matter how much meditation you do. Even people who've been practising meditation for years have plenty of thoughts. The thoughts aren't going to stop. You simply need to change your relationship to thoughts. Seeing thoughts as just thoughts rather than facts makes a world of difference. If the thought 'I'm pathetic' comes up and you believe whatever arises in your mind, you're bound to feel low and uneasy. However, if exactly the same thought comes up and you're mindful of it, you see it as just a thought and not a fact. This takes much of the sting out of the thought, and you're free to dismiss it and carry on with whatever you're doing, relatively untouched. This is freedom. Freedom, or peace of mind, isn't about *stopping* your thoughts, but seeing thoughts as just thoughts and not giving them too much attention, and not believing them as reality. Reality is contained in the here and now, beyond ideas and concepts. You're not your mind – you're the observer, the silent witness, always complete, whole and free.

If you practise meditation regularly, you begin naturally to take a step back from your thinking. Normally, if you have a thought, you act on it, especially if you aren't fully conscious of the thought. In meditation, you observe the thought without acting on it. You see your thoughts as a pattern, as energy moving through your mind.

Be Grateful Every Day

Gratitude is the best attitude! Gratitude is when you discover how to want what you have and not want what you don't have. Usually, people want what they don't have and don't want what they do have. This is bound to lead to a sense of dissatisfaction. You can practise gratitude right now. Think about this book in your hand at the moment – millions of people in the world don't have a single book. Think about the fact that you can read – another skill inaccessible to millions.

Gratitude is an aspect of mindfulness. Mindfulness doesn't just mean concentrating, but an attention suffused with a warm, kind attitude. To be aware as you're cooking of how fortunate you are to have food available to you is to be mindful.

When I'm feeling a bit down, which is sometimes a sign that I'm focusing on things that aren't going well, I find myself practising gratitude. Just reflecting for a moment and trying to think of five things I'm grateful for helps to put things into perspective.

Here are some ways to nurture feelings of gratitude:

✓ **Sleep with gratitude.** Before going to sleep, spend a minute or two thinking about five things you're grateful for. They can be very simple things, and you don't have to feel hugely grateful for them. Just go through each one and see what effect that has on your sleep.

✔ **Say thank you.** This is a simple act but very powerful. Saying thank you is both an act of gratitude and kindness – you're making clear to the other person that you've recognised her generosity.

✔ **Carry out an action to say thanks.** Send a thank-you card or a small gift, or do something like making coffee or helping someone with her work. As the old saying goes, actions speak louder than words.

✔ **Try being grateful for things you wouldn't normally be.** For example, when things are difficult, you can be grateful for the challenge the difficulty offers. Be grateful for access to running water or for your ability to hear. Or try being grateful for being alive in the first place – perhaps this is the greatest miracle.

Here's an extract from a wonderful poem by an unknown author, on thanks and gratitude:

Be thankful that you don't already have everything you desire. If you did, what would there be to look forward to?

Be thankful when you don't know something, for it gives you the opportunity to learn.

Be thankful for the difficult times. During those times you grow.

Be thankful for your limitations, because they give you opportunities for improvement.

Be thankful for your mistakes. They will teach you valuable lessons.

Be thankful when you're tired and weary, because it means you've made a difference.

It's easy to be thankful for the good things.

A life of rich fulfilment comes to those who are also thankful for the setbacks.

Find a way to be thankful for your troubles, and they can become your blessings.

Use Technology Mindfully

Just as plants and animals evolve to better survive and thrive in their environment, technology has also evolved over time. And part of technology's evolution is to become more addictive. With the advent of smart phones, you can use technology from the very moment you wake up until you drift off to sleep. And even if you wake up in the middle of the night, you can find yourself checking Facebook or surfing the web before you know it.

Video games are another form of technology that's highly addictive. Some people spend so long playing games, it affects their work and home lives and has even lead to marriage breakups.

I'm not dismissing the huge benefits of technology, but you need to manage your use of digital devices. Here are some tips:

- **Have a digital detox day or half day once a week.** Give your brain a break.

- **Try keeping your phone away from the side of your bed.** Just try it for a few nights a week. Better still, make your bedroom a technology-free zone.

- **Be courteous.** Switch off your phone at mealtimes or when out with friends and family. Challenge yourself and see whether you can resist the temptation to check your phone at the table, even if your friend does.

- **Go for a walk without your phone.** If you're not used to this, you'll probably find the experience strange at first and then tremendously refreshing. I love doing this regularly.

- **Make a note of how many times you check your phone in a day.** That's an experience of mindfulness in itself. Average users check their phones over 100 times a day! Switch off your phone for chunks of the day and find something more enjoyable to do with your time.

- **Surf the urge to use technology.** When you feel the desire to use technology but don't really have to, notice the feeling in your body. See whether you can ride that urge, just feeling it and relaxing into it. Each time you do that, your addiction will lessen until eventually the urge will disappear completely.

Breathe and Smile!

You'll find that life is still worthwhile, if you just smile.

Charles Chaplin

The muscles in your face link with your feeling of happiness. When you're happy, you smile – you know that of course. But did you know that smiling can make you feel better? Try the process right now, no matter how you feel. Simply hold a subtle, gentle smile as you read these sentences. Continue for a few minutes and note what effect the smiling has. Combine this with feeling your own breathing.

You can apply this technique of feeling your breathing and smiling gently in a systematic way every day for ten minutes, or while you're going about your daily activities. Think of it as yoga for your mouth! In this way you can be mindful doing whatever you're doing, whether washing the dishes, writing a report or waiting in a queue. Each moment is an opportunity to come back to the here and now, the present moment. You don't need anything extra – your breath and smile are both highly portable!

You may feel reluctant to smile right now, because you don't think that the smile is genuine. You'll smile when you're happy, not now. All I can say is, try it out. Yes, you're bound to feel unnatural at the beginning but that soon goes. Just give it a try, even though it feels strange, and see what happens after a time. As someone said to me once: 'Fake it till you make it!'

Mindfulness is not about forcing your yourself to feel better – it's more about bringing a sense of curiosity to your feelings and thoughts and gaining information from them, whatever you're experiencing. Being aware of thoughts or feelings is far more important than trying to *change* your thoughts or feelings.

Chapter 17

Ten Ways Mindfulness Can Really Help You

In This Chapter
▶ Dealing with pain and stress
▶ Improving relationships – including with yourself
▶ Feeling happier and more creative

*M*indfulness provides a plethora of pleasures that I hope you'll experience for yourself. As soon as you start being mindful on a regular basis you'll find mindfulness quite addictive! In this chapter I give you a snapshot of the benefits of mindfulness, many of which are backed up by scientific research.

Training the Brain

Until fairly recently, scientists thought that the connections and structure of the adult brain were fixed, because changing the brain's connections would be far too complex.

Now we know the truth: your brain *can* change! Scientists looked at violinists' brains and found that the part of the brain responsible for finger dexterity was much bigger for violinists compared with non-violinists. They also studied London taxi drivers, who need to know all the complex road networks and 10,000 different streets in London ('the knowledge'). When scientists compared the cabbies' brains with 'normal' brains, they found that the part responsible for location was significantly *bigger*. The longer the drivers worked, the more significant the change.

The evidence proves that through training and simple everyday experience, the physical brain actually changes. Repetitive experience changes the brain more than anything else does. The discovery that the brain changes in response to experience is now called *neuroplasticity*, and it gives everyone tremendous hope – you can *change your brain* through training at any age!

With the help of the Dalai Lama, top neuroscientist Professor Richard Davidson scanned the brains of meditating monks who'd engaged in prolonged meditation for a minimum of 10,000 hours (not all in one go!). The meditation the monks did was a compassion meditation, similar to the metta meditation described in Chapter 6. The monks' brains totally changed through the practice of this meditation. The front left part of the brain (left prefrontal cortex if you're really curious) associated with positivity was activated – in fact, it went off the scale! No scientist had ever seen so much positive effect in a human being before. The scientists found that the monks' entire brains had been rewired to be more positive. This proves that mindfulness and compassion aren't fixed, but are skills that you can train in.

Okay, monks' brains become more positive because they spend most of their time meditating. But what about you and me? We don't have time to meditate for that long. Can short lengths of time meditating mindfully help? Does the brain improve after, say, 30 minutes a day for two weeks?

The incredible answer is yes. Scientists have also looked at short-term mindfulness meditation. People were randomly assigned to two groups. One group trained in cognitive behavioural therapy to show group members how to see challenges in their lives with greater positivity. The other group was trained in metta (mindful loving kindness) meditation. Some of those in the metta group had greater activation in the brain region signifying positivity and also reported greater love for themselves compared with those in the cognitive behavioural therapy group. Helpful changes did indeed happen within a fortnight of practice.

So mindfulness meditation does change the brain, and the more you practise, the greater the positive change within your brain. One more reason to download the MP3 Audio tracks that accompany this book and start meditating!

Improving Relationships

Several studies show that people's relationships tend to improve when they begin to practise mindfulness meditation. Several reasons indicate why this may be the case.

Mindfulness can switch off stress. When you feel threatened by a nasty remark or overly challenged at work or home, your body and mind engage in a stress response. You become less understanding and more reactive and judgemental. Obviously, this can have a detrimental effect on personal relationships. You may snap easily when your partner asks what's wrong, or respond emotionally when you come home to realise that dinner hasn't been cooked. Mindfulness makes you more relaxed in your day-to-day life, making you less likely to react unhelpfully.

Mindfulness develops your capacity to accept your experience from moment to moment. This accepting stance translates itself into improved relationships with others. In knowing how to be more accepting of another person's faults (nobody's perfect!), you're more likely to develop greater understanding and increase the possibility of noticing people's positive qualities.

Being judgemental isn't the greatest relationship booster in the world. However, research shows that meditators are less judgemental and more focused in the moment, even when they're not meditating. This may explain why your relationships improve once you start meditating – you're connecting with what other people say rather than wasting your energy judging them.

Mindfulness leads to higher levels of empathy and compassion for both yourself and others. A more caring attitude naturally leads you to give greater levels of attention and helps you to see from other people's perspective. Ultimately, a feeling of love is at the heart of any meaningful relationship, and, as love grows in meditation, the quality of relationships naturally deepens.

Boosting Creativity

Your creativity depends entirely on your state of mind. You can't expect to have exciting and perceptive ideas if your mind is overworked and jam-packed with opinions and points of view. Creativity requires letting go of the old to make way for the new. Mindfulness meditation is about being aware of your thoughts without judging them; this lack of judgement allows new and unique ways of thinking to arise. In most creativity exercises, the emphasis is always to stop judging ideas and just let them flow – in a mindfulness practice called choiceless awareness, described in Chapter 6, you do exactly the same thing.

Research published in the journal *Consciousness and Cognition* in 2012 was the first study to show that people who rate themselves as being more mindful are better able to solve insight problems – problems that require a shift of perception and novel thinking to find solutions.

Mindfulness, over the long term, leads to a calmer state of mind. When the conscious mind settles down, you begin to access the immense creative capacity and knowledge of the subconscious mind. You normally only access this creativity when sleeping, so doing so is almost totally out of your control. With mindfulness, the creative ideas that arise are more practical. Most of my good ideas have arisen while mindfully meditating. By giving my mind the opportunity and space just to be, I tap into my creativity, accessing idea after idea.

Reducing Depression

Some types of depression are thought to be caused by repetitive negative thinking patterns (rumination) and avoiding uncomfortable thoughts and feelings rather than facing up to them (experiential avoidance). Mindfulness, as part of mindfulness-based cognitive therapy explained in Chapter 13, helps combat depression in several ways. Mindfulness:

- **Develops your capacity to stay with, experience and face difficult experiences and emotions instead of avoiding them.** Avoiding difficult emotions has been found to be the key way in which relapsing into depression occurs. You can gradually develop an attitude of acceptance, kindness and curiosity towards experience through regularly practising mindfulness, enabling a healthier approach towards emotions.

- **Shifts you towards a 'being mode' of mind.** This being mode (described in full in Chapter 5) enables you to witness your depression as something that rises and falls within you, rather than as a core part of who you are. You can step back from your internal experience in a beneficial way and see things from a bigger perspective. This shift in perspective helps to prevent you from seeing the depression as something that'll never end, changing the idea 'I'm depressed' to 'The feeling of depression is here at the moment, but not forever. All feelings have a beginning and an end.'

- **Helps you to understand the patterns of the mind.** Being mindful helps you to see how your mind easily goes into an unaware 'automatic pilot' mode, which leads to negative thinking cycles, leading to further depression. Becoming aware of these habits of mind is the first step to beginning to see them from a different perspective and thereby reducing their potency.

- **Develops healthier habits of mind.** Depression is deepened through rumination. Mindfulness disables this negative thinking cycle by encouraging you to connect your attention to the present moment. This focus reduces the inner resources devoted to rumination. As mindfulness develops into a habit, when mild feelings of sadness arise, your likely response is to focus on the sensations in your body rather than spiralling into major depression.

Turn to Chapter 13 for much more on combating depression with mindfulness.

Reducing Chronic Pain

Incredible as it sounds, mindfulness can actually reduce chronic pain. Participation in Dr Jon Kabat-Zinn's mindfulness-based stress reduction (MBSR) programme has shown, in several research studies, the benefits of mindfulness for those suffering from chronic pain.

In one study, 90 patients suffering chronic pain were trained in mindfulness meditation for ten weeks. Experts observed a significant reduction in pain, negative body image, negative moods, anxiety and depression. The patients also engaged in more activity, including everyday activity such as preparing food and driving, which they'd struggled with before. The use of pain-reduction drugs decreased and feelings of self-esteem increased. These patients did much better than a group that underwent normal pain-management programmes.

The most exciting aspect was the result of a follow-up four years later. The majority of the chronic pain patients reported that most of their improvements had lasted or even improved further. This was probably due to the fact that, incredibly, over 90 per cent of the participants continued to practise some form of mindfulness meditation. This is a major achievement, considering they'd trained four years previously.

All these positive benefits may be partly due to the way mindfulness can train you to accept difficult bodily sensations instead of trying to resist them or pretending the discomfort isn't there. Paradoxically, acceptance seems to reduce the pain. You discover how to feel the pain and experience it as a moment-to-moment feeling rather than avoiding it and tensing up your muscles. You can help the muscles around the painful region relax, thereby reducing the pain itself.

Giving Deeper Meaning to Life

Before I started practising meditation, I found life rather hollow and empty. I had friends and family, a comfortable place to live and a good career, but something was definitely missing. Life was a bit of a grind and lacked zest and vitality. I still remember the first meditation class I attended. The teacher calmly talked about the nature of awareness and how, through regular practice, you can become more aware. This need for awareness resonated with me – the whole thing made sense. However, I lacked discipline to begin with, and discovered that a lack of a regular meditation routine didn't really work. With further practice, many wonderful teachers and good fortune, I was able to deepen my meditation. The practice of meditation itself became a driving force for a more meaningful and authentic life.

When you've touched a sense of deep peace and calmness within yourself, you no longer ask what the meaning or purpose of life is. You're clear in your own mind that peace, kindness, empathy and joy are available to be cultivated in your own being. You know that the suffering, pain and sorrow in the world is partly a reflection of humanity's inability to tap into this inner source of nourishment. You see how your low moods and frustrations are partly due to seeing things from the wrong perspective. Then you know that your purpose is to access your own inner resources as often and as deeply as possible, not just for yourself, but for the sake of everyone around you. Wellbeing is contagious.

Reducing Stress and Anxiety

Stress and anxiety are slightly different. Stress is your response to a threatening situation, and anxiety is one adverse effect of that stress. Anxiety is more fear-based and a reaction to the stress itself. Mindfulness can help with both.

Mindfulness can reduce stress. One key way is by becoming aware of your underlying thoughts and ideas about, and attitudes towards, a particular situation. In doing so, you create the possibility of naturally changing your response to the stressful situation. Responding to stress appropriately is an important way of reducing stress.

Dr Richard Lazarus, world-famous stress researcher and psychologist, defined stress as 'a particular relationship between the person and the environment that is *appraised* by the person as taxing or exceeding his or her resources and endangering his or her wellbeing'. I like his insight. The definition explains how an event may be stressful for you, but not for someone else – the level of stress experienced depends on whether you see the situation (the stressor) as something you can cope with.

Mindfulness reduces stress in many ways and at many different levels. For example, say your boss has a tendency to lose his cool easily and shouts at you often, even though you're doing your best. How would mindfulness help? Read through the three ways listed below.

Firstly, by being more mindful, you'll notice the fact that you're stressed. You may feel your jaw tightening or your shoulders hunching before you even get to work. Then when your boss shouts at you, you're more aware of the choices you have. You know what effect saying nothing, reacting with insults, or storming out would have. The very fact of being aware of your reactions changes them. You naturally begin to move from *reacting* to negative events to *responding* with greater wisdom. You begin to think more creatively, which may include behaving more assertively.

Secondly, through regular practice of mindfulness meditation, you give your body and mind a rest. Instead of spending your time doing and achieving this and that, you provide a space for yourself to simply be. This 'being' mode is tremendously nourishing and uplifts your inner resources for relaxing rather than stressing out.

Thirdly, you begin to see things from a different perspective. Although your car won't start this morning, at least it gives you a chance for a cup of tea while you wait for a mechanic. Even though there's a big queue at the bank, at least you have enough money to live on, unlike many unfortunate people. You may even use the opportunity to practise mindfulness as you wait in the queue.

Mindfulness can also help with anxiety. Everyone experiences feelings of anxiety in their lives, perhaps before an interview or an exam. However, if you suffer from a generalised anxiety disorder, the feeling becomes a part of your day-to-day existence. Anxiety can significantly disrupt activities you found easy to do in the past.

Anxiety and worry are based on thinking about the future. You may be concerned about what will happen later, next month or next year. Your mind drifts into predicting negative future outcomes and thereby generates challenging emotions. Mindfulness counteracts this by encouraging you to live in the here and now, from moment to moment and non-judgementally. You begin to free yourself from your dangerously drifting mind and allow yourself to emerge in the sensory world of the present.

Mindfulness enables you to step back from the contents of your mind and emotions. You discover how to identify less with the thoughts going through your mind and to realise that they're just thoughts, rather than facts. This enables your thoughts to lose their power, which therefore reduces the anxiety.

Surprisingly, research has found that *trying* to stop worrying increases the worry. Through being more mindful, you change your *relationship* to thoughts, being more compassionate and accepting of them rather than trying to eliminate them. This mindful approach seems to be far more effective than trying to prevent worrying thoughts completely. Read Chapter 13 for more about using mindfulness to combat anxiety.

Controlling Addiction

Do you have any addictions? Maybe to coffee or cigarettes? Or maybe you're addicted to shopping, gambling, the Internet? Or are you addicted to reading *For Dummies* books? Joking aside, addiction to substances like alcohol or drugs or to activities like gambling obviously has serious negative consequences for you and your loved ones. The good news is that initial findings on mindfulness are showing promising results.

For example, consider one small study in 2011 on mindfulness for smoking cessation published in *Drug and Alcohol Dependence* journal. The experiment took 88 smokers and split them into either a standard quit-smoking programme or a mindfulness programme. After four months, 31 per cent of the mindfulness group were smoke-free compared with 6 per cent of the standard treatment group. That's five times (over 500 per cent) more effective!

The reason mindfulness works so well is because you learn to root out your craving. In the study, for example, the researchers offered a four-step process for managing craving:

- R – Recognise you're experiencing a craving and allow yourself to gently be with the experience.

- A – Accept the moment as it is – no need to distract or avoid your feeling.

- I – Investigate your experience. Ask yourself: 'What's going on in my body right now?'

- N – Note your experience – perhaps you feel a sense of pressure, tightness, an ache, tension or heat. Realise that these are just bodily sensations which will pass. Ride the wave of this experience until it passes.

For more on mindfulness for addiction, see Chapter 13.

Regulating Eating Habits

Are you aware of what you eat? Do you taste each mouthful and chew it thoroughly before swallowing? Do you give your attention to what you're eating, or do you distract yourself with television, newspapers or books? Do you use food as a way of coping with unpleasant emotions?

If you feel empty inside, you may eat to help try to fill that space. Or every time you're worried, you may grab a bar of chocolate. Perhaps stress drives you to open the fridge door or makes you limit your food to feel more in control. Mindfulness offers a different way of regulating and coping with your difficult and uncomfortable emotions rather than by eating or avoiding eating.

Mindful eating is about becoming more aware of the process of preparing and eating food, being less judgemental and more accepting of your current eating habits. Mindful eating also includes being aware of the messages your body sends to you, and using that awareness to determine how much or little to eat. Through this increased awareness, you can choose what to eat and what not to eat from a wiser state of mind. You're able to savour the taste of the food and enjoy the process of eating. With awareness, you're more likely to be in touch with physical hunger and able to notice when you've eaten sufficiently. So mindful eating can even help you maintain a healthy weight!

Increasing Your Happiness

Everybody wants to be happy. All your actions can be explained as your personal desire for greater happiness. The question is, what's the best way to increase happiness? It turns out that simply trying to think positively doesn't work – you need to engage in something regularly that uplifts your sense of wellbeing in a more authentic way.

Positive psychologists – scientists who study happiness – think that mindfulness is the answer. Mindfulness seems to train the brain to naturally become more positive and increases resilience. Resilience is the capacity to cope with stress and catastrophe in a healthy way. It ensures that you bounce back to your happy self sooner rather than later following difficulties. It also strengthens your capacity to cope with difficulties in the future. Regular mindfulness exercises change the very structure of your brain, helping to increase your resilience in difficult times.

Through practising mindfulness on a regular basis, you also begin to discover that happiness is an inside job. You can have all the money and power in the world, but if your thoughts are very negative and you believe your thoughts to be true, you're not going to be happy. Conversely, you can have very few possessions, but if your mind is naturally open, receptive and positive, having practised mindfulness daily, you're bound to experience a deeper sense of wellbeing.

Here's a simple mindful exercise to help you to happiness. Every day, look at a stranger and think in your mind: 'May you be well, may you be happy.' This makes you notice someone different and creates a positive wish in your mind. It'll probably make you smile too!

Chapter 18

Ten Mindfulness Myths to Expose

In This Chapter

▶ Recognising common misconceptions about mindfulness

▶ Discovering practical ways to overcome unhelpful ideas

▶ Exploring fundamental aspects of mindfulness

When I told a friend of mine that I teach mindfulness, he said: 'I don't think that's for me – my mind's full enough already, buddy!' Mindfulness isn't about filling up the mind, of course. Mindfulness isn't just meditation either. If you want to ensure that you've got the right idea about mindfulness, check out this chapter and do some 'mind emptying' – take this opportunity to root out any wrong ideas you may have about the ancient and modern science and art of mindfulness.

Mindfulness Is All about the Mind

You may have heard this quip: 'What is mind? Doesn't matter. What is matter? Never mind!'

As a human being you have the capacity to think. In fact, you can't help but think. Thinking seems to happen whether you like it or not. Thinking is almost like breathing, and probably happens more frequently. Some experts estimate humans think up to 60,000 thoughts a day! Mindfulness isn't all about the mind; it takes a step back from thinking rather than stops thinking.

Mindfulness can more appropriately be called heartfulness. In ancient Eastern languages like Sanskrit or Pali, the words for mind and heart are the same, so perhaps the word 'mindfulness' is a little misleading. What does heartfulness mean? If you have an open, warm heart you may be: kind, gentle, caring, accepting, understanding, patient, trusting, joyful, honest, grateful, light-hearted, loving and humble. Perhaps you're not all of those things, but I share those words to express the spirit of mindfulness with you. The idea is to bring one or more heart qualities to your mindful awareness. Naturally, you can't bring *all* of them in at the same time, but you can get a sense of the kind of attitude to bring to your awareness.

Mindfulness isn't a cold, harsh awareness. A thief needs to be attentive when planning to steal something, but that isn't mindfulness. Mindfulness has a sense of kindness as well as curiosity about it.

If, when you're being mindful, you sense you're being critical, struggling a lot and being unkind to yourself, or you think that your attention doesn't have a warmth about it, don't beat yourself up. You'll end up frustrated. Simply be aware of whatever you're being mindful of, and in its own time some kindness will naturally grow. You don't need to force things too much – the less you force things, the better.

Some people think that mindfulness means you need to think about whatever you're focusing on. This isn't quite right. If you're being mindful of your breathing, this means you're feeling the sensation of the breathing in your body – you're not trying to think about the breathing.

Mindfulness Isn't for Restless People

Are you a busy, active and perhaps restless person? Always on the go? If so, mindfulness may sound as if it's too passive for you. But actually, mindfulness is great way to uproot restlessness and replace it with an inner joy.

Many of the mindfulness exercises and meditations are about slowing down. But that's not the aim. The purpose is to cultivate a greater level of awareness and warm-heartedness towards yourself and what's happening around you. It's possible to achieve this whether you're sitting still or moving your body.

Restlessness isn't a fixed part of your personality that'll never change. Mindfulness rewires your brain. If you practise mindfulness regularly, beginning with just a few minutes a day, you learn to be with the feeling of restlessness without reacting to it. You discover that the feeling of restlessness arises and eventually passes away. But there's more to discover. You may find that your life was being *driven* by the feeling of restlessness. It doesn't have to be. With time and effort, the feeling of restlessness is replaced with a greater sense of inner peace and satisfaction.

As always, I don't promise it'll be an easy or quick fix, but the journey can begin with just a five-minute daily mindfulness of breath meditation. So do have a go if you'd like to overcome restlessness.

If you find it difficult to sit still for even a few minutes, try mindful movement. Be aware of your bodily sensations as you stretch up, try to touch your toes or as you go for a run in your local park.

Mindfulness Is Positive Thinking

You can interpret all situations in a positive or negative way, but it's helpful to regard situations optimistically rather than always expecting the worst. Through your regular practice of mindfulness you become more aware of your own thought patterns, both negative and positive. When negative thoughts arise, mindfulness helps you to recognise your own habitual reactions. You may try seeing the situation differently, whether positively or more realistically, and see what effect that has. Mindfulness doesn't tie you into any positive thinking rules – you just bring a sense of curiosity to the experience.

I don't recommend fighting with negative thoughts. Battling with your own mind creates a struggle, and you can end up increasing the level of negativity in yourself. The more you fight a thought, the stronger the thought becomes.

Ultimately, mindfulness takes a step back from all thoughts, both negative and positive. Thoughts are thoughts, not facts. You can't control thoughts completely – all you can do is watch, take a step back, and stop reacting to your thoughts. The more you can do that, the more you feel in control and the less you feel helpless and stressed. Chapter 5 has more about detaching yourself from thoughts.

Mindfulness Is Only for Buddhists

Buddhists don't have the exclusive rights to mindfulness. Mindfulness, or a mindful awareness, is a universal human attribute and skill, a fundamental quality of being alive, just like eyes, ears and a stomach are part of a human body. To be mindful is to be aware, and awareness is not and cannot be attributed to any one religion.

However, mindfulness *was* investigated and developed by Buddha and followers of Buddha. Therefore, if you want, you can read and study more about mindfulness in Buddhist texts, no matter what your religious beliefs. You can also find out about mindfulness in several other religions and philosophies such as Hinduism, Taoism, Advaita, Sufism and many more. However, you find out far more by just being mindful yourself and exploring and learning through your own experience.

As one modern sage, Nisargadatta, said: 'The greatest Guru is your inner self.' Even the Buddha often said: 'Don't simply believe what I am saying – find out for yourself in your own experience.'

Mindfulness isn't a religion or belief system. If anything, mindfulness points towards an approach to living. The mission of the Center for Mindfulness in Massachusetts is simply 'an awakened and compassionate world'. If you really want a goal for your mindfulness practice, I think that to become more awakened and compassionate is a good one.

If you're religious and look deeply into your own faith, you're likely to find some way or system to strengthen the capacity to let go of conceptual thinking and train your quality of attention. So, you don't need to change your religion to find mindfulness a meaningful discipline. To be mindful is to develop the innate human capacity to be aware – you can be of any faith or no faith at all and be mindful.

Mindfulness Is Only for Tough Times

Mindfulness is used to alleviate depression, chronic pain, anxiety, addiction relapse, stress, and high blood pressure, and even to manage the stress and treatment of cancer. Initial results in these areas are very encouraging, and the application of mindfulness is sure to develop along with all the other treatments.

However, mindfulness isn't only for the hard times. Consider this: you can't just start saving money in a recession. You need to save money in the good times too, so when things are really difficult you have some cash to help you out. In fact, saving money is much easier and more effective when times are good. In the same way, you can benefit by developing your mindfulness discipline when things are going relatively well. When the going gets tough, you can naturally bring your mindfulness skills to the challenge, and dip into your inner resources to help you cope.

When I first began practising mindfulness, partly for managing stress, I never understood the far-reaching effect of the practice. For example, I used to struggle if I had to speak to more than a small group of people; now I'm lucky enough to feel able to deliver lectures to hundreds of people. This isn't so much due to my own courage, but to the power of mindfulness. Although your mindfulness practice may be used to fix a problem to start with, if you persevere, mindfulness goes on to nurture all sorts of different areas of your life.

As you begin to understand and practise mindfulness, you notice benefits. At this stage, some people stop practising. Life seems to be going well, you've resolved the issues, and you kind of forget about the mindfulness and meditation . . . until the next disaster strikes! And then you reach out for help again. Coming and going to and from mindfulness meditation is part of the natural process, but in the end you come to realise that without a daily discipline, your life is a bit of a rollercoaster. The meditation makes the ride that little bit smoother.

Mindfulness Is a Set of Techniques

A technique is usually a quick method of achieving a certain outcome, like counting to ten to help calm yourself down when you feel angry. You may have a certain technique for hitting a golf ball, or a technique for reducing conflict in a conversation. Techniques are great for achieving certain results, but they have their limitations too. If you get too stuck on one technique, you can't branch out to new ways of doing things. Sometimes you may get defensive about your particular technique and become actively unwilling to try something different – in this way, techniques can stifle development.

Mindfulness isn't a technique, because fundamentally mindfulness isn't goal-orientated. This is quite a difficult concept to grasp, because you're probably used to doing things to achieve something. Why would you bother doing something to achieve, ultimately, nothing? Mindfulness has benefits, but if you practise to achieve a particular outcome, you limit its potency. A good scientist does an experiment without forcing a certain outcome – all the scientist wants to do is find the truth of the situation by observing the outcome. If the scientist is looking for a particular outcome, perhaps if the experiment is sponsored by a drug company, you're wary of the results because they may be biased. In the same way, if you look for a certain outcome with mindfulness, you're being biased and not really trying the mindfulness wholeheartedly.

Mindful awareness is about being aware of your inner and outer experience, *whatever that experience is.*

Paradoxically, mindfulness underlies and enhances the quality of all other techniques. Without awareness you can't use a technique. The less aware you are, the less likely it is that whatever technique you're using will work. For example, if you use a technique to reduce stress by letting go of negative thinking, but you're not really aware of your thoughts, how do you hope to succeed?

This book does contain lots of tips and techniques to encourage mindfulness, but ultimately mindfulness itself isn't a technique.

Mindfulness is about letting go of doing. It is about simply being as you are. Being yourself, whatever you think of yourself. Being yourself isn't a technique. You can't *do* non-doing. Non-doing means letting go of all techniques with their desired outcomes and just *being*.

Mindfulness Isn't for Me

Some people may not be keen on mindfulness, perhaps due to misconceptions and stereotypical views about the practice. Mindfulness doesn't even have to be connected with the typical picture of a meditator: someone sitting cross-legged, perhaps burning incense, aimlessly navel-gazing for some future spiritual high. But mindfulness is for anyone interested in becoming more aware, more awake, more alive, more connected. Although meditation is an extremely helpful way of developing greater mindfulness, you can also simply pay a bit more attention every time you go for a walk, have a chat with your colleagues or play sport. You may spend a few minutes feeling your breathing as you rest on the sofa before switching on the television. These are simple ways of waking up to your life and letting go of automatic pilot. I don't know anyone who can't do with a greater dose of awareness.

You may think that you can't do mindfulness because you're too impatient, too stressy or too anxious. But mindfulness develops your capacity to be patient, kind, attentive, calm and happy, so you may be the perfect person to try mindfulness! To say you're not patient enough to do mindfulness is like saying you're too unfit to exercise. If you don't exercise at all, you'll never be fit. However, take things easy to begin with – try a short, five-minute meditation every day and build from there. Or try some mindful walking for a few minutes. Go to Chapter 6 for ways to practise walking meditations.

Some people think that mindfulness is something weird to do with religion, or some cultish idea. Mindfulness is feeling your own breathing, or listening to the sounds around you, or really tasting the food in front of you. Mindfulness is another word for kindly awareness – nothing mysterious in that sense. You can make mindfulness whatever you want – there are no rules in this game. Some people practise mindfulness for spiritual or religious reasons, just as some people burn incense for religious reasons – that doesn't mean incense is for religious people only!

Mindfulness Meditation Is Relaxation

Relaxation exercises are often designed to loosen the muscles in your body, and the aim of relaxation is to become less tense. So relaxation has a clear goal, and you have various methods for achieving it.

Mindfulness is ultimately goalless. You can't really say you had a 'good' meditation or a 'bad' meditation, because that would presuppose the kind of experiences you're supposed to have. Meditation is about experiencing whatever the content of experience is, from moment to moment. Your intention and attitudes behind the meditation are key. Meditation is about understanding and growing in wisdom by looking within.

Relaxation is often, but certainly not always, a very welcome side effect of meditation. However, when you first practise meditation, you may feel more tense by the end. When I first began to meditate, I was trying to do it well and my attention was overly intense. My body became tense trying to focus, as I tried in vain to force thoughts out. This led to more tension, but was part of the learning process.

Meditation can sometimes release deep-seated trapped emotions that your subconscious mind has hidden away and works hard at keeping out. The process can create more tension temporarily as you face your demons. However, the sooner you release the emotion, the better. As the emotion rises into your conscious mind, the feeling can dissolve, sometimes relaxing a part of the body that has been tense for years. (Chapter 10 has more about dealing with mindfulness bringing up painful emotions.)

Mindfulness Can Be Used Instead of Therapy or Medicine

Mindfulness certainly can't be used *instead of* therapy or medicine. If you suffer from a clinical condition, you need to follow your doctor's recommendations. However, *in addition to* medical advice, you can normally develop a mindfulness practice to support your healing process. Mindfulness helps to manage your stress levels, and can reduce your blood pressure and boost your body's immune function.

Doctors can refer patients to a mindfulness-based stress reduction (MBSR) course, empowering patients to take a more proactive part in looking after their own health and wellbeing though the application of mindfulness. This way of developing inner resources and enhancing resilience to stress has been found to be profoundly wholesome. Chapter 9 goes into more detail about MBSR.

Mindfulness Is Complicated and Boring

How you view mindfulness depends on the rules you create in your head about the process: mindfulness should be relaxing and enlightening; my mind should be blank; I should feel comfortable; I shouldn't feel emotional; if I don't do it every day I've failed; if it feels difficult I must be doing it incorrectly.

You need to be aware of the kind of rules you've created in your head about mindfulness. Any 'must', 'should' or 'ought' is the sign of a rigid rule laid down in your mind. Life has the tendency to flow wherever it wants to go, therefore you find, time and again, your inner rules being broken and frustration and boredom arising.

Mindfulness is simple but not easy. The simple bit is that mindfulness is about being aware and paying attention. The not-so-easy bit is having the discipline to practise regularly and the ability to trust in the process, no matter how wild your mind appears to be.

Mindfulness has a sense of simple flow about it: doing less rather than more; thinking less rather than more; going with the flow of life rather than spending life wrestling with complications created by the mind.

I'll give you an example of the simplicity yet difficulty of mindfulness. Right now, if you're aware of the weight of this book in your hand, you're being mindful. If you walk out of the room you're in and feel your feet on the ground, you're being mindful. So mindfulness is simple. However, the difficult bit is overcoming your current habitual thought patterns, which have been strengthening for however long you've been on this planet, and are naturally very powerful. When you put this book down and walk off, notice how long it takes before you're lost in an ocean of thoughts, feelings, stories, frustrations and desires.

If you find meditating boring, you have a few choices:

- ✔ Reduce the length of time for which you meditate.
- ✔ Become curious about boredom.
- ✔ Let the feeling of boredom go, and re-focus on the present moment again and again.
- ✔ Accept the boredom as part and parcel of life and keep meditating – the boredom will soon pass.

Ultimately, no matter how much trouble you have being mindful, and no matter how confused or bored you may be occasionally, you have a deep and powerful aspect of yourself that nothing can ever touch. Awareness is a mysterious aspect of being human that remains beyond the understanding of science. Awareness is always there, at the root of your being – ever shining, ever knowing. Even when you're lost in thought or caught up in the darkest, most frightening emotion or situation, you're aware, at some level, of what's going on, both inside and outside yourself.

Chapter 19

Ten Paths to Further Study

So, you've begun the exciting journey into mindfulness and want to find out more. Well, you're in luck. Mindfulness is a hot topic, and you can find all sorts of different resources to support your mindfulness practice. Browse through this chapter to see whether anything catches your eye.

Websites

You can find out just about everything you need to know about mindfulness on the Internet. The problem is there are so many different websites, it's hard to know where to start. Here are a few to help you to begin mindfully exploring.

ShamashAlidina.com

If you like my approach in this book, you may enjoy spending a few minutes browsing my website and subscribing to my electronic newsletter. My organisation offers training and online teacher training in mindfulness. I also work with other experts in the field of mindfulness, offering their specialities to my electronic newsletter subscribers. My mindfulness courses are offered online or I can come and run a workshop or retreat near you if you or someone in your area invites me.

Visit www.shamashalidina.com to contact me, for training or for free resources, including:

- ✔ **Online free 21-day online course in mindfulness**
- ✔ **Online eight-week mindfulness course**
- ✔ **Mindfulness teacher training online**
- ✔ **E-mail newsletters and 'weekly wisdom' e-mails when you subscribe**

If you're on Facebook or Twitter, have a look at my online community which will support and inform you with quotations, tips, offers and free resources that I add regularly. It's a great way to remind yourself to be mindful. See www.facebook.com/shamashalidina or www.twitter.com/shamashalidina.

Greater Good Science Centre

The mission of The Greater Good Science Centre is to 'study the psychology, sociology, and neuroscience of well-being, and teach skills that foster a thriving, resilient and compassionate society'. It sounds very grand, but the centre's website is fantastic and the web pages are enjoyable to read.

Visit the centre at greatergood.berkeley.edu and browse through the core themes, which are: gratitude, altruism, compassion, empathy, forgiveness, happiness and, last but not least, mindfulness. The articles are well written and well researched.

Mindful.org

Mindful.org celebrates being mindful in all aspects of daily living. It's an ideal resource if you're interested in various forms of mindfulness practice. The website offers a range of stories, practical news, insights and tips.

Visit www.mindful.org and read sections on:

- ✔ Body and mind
- ✔ Love and relationships
- ✔ Home and work
- ✔ Mindfulness practice
- ✔ The science behind mindfulness

Books, Magazines and Films

I recommend that you continue to nourish your mindfulness practice with a range of different writers to help deepen your understanding of yourself. Here are some resources that I have enjoyed and still do.

Book: Wherever you go, there you are

This book by Jon Kabat-Zinn (published by Piatkus) is simple and easy to read, covering a wide range of topics on mindfulness. Kabat-Zinn developed the mindfulness-based stress reduction course detailed in Chapter 9, so he definitely knows a thing or two about mindfulness!

The chapters in this book are nice and short, so it's ideal to pick up and read for a few minutes before or after doing a mindfulness meditation. The book is perfect for beginners and contains something for more experienced practitioners too.

Book: Peace is every step

Thich Nhat Hanh (pronounced Tik N'yat Hawn) is a Vietnamese Zen Buddhist monk, poet, scholar and peace activist. Nhat Hanh has written many books, and I particularly enjoyed reading this one (published by Rider).

Everything is connected

Part of the purpose of mindfulness, according to Thich Nhat Hanh, is to see how you're interconnected with everything else and not a separate entity that exists in isolation. This *interbeing* leads to a sense of peace and wellbeing and reduces feelings like anger and frustration. You come to see that if you're angry towards another person, you're in a way being angry towards yourself. If you're hammering a nail into a piece of wood and accidentally hit your left hand with the hammer in your right hand, your left and right hand don't start fighting each other! On the contrary, your right hand cares about and soothes the pain in the left hand, because the two hands are one. In the same way, if you begin to see how you're interconnected with everything else, you experience greater compassion (one of the most positive emotions you can have) and respect for things and people around you.

The author begins the book with:

> *Every day, when we wake up, we have twenty-four brand new hours to live. What a precious gift! We have the capacity to live in a way that these twenty-four hours will bring peace, joy and happiness to ourselves and others.*

Thich Nhat Hanh is probably one of the world's most famous teachers of mindfulness. Because of his lifelong commitment and efforts for peace in Vietnam, he was nominated for the Nobel Peace Prize in 1967 by Martin Luther King, Jr.

You can find many gems in this book to help transform your daily life and achieve conscious awareness of, and gratitude for, what you do. The simplicity and poetry of Thich Nhat Hanh's words make them a joy to read. The book is in short sections that you can read in a few minutes and then reflect on, – ideal before or after meditating to set you up for the day.

Book: Mindfulness – a practical guide to finding peace in a frantic world

This is currently a very popular book – in fact, one of the bestselling books in the world!

Co-authored by Professor Mark Williams, former head at Oxford University's Mindfulness Centre, and Danny Penman, a journalist, this book details an eight-week mindfulness course for people suffering from the challenges of everyday stress. The book includes short mindfulness exercises, 10–15 minutes long, so it's ideal if you lead a busy life and don't have time for the longer mindfulness meditations.

Do take a look and see whether it appeals to you.

Magazine: Mindful

This is the only quality monthly magazine that I know dedicated to celebrating the 'mindfulness movement'. Packed with well-written articles, the magazine contains ideas for applying mindfulness at home and work, as well as the latest research findings on mindfulness, fascinating interviews, recommended mobile apps and more.

Currently, both digital and print versions are available, so you can access *Mindful* wherever you are in the world.

DVD: Room to breathe

This documentary film is about the transformation of a struggling school in San Francisco as the students are introduced to the practice of mindfulness meditation. Stressed-out teachers face the option of either continuing the battle to gain the focus of frustrated students or trying to share the ancient practice of mindfulness to help develop the students' ability to be present. Find out how a young mindfulness teacher from Berkeley, facing the students' lack of discipline, lack of respect for authority and little interest in learning anything works through the challenge.

The DVD is particular interesting for anyone who works with children or has any interest in the power of mindfulness.

Retreats

You can deepen your experience of mindfulness by attending a retreat. Retreats offer you an extended period away from your usual environment and responsibilities – often in silence. In this setting, your mind has more time to settle, and through the practices of mindfulness meditation you gain insights and grow in wisdom as you meditate.

This sort of opportunity is rare, so if you get such a chance I encourage you to have a go. If you're never spent a day not talking, why not try it out and see what happens? You may find it fascinating how your mind reacts to the experience. For many people, the experience is restful, energising and a bit like a mental detox.

Mindfulness-based retreat centres worldwide

The following retreat centres offer mindfulness-based silent retreats:

- ✔ Insight Meditation Society, Barre, Massachusetts, USA
- ✔ Spirit Rock, Woodacre, California, USA
- ✔ Insight Meditation Community of Washington, Cabin John, Maryland, USA
- ✔ Southern Dharma, Hot Springs, North Carolina, USA
- ✔ Boundless Way Zen, Worcester, Massachusetts, USA

- San Francisco Zen Center, San Francisco, California, USA
- Zen Center of San Diego, San Diego, California, USA
- Zen Community of Oregon, Clatskanie, Oregon, USA
- Karme Choling, Barnet, Vermont, USA
- Shambhala Mountain Center, Red Feather Lakes, Colorado, USA
- Gaia House, Devon, UK
- Amravati, Hertfordshire, UK
- Vipassana Meditation Centers (worldwide)

This is not an exhaustive list, but it gives you some ideas of places to look. Most of these centres are in the USA, but when you look on their websites you may find links to recommended centres near your country or even near where you live.

Vipassana Meditation Centers are located worldwide and are based on the SN Goenka tradition. In my experience, people tend to either love these centers or find them a bit too intensive. Check the website or speak to someone who's been there to see whether it's for you.

If you're looking for a centre completely not associated with religion, get in touch with a secular mindfulness teacher like me. Many secular mindfulness teachers now offer retreats. The easiest way to find a such a teacher may be to search on the Internet for one in your area and then check the credentials and experience of the teacher on the associated website.

Check the timetables and schedule for the retreat. If you're a beginner and think you may feel intimidated with a whole week or more, try to start with just a day or weekend retreat. And don't feel you have to attend every meditation session: take some breaks if you need to, and go at a gentle pace rather than pushing yourself too much. It is a re*treat* after all, not a re*torture*!

Plum Village and related centers

Plum Village is a Buddhist retreat centre founded by Thich Nhat Hanh in southern France. I attended a retreat there and enjoyed the light-hearted atmosphere mixed with the incisive and fascinating talks by Thich Nhat Hanh every morning. The retreat was partly in silence, especially at meal times. Everyone seems to enjoy the silence. The summer retreats are also family friendly, so you can bring the kids along too!

Other retreat centres now follow the same approach. They are:

- ✔ **Blue Cliff Monastery:** In 80 acres of beautiful woodland, about one and half hours north of New York City, USA, this is home to 12 monks and 17 nuns, who welcome you to come and practise mindfulness with them.

- ✔ **Deer Park Monastery:** On 400 acres in the glorious mountains of southern California, USA, Deer Park is a place of serenity, home to 17 monks and 19 nuns. Visit and practise mindfulness there.

- ✔ **Magnolia Grove Monastery:** In Batesville, Mississippi, USA, more than 30 monks and nuns in residence, welcome visitors who wish to practise meditation and mindfulness with every breath and every step.

Check the respective websites to find out the best time to arrive and leave.

If you attend a summer retreat, here's a typical schedule:

5:30 a.m.	Rise
6:00 a.m.	Sitting and walking meditations
7:30 a.m.	Breakfast
9:00 a.m.	Lecture by Thich Nhat Hanh
12:30 p.m.	Lunch
2:00 p.m.	Rest
3:00 p.m.	Class/study time
6:00 p.m.	Dinner
8:00 p.m.	Exercise
9:30 p.m.	Silence begins
10:30 p.m.	Lights out

If that sounds appealing and you like Thich Nhat Hanh, look out for his summer retreat and book yourself in! Visit www.plumvillage.org or the websites of the other retreat centres for more details.

Index

• C •

• *F* •

• J •

• K •

• L •

• N •

• O •

• U •

• V •

• W •

About the Author

Shamash Alidina has been teaching mindfulness since 1998. He was invited to experiment with a short mindfulness exercise whilst studying in a 'practical philosophy' evening class, and caught the mindfulness bug! He was amazed at the power of mindfulness to transform his state of mind, both during the meditation itself, and through exercises in day to day life. He decided to dedicate his time to learn and teach mindfulness to others. He taught mindfulness to groups of adults, and then additionally taught in a children's school in London for eight years which integrated mindfulness and meditation into the curriculum. He's been working in the field of mindfulness on a full-time basis since 2010.

Shamash formally trained at Bangor University's Centre for Mindfulness in Wales. He runs his own successful training organisation, *ShamashAlidina.com*, to introduce mindfulness to the general public, as well as training mindfulness teachers and business organisations, both in-person and often through live online learning. He has trained in managing workplace health with the Health and Safety Executive and regularly coaches executives in stress reduction. He has taught mindfulness all over the world, including the USA, Australia, New Zealand, the Middle East and Europe.

Shamash has been interviewed by many national newspapers and magazines and has appeared on radio and television. He has featured in mindfulness campaigns, and regularly blogs on his main passions: mindfulness, compassion, wisdom and happiness. He currently lives in London.

Dedication

This book is dedicated to you, dear reader. May the practice of mindfulness be of benefit to you, and your loved ones.

Author's Acknowledgments

I would like to say a special thank you to my editor Iona Everson who I've had the pleasure to meet and work with — I'm proud to have had her insightful eye over the production of this second edition. I would like to thank Jennifer Prytherch and Nicole Hermitage who originally commissioning me to write the first edition of this book. And I would also like to wholeheartedly extend my thanks to the whole production team at Wiley — this book is certainly a team effort!

I'd like to thank all my family members. In particular, thanks to my brother, Aneesh, who first suggested the idea of *Mindfulness For Dummies*, and my parents Manju and Fateh, who support me throughout my life.

Big thanks to my wonderful friends for their support (together with why I think they're great!): Joelle (bright enthusiasm), Vicky (glowing positivity), Michal (visionary outlook and kindness), Patrycja (compassionate being), Alma (my inspiration), Garry (full of laughter), Marc (so wise and fun), Harpal (friendly and funny), Oskar (pure spiritual), Maneesh (big thinker), Joe (friendly and fun), Richard (makes things happen), BKC (deep thinker), Sid (keeping it chilled), Leroy (hilarious) and Waqas (a great friend). I don't have a chance to see some of you often, but rest assured, I often think of you. And apologies to any of you I've forgotten — it just means mindfulness has not improved my memory!

Gratitude to my Chief Technology Officer and friend Paul who has helped me SO much with turning my passion into my work. And to Teresa, my friend and Chief Happiness Officer, who you'd chat to if you contact us.

I would like to thank Steven Hickman, Director of the UCSD Center for Mindfulness, for his support of my work, and for writing a beautiful foreword to this book.

Finally I'd like to thank the teachers who continue to inspire me with mindfulness, wisdom and compassion through their talks and writing: The Dalai Lama, Matthieu Ricard, Jon Kabat-Zinn, Mark Williams, Steven Hayes, Russ Harris, Ramana Maharshi and Nisargadatta. Thank you for inspiring others to look deep within and for sharing the beauty of this mysterious gift we have — life itself.

Publisher's Acknowledgements

We're proud of this book; please send us your comments at http://dummies.custhelp.com. For other comments, please contact our Customer Care Department within the U.S. at 877-762-2974, outside the U.S. at (001) 317-572-3993, or fax 317-572-4002.

Some of the people who helped bring this book to market include the following:

Acquisitions, Editorial and Vertical Websites

Project Editor: Iona Everson

Commissioning Editor: Ben Kemble

Proofreader: Mary White

Publisher: Miles Kendall

Composition Services

Project Coordinator: Melissa Cossell

Indexer: Potomac Indexing, LLC